The Two Worlds of Nineteenth Century International Relations

This edited volume presents a new, grand, and global narrative for international relations (IR) history in the pivotal nineteenth century. Typically considered by IR scholars to be a long century of relative peace after 1815, the contributors offer a reconceptualization of IR in this century, arguing that it is temporally bifurcated, with very different patterns of behavior in the first and second halves.

A mid-century discontinuity – a "pivot period" – marks the transition phase in Europe and globally when, in the space of a few years, a shift occurred from a comparatively calm, politically disconnected world under loose British free trade hegemony to one of scrambles for territory and keen interest in imperial possessions and conquest. All the book's chapters deal with characterizing patterns of relations in the first half of the century or the second, with two addressing the discontinuity in the middle. In the first half, aspects of regional orders are described (in Latin America, East Asia, and Europe) alongside crucial developmental processes (missionaries and colonial expansion, the agency of regionally localized actors, of leading elites). In the second half, there is again discussion of regional developments (East Asia, Europe), but now under the onslaught and pressures of the latter half of the century, and spotlighting industrialization's impact and the role of status competition and international law.

In presenting this new narrative for the nineteenth century, it becomes clear that an era long considered uninteresting on Eurocentric grounds is in fact crucial and pivotal in global terms. This work will be of particular interest to students and scholars of the history of international relations.

Daniel M. Green is Associate Professor of Political Science at the University of Delaware. Trained as a comparativist and Africanist, he turned his focus to international relations theory and history in 2004 and was the Founding President of the Historical International Relations (HIST) Section of the International Studies Association in 2012. He is also the ongoing organizer of HIST's Nineteenth Century Working Group. He has published in several journals and edited volumes and is the editor of *Constructivism and Comparative Politics* (2002) and of *Guide to the English School in International Studies* (2014, with Cornelia Navari). He is currently completing a book project entitled *Order Projects and Resistance in the Global Political System: A Framework for International History*.

The Two Worlds of Nineteenth Century International Relations
The Bifurcated Century

**Edited by
Daniel M. Green**

LONDON AND NEW YORK

First published 2019
by Routledge
2 Park Square, Milton Park, Abingdon, Oxon OX14 4RN

and by Routledge
52 Vanderbilt Avenue, New York, NY 10017

Routledge is an imprint of the Taylor & Francis Group, an informa business

© 2019 selection and editorial matter, Daniel M. Green; individual chapters, the contributors

The right of Daniel M. Green to be identified as the author of the editorial material, and of the authors for their individual chapters, has been asserted in accordance with sections 77 and 78 of the Copyright, Designs and Patents Act 1988.

All rights reserved. No part of this book may be reprinted or reproduced or utilised in any form or by any electronic, mechanical, or other means, now known or hereafter invented, including photocopying and recording, or in any information storage or retrieval system, without permission in writing from the publishers.

Trademark notice: Product or corporate names may be trademarks or registered trademarks, and are used only for identification and explanation without intent to infringe.

British Library Cataloguing-in-Publication Data
A catalogue record for this book is available from the British Library

Library of Congress Cataloging-in-Publication Data
Names: Green, Daniel M., 1961- editor.
Title: The two worlds of nineteenth century international relations : the bifurcated century / edited by Daniel M. Green.
Description: Abingdon, Oxon ; New York, NY : Routledge, 2019. | Includes bibliographic references.
Identifiers: LCCN 2018031091| ISBN 9781138737204 (hardback) | ISBN 9781315180557 (ebook) | ISBN 9781351719674 (epub3) | ISBN 9781351719667 (mobipocket)
Subjects: LCSH: International relations--History--19th century.
Classification: LCC JZ1329.5 .T96 2019 | DDC 327.09/034--dc23
LC record available at https://lccn.loc.gov/2018031091

ISBN: 978-1-138-73720-4 (hbk)
ISBN: 978-1-315-18055-7 (ebk)

Typeset in Times New Roman
by Taylor & Francis Books

Printed and bound in Great Britain by
TJ International Ltd, Padstow, Cornwall

Contents

List of contributors   vii

1 Introduction: The two worlds of nineteenth-century
   international relations   1
   DANIEL M. GREEN

2 Missionaries and the civilizing mission in British colonialism   25
   ANDREA PARAS

3 Republican privateering: Local networks and political order in
   the western Atlantic   43
   JEPPE MULICH

4 Limits of cooperation: The German Confederation and
   Austro-Prussian rivalry after 1815   60
   TOBIAS LEMKE

5 Rejecting Westphalia: Maintaining the Sinocentric system,
   to the end   80
   DAVID BANKS

6 Ordering Europe: The legalized hegemony of the
   Concert of Europe   101
   GEORGE LAWSON

7 Industrialization and competitive globalization after 1873:
   International thought and the problem of resources   119
   LUCIAN M. ASHWORTH

8 Between European Concert and global status: The evolution of
   the institution of great powers, 1860s to 1910s   138
   THOMAS MÜLLER

9 Reordering East Asian international relations after 1860 157
SEO-HYUN PARK

10 An evil of ancient date: Piracy and the two Pax Britannicas in nineteenth-century Southeast Asia 177
MARK SHIRK

11 Conclusions: The value of our new historical narrative 196
DANIEL M. GREEN

Index 207

Contributors

Lucian M. Ashworth is a Professor of Political Science at the Memorial University of Newfoundland, St. John's Canada. His main area of research interest is the history of international thought, and he has published widely on the topics of international thought and the disciplinary history of International Relations (IR). His latest book is *A History of International Thought* (Routledge, 2014), and he is currently working on a new book for Routledge, scheduled to be published in 2019, on the different origin stories in IR.

David Banks is a Professorial Lecturer at American University, where he focuses on International Order, Great Power Politics, and Diplomacy. His current book manuscript researches the motivation for, and political consequences of, state violations of diplomatic practice. He has recently finished a two-year research project funded by the Center for Long-Term Cybersecurity at Berkeley that used wargames to investigate US and Chinese cyber strategies in the event of a war in the South China Sea. In addition to these projects he has a number of articles in development regarding great power conferences, diplomatic practice, coercive diplomacy, and symbolic diplomacy.

Daniel M. Green is Associate Professor of Political Science at the University of Delaware. Trained as a comparativist and Africanist, he turned his focus to international relations theory and history in 2004 and was the Founding President of the Historical International Relations (HIST) Section of the International Studies Association in 2012. He is also the ongoing organizer of HIST's Nineteenth Century Working Group. He has published in several journals and edited volumes and is the editor of *Constructivism and Comparative Politics* (2002) and of *Guide to the English School in International Studies* (2014, with Cornelia Navari). He is currently completing a book project entitled *Order Projects and Resistance: A Framework for International History*.

George Lawson is Associate Professor of International Relations at the London School of Economics. He works on the relationship between history and theory, with a particular interest in historical sociology. He applies these interests to the study of revolutions and debates around global modernity, with a particular concern for how 19th-century developments have shaped contemporary world politics. His books include *Global Historical Sociology* (edited with Julian Go), *The Global Transformation* (co-authored with Barry Buzan), *The Global 1989* (edited with Chris Armbruster and Michael Cox), and *Negotiated Revolutions*. He is currently completing a book entitled *Anatomies of Revolution*.

Tobias Lemke is a Ph.D. candidate in Political Science and International Relations at the University of Delaware. His research examines the emergence and diffusion of nationalist movements and their impact on foreign policy, international relations, and order. His dissertation, *Nations in Narrative: Mass Politics and International Orders in the Short Nineteenth Century, 1830–60,* traces the rise of nationalist rhetoric and identity movements in Great Britain, France, and Prussia, unpacking how sociopolitical developments contributed to the disruption and transformation of established diplomatic practice. He has also written about the role of collective identity, strategic narratives, and digital communication networks in historical and contemporary international relations, work recently published in *International Relations*.

Jeppe Mulich is a Teaching Associate in Global History at the University of Cambridge. He has published work in the *Journal of Global History, Review of International Studies,* and *Political Power and Social Theory.*

Thomas Müller is a postdoctoral researcher in the Collaborative Research Centre 1288 "Practices of Comparing" at Bielefeld University (Germany). In his research, he is particularly interested in the interplay between the stratification of international society and the design and practice of its governance institutions. He additionally focuses on the history of the practices through which states and other actors – in particular international organizations and think tanks – have comparatively assessed the distribution of (military) power in the international system. He is currently working on a monograph that reconstructs and analyses the co-evolution of great power status and great power management from the middle of the 18th century to the present.

Andrea Paras is an Associate Professor in the Department of Political Science at the University of Guelph. She is a cross-disciplinary international relations scholar whose research contributes to political science, international development studies, history, intercultural studies, and the scholarship of learning and teaching. Her research investigates how different international actors derive their legitimacy through languages of morality. Her forthcoming book, *Moral Obligations and Sovereignty in International Relations: A Genealogy of Humanitarianism* (Routledge, 2019), examines the evolving relationship between moral obligations and sovereignty from the sixteenth century to the present, and argues that humanitarian norms act just as much to reinforce the logic of sovereignty as they do to challenge it.

Seo-Hyun Park is an Associate Professor in the Department of Government and Law at Lafayette College. Her research interests include hierarchy and regional orders, national identity politics, state sovereignty, state-building, and history and international relations, with a regional focus on East Asia. She is the author of *Sovereignty and Status in East Asian International Relations* (Cambridge University Press, 2017). Her work has appeared in the *Review of International Studies, International Relations, Journal of East Asian Studies, Strategic Studies Quarterly,* and *Chinese Journal of International Politics.*

Mark Shirk is a Lecturer in International Relations at the University of Cambridge. He has previously taught at Stonehill College, Dickinson College, American University, the Universities at Shady Grove, and the University of Maryland. He holds a Ph.D. in Government and Politics from the University of Maryland. His research centers on trans- and sub-national violence such as terrorism and piracy as a site for the making and remaking of the state and global order across history. He has also written about empires, narratives, and surveillance. You can find more of his work on piracy in *International Studies Review; Global Change, Peace, and Security*; and *Terrorism and Political Violence*. His current project is tentatively titled *Pirates, Anarchists, and Terrorists: Violence and Global Order in the Modern Era.*

1 Introduction

The two worlds of nineteenth-century international relations

Daniel M. Green

The nineteenth century is now enjoying a burst of attention from those interested in international relations history (Bell, 2014; Buzan and Lawson, 2013, 2015; Keene, 2007; Mitzen, 2013; Osterhammel, 2014), and deservedly so. As historian Jürgen Osterhammel has observed, "[t]he nineteenth century saw the birth of international relations as we know it today" (2014: 394). This provokes us, however, to explore further why it is an important era, and ask how we should understand the century as a whole and its place in international history.

This volume presents a somewhat novel grand narrative for international relations history in the nineteenth century, with a more global approach. Often characterized by IR scholars as a long century of relative peace after 1815, perhaps the age of a *Pax Britannica* before WWI, our reconceptualization argues that it was in fact a 'bifurcated' century, with different 'worlds' of relations in the first and second halves. This posits a *temporal* division of the century into two – with a discontinuity in the middle fifteen years (1856–1869) – and a *geopolitical* division in the first half that was erased in the second via intensifying global connections and the integration of regional systems after 1856 into a united political-strategic world.

In the first half of the century the world was divided into several circuits with varied sets of rules, practices, and pressures – a European arena and the regional systems of the rest of the world. Europe had its own complexities, including the great power management of the Concert system at fluctuating levels of functionality. Globally there was a tacit acceptance of British hegemony – as the strongest power with global presence to emerge from the struggles of 1789–1815 – in a *Pax Britannica* which restrained European actors (Darwin, 2011: 26–27; Fregosi, 1990; Keene, 2002; Kennedy, 1986: 149–158; Schroeder, 1986). This was a more open age of differing sociopolitical trajectories, zones of insularity, and expanding interactions after the tumult of the Age of Revolution; an age largely before steamships, railways, and rapid-fire artillery from rifled barrels.

In the second half of the century, in processes accelerating after 1856, disconnected regional systems became integrated into a single competitive international system. Several major powers, some newly on the scene, became involved in competitive global imperialism: Britain, France, Germany, Italy,

Russia, the United States, Japan. The Sinocentric system fell in East Asia as a 'Scramble for Asia' of sorts began in 1857; a 'Scramble for Africa' has beginnings in the 1860s and accelerated in the early 1880s. Something of a 'West and the rest' division remained, but with increasing competition and differentiation, in a different era of intensifying global contestation and heightened resistance from non-European peoples. While industrialization in the West facilitated its expanding domination of the rest of the world, key policy choices were also made before economic changes crystallized. Expanding, Eurocentric international law produced legal-order breakthroughs, also codifying a 'Standard of Civilization' applied to the non-West (Gong, 1984), to press for conformity with European expectations or suffer colonization.

Finally, a mid-century disruptive discontinuity – a discernable 'pivot period' – is the transition phase in Europe and globally when, in the space of a few years, there is a marked shift from a comparatively calm, less imperialized world to frenzied scrambles for territory and a qualitative shift in the interest in colonial possessions and conquest. Some great powers (France, Russia, Japan) became ambitiously expansive, while Britain learned new lessons about the potentials of its laissez-faire hegemonic order project. The first full political-military-strategic connectedness of all the world occurs in these years, as several major powers pitted themselves against each other in a globe-encompassing struggle. This also energized movements of conformity and resistance to such cultural and military predations, gelling a single competitive system into place that still endures today.

Our chapters examine patterns of relations in the first half of the century or the second, and a few address the discontinuity in the middle. The first half of the book describes aspects of regional orders (in Latin America, East Asia, and Europe) alongside crucial developmental processes (missionaries and colonial expansion, the agency of regional actors, of leading elites). In the second half, we again discuss regional developments (East and Southeast Asia, Europe), but now under the onslaught and pressures of the second half of the century and looking more closely at the role of industrialization's impacts and international law. In this account it becomes clear that standard IR narratives are Eurocentric when marking 1815–1914 as an unusual era of peace. That rendering misses 'the global transformation' described in Buzan and Lawson (2015), the pivot period we discuss, and the important differences between the first and second halves of the century. On the other hand, our purpose is not to enter into the debate about explaining the causes of a 'global transformation', a 'great divergence', or a 'power-flip' between the West and the rest. That has been widely studied (see Buzan and Lawson, 2015: 24–42, for a recent and thorough literature review; Philips, 2013). Instead, we offer a new IR periodization of the entire century and discuss the international relations on either side of the pivotal middle years.

This introductory chapter provides a literature review to situate the 'two worlds' argument, discusses events in the hinge portion of the century, the pivot period, and introduces the chapters to come. The 'two worlds' idea provides a corrective for other approaches to this century and to international relations history as a whole, for which the notion of two very different halves of the century is something new. Many argue that the key founding date of the modern international system is 1648, and 1918 or 1945 are the key dates thereafter (Buzan and Lawson, 2013, 2015). We find that the world becomes one political system in the middle years – the 1860s – born at a particular historical moment and burdened with remarkable violence, cultural arrogance, and racism, from which it has only begun to recover.

The nineteenth century in international relations history

IR's historical narratives structure the very fundamentals of our research agendas (Green, 1995; Reus-Smit, 2016), yet it is surprising how little we worry directly about them. The nineteenth century has been most typically ignored by IR (Buzan and Lawson, 2015: 48–55), and certainly has missed a mid-century turning point and the two worlds on either side of it. This includes the neorealist literature on hegemonies, hegemonic cycles, and hegemonic stability, much of the literature that uses balancing configurations as a lens, the literature on Eurocentric civilizational hierarchy, and the historical literature on British hegemony and *Pax Britannica*. Ours is not a breakthrough insight for the English School, however, which has noted this turning point (and continues to explore it in work such as Buzan and Lawson 2013, 2015; see also Doyle, 1986). But we feel we can add to such insights, recharacterizing the entire century and speaking to accounts of international relations history generally. Before presenting our responses to this century-of-continuities tendency, I review several of its themes.

A century of continuities?

Multiple factors contribute to the neglect of the nineteenth century but one we highlight here is that, from several different IR perspectives, the century is too easily summarized and dismissed, as an age of monotone continuities with turning points elsewhere.

A common account of the century is as an era of relative peace – 'the long peace' – broken significantly only once, with the Crimean War in the middle (Anderson, 2007; Gilpin 1981, 1988; Matzke, 2011: 2–3; O'Brien, 2002; Sheehan, 1996: 121–144; Spiezio, 1990; Watson, 1992). It is a stable world globally, provided by a *Pax Britannica* of British hegemony (most recently Keefer, 2013; Gilpin, 1981; Goldstein, 1988; Morgenthau, 1960); indeed, Gilpin (1981) is the place where the reputation of British hegemony is most bluntly asserted. This makes it a model century of several great powers that showed restraint and largely kept the peace, amongst themselves, thanks to crucial British leadership. This is the portrayal of Britain in 'hegemonic stability theory' that became popular in the 1980s (Gilpin, 1981; Kindleberger,

4   *Daniel M. Green*

1973). By this account the nineteenth century is stable and undifferentiated, thanks to British provision of global order.[1]

A second continuity theme is the assumption of an unfluctuating civilizational, cultural, and racial hierarchy (Bowden, 2009, 2014; Gong, 1984; Keal, 2003; Keene, 2002), and related depictions of the century as one of constant imperial conquest. Europe's arrogance and cultural and racial hierarchies are dated to previous turning points, such as the Enlightenment (Bowden, 2014; Zarakol, 2011), sidelining crucial mid-nineteenth-century ideational developments.[2] Or the beginnings of continuity are even earlier, as in Keene's account (2002) of a world divided in terms of civilized vs. non-civilized since the 1600s, only united in the 1914–1945 period (p. 143). The nineteenth century can also be cast as an undifferentiated century of colonial conquest. Rod Hall (1999: 214–247), for example, discusses how the new 'national sovereignty' in the nineteenth century produces expansive imperialism, but is not concerned with dating this – there is just a lot of imperialism in the century. Similarly, Osterhammel (2014: 450–461) attributes some limited importance to a *Pax Britannica*, but also gives the impression of constant, unbroken nastiness: "Everywhere and at every moment it was embroiled in rivalry with other powers" (p. 460).

One perceived continuity in the global nineteenth century we find accurate has been labeled 'Global Dualism' (e.g., Osterhammel 2014: 483–493): that the European sphere is separated from the rest of the world, with a general "shielding of European politics from extra-European quarrels" (Schroeder, 1986: 15; Keene, 2002). This creates a distinction between a European and an extra-European order, with different rules and expectations in each (Keene, 2002; Osterhammel, 2014). Global Dualism occurs initially because the Concert was specifically focused on Europe and the rest of the world was not to be subject to its great power conference management (Osterhammel, 2014: 473–475). Europeans did not take the initiative to establish a new global legal order, just spread their own, and overseas conquests were not subject to the same limits that were observed in Europe (2014: 474).[3] Nonetheless, we have new things to say about this continuity.

The IR literature which most regularly identifies a disjuncture in the nineteenth century is that focused not on peace and hegemony but on tracking the mix of powers and balancing developments (Little, 2007; Mearsheimer, 2001; Sheehan, 1996), though even here some emphasize continuity, in the face of constant balancing. In this view the nineteenth century is best understood as simply an age of balancing, and not much more need be said (Morgenthau, 1960: 178–223). Again, according to this narrative the key dates are not in the nineteenth century. Morgenthau fixes 1789 as a turning point that introduces raw power politics and then that system steadily strengthens over the century (1960: 190–192). For Mearsheimer (2001), this is most simply the era of six European powers, 1815 to 1902.

The two worlds: a bifurcated century

We challenge these continuity arguments for ignoring a crucial 1856–1869 turning point and the differences on either side of it. As to the hegemony/pax narrative, one must ask for whom was this an ordered and peaceful century? There was relative peace and stability for some, and catastrophic cultural holocaust for others. When, where, and for whom was the *Pax Britannica*? The pax perspective cares almost entirely about great power war, not colonial predations, missing the shifts in Europe that led to global imperialism. A better approach would problematize and historicize British hegemony, to see what it achieved and when. Historians (e.g. Gough, 2014) find that British hegemony was important but limited. It was predominantly maritime-based, and its main goals were to maintain open seas, suppress the slave trade, combat piracy, and open global markets, especially for British goods. Britain strived for this, but what might they have done? British influence in the world did not prevent a great disaster being visited upon the non-West, though British policy for a time was to prevent exactly that – they failed, and revised their goals (Mantena, 2010). The hegemony/pax argument downplays global conquest after 1856, except perhaps to note that it was done in an orderly fashion.

As to the continuous cultural hierarchy and conquest argument, we agree that there always was a Christian and later a European sense of superiority and a cultural hierarchy, in European eyes. But there were notable changes in this discourse and the ways that Europeans acted upon them, such that a periodization is quite useful. There are crucial developments at mid-century in the appearance of Social Darwinism and key rebellions in the colonies (India, Jamaica) that hardened European attitudes and stoked confidence about the civilizing mission and the superiority of European ways. Second, European arrogance was not necessarily globally impactful until the Sinosphere collapsed and new locales were suddenly forced to deal with intensifying Western sociocultural pressures. Relatedly, it is crucial to look at local reactions to the final linking of regional systems in the 1860s. When the world became one political space it was a highly contested one, in which global answers to issues have been constantly in dispute (Bayly, 2004; Mishra, 2013).

We agree with the claim of a persisting Global Dualism, but seek to better understand its evolution over the century. A constant Dualism obscures the different eras of Great Power tensions in Europe and changes there (see Müller chapter). Dualism was maintained by different means at different times – first by leaving British hegemony lightly in charge, later by extending great power territorial compensation norms into extra-European arenas. Also ignored is the creation of one world political system: positing a lasting split between the West and the rest does not track the great changes in that relationship, and implications for the globe's regional systems. Similarly, the balancing perspective also tends to Eurocentricity, and acknowledging a mid-century change in the European balance still neglects the other developments in the 1860s – cultural, normative, and ideational – that made that shift in the balance have the impacts it did.

Fellow travelers

We also acknowledge work of scholars in agreement with the basics of our 'two worlds' narrative, to whom we are indebted; we hope to advance their arguments still further. Portions of the realist-balancing literature notices the changes in the European balance in the 1860s, and therefore that aspect of the pivot period and what came after, if not before.[4] Second, some in the English School come close to our arguments in the dating and the historical narrative. Arguably the IR approach with the richest account of history, the English School early on cared about the wave of imperial conquests in the late nineteenth century and theorized them as an expansion of the rules of European international society out to a global international society. Hedley Bull (1984), for example, argues that the merging of regional systems into one takes place around the mid-nineteenth century, in a brief chapter entitled "The Emergence of a Universal International Society" (1984: 117–126). Indeed, among other things the English School's expansion narrative is about unfolding global political connectedness (see Buzan and Little, 2014).[5] Gong's work on the standard of civilization (1984) provides considerable detail on the incorporation into international society of countries not formally colonized (the Ottoman Empire, Japan, Siam, China), beginning around mid-century. (Though the standard itself, as manifested in international legal texts, is more a late-century phenomenon.)

Buzan and Little (2000) provide a fuller description, employing a useful distinction between political-military and economic interaction. However, they focus heavily on unit-type and the development of a state-system, dating its origins to 1500 and the emergence of modern states in Europe (2000: 243–246). Like our conceptualization, their 'modern international system' is that which achieved "global scale and geographic closure" (p. 344). Around 1850 "a full, military-political international system reached global scale, and thus geographical closure, with the defeats of China and Japan by the Western powers" (2000: 403). Still somewhat within the English School perspective, the new Buzan and Lawson book, *The Global Transformation*, fleshes this out much further, discussing changes in Western economies, technology, and new ideologies of progress that created a core-periphery dynamic and a basic economic inequality. The approximate date of 1860 is when the East-West power-flip takes place and a core–periphery model of the global system emerges.[6]

Lastly, our account also builds upon important books by Michael Doyle (1986) and Rod Hall (1999), two of IR's few accounts of the New Imperialism. Doyle's rendering of the nineteenth century (pp. 234–248) has basically the same dating and periodization as ours. Hall's landmark book is one of the best in IR at grappling with explaining origins of the New Imperialism. While occasionally cited, the arguments of these two books about history – their historical narratives for the century – are generally forgotten. Why? Because IR scholarship is not interested in periodized accounts of international relations history. (See more on this in this volume's conclusions.)

In sum, we broadly agree with the above accounts of the nineteenth century, but say more about the details of events in the pivot period and describe the international relations on either side of it as discreet, unique 'worlds' of international relations history. We have little to say about structural socioeconomic changes and debates about the causes, though the below account of the pivot is political rather than economic. Relatedly, our book is not amenable to any civilizational triumphalism, for several reasons: 'Europe' is itself a product of global exchanges (Hobson, 2004); 'European miracle' narratives tend to over-appropriate exceptionalisms (Sabaratnam, 2011; Seth, 2013); and finally, European hegemony within a single global political system did not last that long (less than 100 years? 50?) and was resisted intensely from the outset and throughout (Bayly, 2004; Husain, 1995; Mishra, 2013).

Our arguments and contributions

We do not argue that there was no colonial conquest before 1856, obviously, but that there is a qualitative difference in dynamics after that date. The final connecting of the world happens due to the breakdown of the Sinocentric system, increased great power competition in the Western Hemisphere, and overlooked early colonial expansion into Sub-Saharan Africa.[7] This integrated political-strategic system created the predatory environment that made possible crucial later developments considered watersheds of the late nineteenth century: the standard of civilization (Gong, 1984) and 'drawing the global color line' after 1890, both more fully cementing a global racial-cultural hierarchy in place (Lake and Reynolds, 2008).

The first half of the century, 1815–1856

This is the era appropriately described as the age of global *Pax Britannica*, before Britain's decline in Europe, the eclipse of their laissez-faire order model, and the unleashing of competitive imperialism. This account is difficult to locate in the IR literatures, as we have seen. Schroeder (1986) argues that there was a global British hegemony or *Pax Britannica* in this era, in part because British hegemony was not very offensive to others – they were more open and provided order for all. The years 1799–1814 made British global dominance possible. Revolutionary France failed to establish a sizable empire overseas – Egypt was conquered in 1798 but given up three years later (Fregosi, 1990). Thereafter, British hegemony was made possible by the self-limiting of France under Napoleon's 'Continental System' (Schroeder, 1986: 14). Britain refused to make concessions on colonial territory in the peace settlement of 1814–1815, and eventually the other powers agreed (p. 14). It could thus be said that the French empire disappeared, and would have a third beginning in 1830 with the invasion of Algiers (Osterhammel, 2014: 437); but even then there is not much French expansionism until after 1856. British hegemony undertook to provide an open system, with an unrivaled navy, and serve as a 'global maritime police' to fight slavery (Osterhammel, 2014: 451). The overall British operating principle was that "influence should be exerted for as long as possible and formal colonial rule be introduced only after the exhaustion of such informal options" (Osterhammel, 2014: 458).[8] In Africa in the 1830s–1850s, for example, Britain's main concern was wiping out the slave trade and hoping that a bountiful and beneficial 'legitimate trade' in other commodities would take its place (Braithwaite, 1996).

This is an era before intense global competition for territory and colonies. Much of the world was still not colonized, and Latin America was walled off by the Monroe Doctrine, which Britain cooperated with. There was some imperial expansion and contestation, certainly. The Great Game in Central Asia between Britain and Russia had already begun in the 1820s, for example. Britain fought simultaneous wars in Afghanistan and China 1838–1841 to protect India and expand trading opportunities; Britain and France were in competition at times in North Africa and the Levant by the late 1830s. But much of Asia was out of these circuits of competition, as was Africa and much of Latin America.

Chapters in the first half of our book describe and examine aspects of international relations in precisely these conditions of loose British hegemony globally, of pockets of informal empire, of cultural imperialism, but with a less intrusive hand, as different regional systems contained their own dynamics. Andrea Paras writes about the role of British missionary movements and organizations as independent and sometimes fickle non-agents of British influence, for the most part, in the decades up to the 1840s. They are promoting the famous package of 'Commerce, Christianity, and Civilization', but as a sort of cultural imperialism that fit nicely with the pre-imperial-scramble environment. She describes an important transition to British overseas interest around 1800, an explosion of missionary activity, and the ways in which this shaped British understanding of the world in the first half of the century, before the New Imperialism phase.

Our chapters also discuss the various mechanics of regional systems before the 1860s. Jeppe Mulich's chapter, which includes a case study of privateering in 1828, exemplifies the need to examine with care varying regional systems under the loose, British laissez-faire hegemony of the first half of the century. It is a study of region-construction after the Age of Revolution, in this case by Latin American republics and the disparate imperial presences in the Caribbean, when the world was still divided in colonized and sizable non-colonized spheres. The Caribbean was an arena of modest imperial rivalry, filtered through local dynamics, and also of 'imperial transience' as islands shifted from one power to another. Likewise, David Banks' chapter shows how the separateness of the Sinocentric system was maintained by specific diplomatic practices and staunch imperial Chinese resistance. However, Britain and the Europeans did press China for trade openness and other concessions, and that was vastly damaging in itself, as he documents.

Our approach also raises new issues about the European regional system, whose power dynamics were unusual and distinctive in the first half of the century. Tobias Lemke shows another side to the European regional system in his discussion of the efforts at Vienna to deal with 'the German Question' in 1814–1815 and tensions between Austria and Prussia over control of Central Europe. The issue was not ultimately taken care of and ended up bringing Europe's self-management into crisis in the 1860s. George Lawson's chapter illustrates similar themes of European separateness and informs us of the general contribution of the Concert era to the management of Europe's politics. The Concert helped create a 'de-globalized' Europe that was somewhat compartmentalized and was constitutive of the difference of the first half of the century – as he phrases it, "the Concert was something of a period piece".

We also see the ways in which regional dynamics in the first half were leading to the breakdown of first-half patterns of international relations. Lemke most directly deals with the serious tensions surrounding the German Question, which explodes in Europe's face in the 1848–1863 period. Lawson finds that three deepening tensions in Europe were undermining its settlement: the harsh repression of reform movements, the challenge of pressures for constitutionalism, and the disconnect between Europe and issues globally. Banks, of course, has a great deal to say about the stakes for the Manchu-Qing Imperial order in the breakdown of the Sinosphere. These papers are an appropriate prologue to our discussion of the second half of the century.

The second half, 1870–1914

The second half of the century gets more attention in the IR literature, as global competition takes off and especially in work on the prelude to WWI. IR scholars have noted important developments in the international system in the second half of the nineteenth century, sometimes linking them together: breakthroughs in international law, the formulation of a 'standard of civilization' for judging the non-West and legitimizing colonization, the spread of a more virulent strain of nationalism, and a New Imperialism. There is also a common tendency to focus on WWI as the endpoint and count down to it. However, this again keeps us focused on Europe, making decades of devastating imperial conquest a side event. Interesting questions remain. Going beyond Eurocentrism, what has IR said about relations in different regions of the world after 1870, when outside pressures came to impinge so harshly? How do crucial developments in these years interrelate, and is their timing and sequencing interesting? If Europe was able to insulate itself from destabilization sourced in the extra-European world, what developments inside Europe accompanied the new global competition and how were they handled? Our focus for the second half of the century addresses some of these questions. We are interested in the political and status dynamics of jockeying for power in Europe (Müller), the breakdown/penetration of regional systems (Park), and the impacts of breakdown at the regional level upon powerful and weaker regional actors (Park, Shirk). This also brings forward new aspects of the international culture of major powers, regarding status categories, legal developments, and the impact of industrialization in Europe on IR thinking after 1880 (Ashworth).

We might offer less in the way of new insights for the second half of the century, since scholars across disciplines recognize the New Imperialism, the rise of revisionist great powers, and the tensions that lead to WWI. But our periodization draws attention to some somewhat novel issues nonetheless, which encourage addressing the second half of the century as an environment unto its own. In his chapter Mark Shirk provides a glimpse at what happened on both sides of the pivot period – the sudden decision to address a problem that had been festering for decades, piracy, even a re-envisioning of that problem. The two worlds are in evidence as well. The British got along well with the Dutch and Spain, and there was empire in the region but not expansive competition – when that changed, everyone activated. The chapter by Seo-Hyun Park concerns the new competitive pressures in East Asia in the 1860s and after, alongside lingering Chinese influences, and how these alter politics inside Korea and Japan, which are left reeling and forced to adapt quickly. An odd hybrid and pluralist systemic order lasts at least until 1895, one which elicits differential responses from Japan and Korea.

Thomas Müller's chapter addresses how great power relations took place late in the century, after more new countries were joining in. He counters the narrative that says great power cooperation more or less ceased by the 1860s – it did not, but changed in circumstances and content. His chapter explores how European actors conducted their rivalries back in Europe. What did they do with new statuses like 'world power' that emerged as the great colonial expansion took place? Also grappling with the new power dynamics, the subject of Luke Ashworth's chapter is the wave of industrialization as it deepened in the 1870s and 1880s, producing a "new, two-tiered global order". His particular focus is the impact upon the thinking of major figures – Norman Angell, Henry Noel Brailsford, J.A. Hobson, Alfred Thayer Mahan, Friedrich Ratzel – in what amounts to a second founding moment for IR thought after the 'second industrial revolution'. The temporal focus is after 1870, but especially on the later thought of 1890–1904, as these thinkers came to perceive the two worlds, and developed a new appreciation for how global political economy made lesser powers subservient in new ways.

Overall, we take steps toward two worthy goals. We expand IR's traditional notion of violence in the way Robert Cox advocated long ago (1981: 134), to include imperialism – 'vertical' accounts of power and the damage done, not just the horizontal jockeying of great powers. Obviously IR's post-Coxian hierarchical and postcolonial turns do that too, but we also embrace it. Second, ours is a narrative of the linking of the different regional arenas together. Osterhammel argues that there is a disconnect in our histories of the nineteenth century: "Diplomatic history and colonial history have seldom really converged" (2014: 402). While he underestimates the literature, historical IR can certainly work to alleviate this, by showing how European power-plays implicated the world, as well as how European leaders viewed the non-European world, by understanding great power order projects and their impacts, and by recognizing the different phases in nineteenth-century history.

The pivot period

Dividing the century in two requires an account of the hinge of changes in the middle, to provide an origin story for the era of competitive imperialism and explain the fate of the British laissez-faire order before it. This section sketches out this pivot period, dating it to specific years, events, and turning points based on the conviction that timing and details are important to unpacking explanatory arguments. Our book is in one sense simply highlighting and problematizing the New Imperialism, a phenomenon commonly recognized, especially by historians (Hall, 1999; Hobsbawm, 1989; Osterhammel, 2014), but whose dating varies widely. Dating questions are not trivial, since they encapsulate disputes about political or economic origins, agentic and structural causes, and country blame.

What made the New Imperialism outburst possible? Engaging in the debate on the sources/causes of the New Imperialism is not possible here. A recent, advanced macrostructural account is the multipronged explanation of Buzan and Lawson (2015): a new mode of power, progressive ideologies, changes in state capacity. The arguments nearest our own highlight relatively sudden new 'geostrategic' competitive pressures that fueled imperial frenzies (Hall, 1999: 241) and of "competitive imperialism" (Bayly, 2004: 230), a launching of a globe-wide scramble for territory that was not necessarily materially rational, but faddish and driven by status competition. The predominant unit in the system became empire, and a culture of empire developed.

Intensifying pressures for global territorial competition caused the abandonment of a previous order, of British laissez-faire hegemony, and this was well in course by the early 1860s, such that oft-cited turning points like the Austro-Prussian War of 1866 or the Franco-Prussian War of 1871 were actually symptomatic of the aggressive behavior this new environment enabled. Larger factors making this happen include the rising strength of a global dynastic-conservative project after 1856, the eclipse of British geopolitical influence in important ways, and changes in Britain's own policies and attitudes. Looking at three periods in these years – 1856–1861, 1862–1864, and 1865–1869 – clarifies developments.

First steps, 1856–1861

The groundwork for the pivot period was laid in 1856–1861, in Europe and globally, as Britain's relatively inactive offshore balancing strategy and non-interventionism in Europe was losing out to more active and ambitious powers. Key developments were 1) a remarkable but largely unnoticed French revisionism under Napoleon III after the Crimean War, in Europe, and outside; 2) the deceptive success of British free trade ideas, precisely when the British model/order was actually in decline; and 3) scrambles for territory and power in the greater Americas sphere, and Central and East Asia, due to the American Civil War, a Russian turn to Asia, the opening of Japan, and the Second Opium War.

Britain's was still a 'cautious' colonialism in the 1850s and 1860s, explained by her penchant for laissez-faire (Go, 2011: 110–117). Chamberlain describes a theme in British policy discourse after 1846, especially among liberal factions (1988: 125): "With the triumph of free trade it became the received political wisdom to say that colonies were expensive burdens of no benefit to the mother country which should be disposed of as soon as possible." Faith in the wondrous benefits of free trade was extreme – it was a panacea for all problems, able to pull humanity to civilization, morality, and sensibility the way gravity acted physically, without the need for any other intervention (Hyam, 2002: 109–111): eliminate slavery and the slave trade, make lands productive, promote peace among all, etc. The crucial point, however, is that while predominant in British policy for some time, it was precisely this doctrine that was being undermined by 1856–1861, soon to be viewed as tested and failed and then outpaced by newly expanding colonizing activities.

Within, the British Empire was shaken by the Indian Rebellion of May 1857. The East India Company was liquidated and India annexed directly by the Crown, a huge new commitment, territorial expansion in India accelerated, and the administrative apparatus expanded. There was a parallel upswing in missionary and evangelical movements, for more proselytizing and more of a lasting presence, to spread British values and 'civilization' (Stanley, 1983; Porter, 1985); David Livingstone returned to Britain from his travels, for a year-long stay that generated excitement about African possibilities. This was a new beginning for British interest in a more permanent presence in existing or new colonial acquisitions.

Conservative forces were mobilizing in Europe and interested in games of territorial acquisition, in Europe and elsewhere. On this note, it is startling that the IR literature's accounts of the nineteenth century – aware of Germany and Japan's effects on imperialism later in the century – is oblivious to Napoleon III's expansionist adventurism in the 1856–1865 period (for a little bit, see Hall, 1999: 178–179). France had done a great deal of the land-based fighting in the Crimean War and emerged from it newly confident and assertive. This translated almost immediately into France as an aggressive new player in colonial expansion, at times with British cooperation or tacit approval, but often without. Napoleon sought to avoid scaring the British and to work with them, but British leaders were put off by his ambitious schemes (Echard, 1983: 82–84; Milza, 2007: 399–400). Also noteworthy was official learning in Russia from the outcomes of the Crimean War around the same time, and strategic revisions. As an internal report of 1856 phrased it: "Russia's future is not in Europe; it is toward Asia that Russia must look" (Volodarsky, 1983: 75).

Britain was losing its ability to shape outcomes in Europe. Britain was largely sidelined in events in the Italian crisis of 1858–1859, which were brokered by France and went in a conservative rather than Mazzinian republican one (Beales, 1961). The Italian peninsula might have ended up as a liberal republic loosely federated, like 'Germany' was until unification (also becoming very centralized in these years under Prussian control). The two major national unifications in Europe, already percolating by 1858, might have gone in a liberal-democratic direction but did not.

French adventurism penetrated every regional subsystem. In Latin America, France and Spain were coordinating to aid in the conservative fight against Liberals in the Mexican civil war (Hanna and Hanna, 1971: 24). Evidence of Napoleon 'unleashed' are his plans for putting a European monarch on a throne in Mexico, in the offing by 1858 but delayed until the US Civil War broke out (Hanna and Hanna, 1971: 28–33). This was a chance to both strike a blow against Mexican republicanism and build a bulwark against North American expansion. Another revisionist power in the Caribbean was the US under President Buchanan, elected in 1856 by courting Southern electoral support with pledges to annex Cuba and achieve "ascendancy in the Gulf of Mexico" (Kagan, 2006: 242–243).

Napoleon III also held revolutionary ideas about the Middle and Near East (Echard 1983: 168–171), wishing to eliminate the Ottoman Empire entirely and make the Mediterranean into a 'European Lake' – he felt that Islam could not coexist with European civilization. He undertook French sponsorship of construction of the Suez Canal in 1859, over British objections (Milza, 2007: 632); he had already proposed that Britain and France simply partition Egypt amongst themselves, but Palmerston rejected the idea (Hyam, 2002: 108). Then France intervened forcefully in sectarian violence Syria/Lebanon in 1860–1861, as a protector of Middle East Christians; a multilateral Control Commission monitoring the intervention had to insist that the French occupation force leave Damascus (Ridley, 1971). This was a notable contrast with British policy since the 1830s, driven by cautious balancing, to keep the Ottoman Empire together at all costs and help it to internally reform and become more liberal. The French also expanded out from Dakar into Senegal and neighboring West Africa, interested in using new lands under their protection to encourage the cultivation of cotton to replace that of the Southern US (Pomeroy, 1943). French encroachments in West Africa prompted Britain to annex Lagos in 1861 (Hyam, 2002: 105; McIntyre, 1967).

In Asia, in addition to renewed British commitment after the Indian Rebellion, one can discern a new 'Scramble for Asia,' in effect (predating the more infamous Scramble for Africa), ending the Sinocentric system and unleashing regional powers. The Crimean War's Pacific Ocean theater – the 'First Pacific War' (Grainger, 2008) – introduced global military competition there, but breakdown was also enabled by the chaos in China due to the Taiping rebellion (Bayly, 2004; Phillips, 2011). Japan broke out onto its own, becoming an ambitious revisionist power in short order. A war for control of

14 *Daniel M. Green*

Vietnam was also taking place, pitting a French-Spanish combine against local forces. And in late 1860, as the Treaty of Peking was ending the war between China, France, and Britain, Russia swooped in to take a new province south of the Amur River, obtaining the harbor of Vladivostok and "making Russia a Pacific power" (Gough, 2014: 128). In a war for control of East Asia in 1857–1861 Asians lost, and things changed drastically thereafter. This is the context for the Meiji Restoration of 1868 and all that comes after it (Suzuki, 2009). Contemporary Japanese observers were well aware of what was happening – they were "entering a world of war" (Suzuki 2005: 145–146), an apt description of the competitive new imperialism then igniting.

Finally, another element laying the groundwork for colonial competition was new Western concern and changed attitudes about non-white peoples in the rest of the world. This includes British reactions to the shock of the Indian Rebellion of 1857 (Darwin, 2011: 53–54; Hyam, 2002; Mantena, 2010), but also slave-owners in the American South. The latter's fears of changes in the Caribbean, the liberation of slaves, the growing power of blacks in Cuba and the Caribbean islands, all fed Southern expansionist interests and 'filibustering' activity (Kagan, 2006; Karp, 2016; May, 1973). These are paralleled by breakthroughs in racist ideology, J.S. Mill's influential 1859 endorsement of colonies, etc. Charles Darwin's *Origin of Species by Means of Natural Selection* in 1859 changed how people thought about the adaptability and malleability of racial characteristics, fueling skepticism about the ability of non-European peoples to catch up with whites quickly (Hobsbawm, 1989: 252–258; Hyam, 2002: 156–157; Mantena, 2010).

Dark and portentous years, perhaps, but one might counter that the 1860 Cobden-Chevalier free trade treaty between Britain and France and a general spread of free trade agreements in the years 1859–1865 was the antidote (e.g., Howe, 2007). While the British order project, reliant on free trade laissez-faireism, does have victories in the spread of free trade in Europe, this did not defuse conflicts in the European regional system at all. Indeed, there is evidence that free trade agreements were signed to dupe and placate Britain, as *Realpolitik* measures (Milza, 2007: 453–454; Marsh, 1999), not the Manchester School's utopian plan. The result globally is that by 1860–1861 a new, higher level of competition for territory in Latin America, the Caribbean, East Asia, and parts of Africa had emerged.

Conquests and power shifts, 1862–1864

The middle years see crucial changes in all the world's regions, more dramatic steps in the rise of conservative aggressive powers, and the weakening of British influence to check imperial expansion. The onset of the American Civil War in 1861 was a key enabling factor, especially in Latin America, but also the cause of a scramble for territory to replace the cotton supplies now lost (attention turned to Egypt, West Africa, India). Napoleon's plans for Mexico activated in 1862–1863, eventually implanting a new European monarch there, Archduke

Maximilian of Austria (Hanna and Hanna, 1971). Napoleon's 'Grand Design' was to recognize the Southern Confederate States, split the power of the US, make the South an ally and bulwark against Northern aggression, tear up the Monroe Doctrine, and open up all of South America to French commerce and influences, protecting and reinvigorating 'the Latin race' there (Hanna and Hanna, 1971: 58–68). In parallel, Spain undertook a 'reannexation' of the Dominican Republic as a protectorate, re-establishing control over her former colony; it was speculated that soon France would return to Haiti as well (Hauch, 1947). In West Africa, French policy had been laissez-faire commercialism like the British to this point, but now shifted to empire-building, taking territory and establishing fortress outposts (Newbury and Kanya-Forster, 1969: 255–257).

In Europe, most developments were heading in the direction of conservatism, nationalism, and monarchy rather than liberal federalist solutions. The Italian question resolved itself in 1861 with a relatively conservative, centralized, and monarchical unified state under Piedmont-Sardinia and King Vittorio Emanuele, rather than the more liberal confederation many had expected (Beales, 1961: 101–104, 138–139). We also see a weakening and exclusion of liberal movements in Germany in 1861–1862 (Clark, 2006: 510–517). The boldness of Bismarck's moves beginning in 1862 were made possible by the new possibilities in the air.

With the defeat and taming of China by both Britain and France in the war that concluded in 1860, France began territorial acquisitions in East Asia for the first time (Milza, 2007: 635–636): in 1863 France established a protectorate over Cambodia; Cochinchina was taken under control between 1862 and 1866. New Caledonia in the Pacific had already been annexed in 1860. In 1863 Russian predations on Korea began and, after decades of inactivity, Russian expansion into Central Asia resumed as well (Mahajan, 2002: 22). The 'Scramble for Asia' was accelerating.

If British influence over other European powers had a restraining impact on intra-European competition and colonial expansion, a crucial watershed came in 1864, in Austria and Prussia's confrontation with Denmark. Prime Minister Palmerston and Lord Russell tried to rescue Denmark, with diplomacy and loud denunciations, but these were ignored. The crisis devolved into a Prussian war with Denmark over the Schleswig-Holstein provinces, with Russia backing Prussia, and marked the collapse of the Western dimension of Palmerston's system in Europe, and an overall crisis of British standing. Palmerston tried to concoct a grand satisficing arrangement like the Belgian settlement of 1830, but Britain had lost its pull in Europe (Shannon, 1976: 44–45). As Parry has observed (2006: 240): "[M]oralistic hectoring looked artificial. In fact, the confusion of 1864 really marked the end of the Palmerstonian era, in which opposition to autocracy had dominated British political language." It was "a humiliating set-back for the foreign policy of Palmerston and Russell, who found themselves impotent in the face of Prussia's attack" (Jenkins, 1994: 99). Indeed: "The shock of the events of 1864 induced a kind of paralysis of will, an unwillingness to commit British policy in any positive direction for fear of further failures and humiliations. Hence there was a period of well-defined recoil from Europe. But this was an isolation not, as the Cobdenites congratulated themselves it was, of calculation, but of bewilderment, of an inability to understand why" (Shannon, 1976: 41).

Finally, the epitome of the imperial resurgence in these years was the placing of a Habsburg archduke on a new throne in Mexico in 1864.

The route is marked, 1865–1869

The final steps cascade down in 1865, a year packed with pivotal events, and after. France created the new Department of Marine and Colonies, signaling a new focus on naval capacity, to pursue colonies. While the American Civil War was a time of opportunistic imperial expansion, the end of that conflict and the victory of the anti-slavery side did not produce a new liberal moment of amity. The US did reassert itself in the Western Hemisphere, helping to drive the French and Austrians out of Mexico and taking that regional system out of imperial contention; the final step was the purchase of Alaska from Russia in 1867. But many in Britain had believed that the US would be an ally afterwards, in a future world of free trade harmony; instead the US emerged as an invigorated competitor and sometime rival to Britain (Howe, 2007: 40; Parry, 2006). High tariffs put up by the North during the war were scarcely lowered afterwards, and there was resentment of the remaining British colonies in the hemisphere (Chamberlain, 1988: 124).

In addition, 1865 saw the death of Palmerston and Cobden within weeks of each other. This was the passing of a generation in British politics, and the old laissez-faire liberal project was dying with it, replaced in Britain to some extent by conservatism, a modicum of nationalism, and new attitudes to imperial expansion. In Europe, Cobden might have been heartened by the signing of new free trade treaties in 1865, between France and Prussia and Britain and Prussia, but these were in fact largely aimed at the further aggrandizement of Prussia in excluding Austria from Germany and a preface to the Austro-Prussian War of 1866; free trade was not driving out war but enabling it (Marsh, 1999: 62–63). Napoleon III simultaneously prepared for more expansionism, visiting Algeria in 1865 (Milza, 2007: 630–632) and announcing plans to extend French influence and power 'from Tunisia to the Euphrates'. France was already establishing a presence in Tunisian politics and working with Ismail Pasha in Egypt.

Experiments in social engineering were also yielding poor results. A British Parliamentary Select Committee on Africa found that the laissez-faire model was not working. The legitimate trade and missionary activities were not naturally pushing out the slave trade, and so either Britain should give up or be more forceful and interventionist (Huzzey, 2012). October 1865 saw the infamous suppression of the rebellion in Jamaica and the ongoing 'Governor Eyre controversy' – more hardening of attitudes towards non-whites (Holt, 1971; Pitts, 2006: 150–160; Smith, 1995), which prompted some recentralization of authority back to London. The lesson gradually learned was that freed slaves could not be counted on to improve and flourish, and that racial identity might also dictate destiny (Brantlinger, 2011: 111–119).

In Africa, not technically 'scrambled' for until 1885, by 1865 the pattern of competition for territory was emerging. At the end of 1865 the new king of Belgium, Leopold, assumed the throne, and he was very keen on acquiring colonies either for himself personally or for Belgium. A Franco-British rivalry for territory in West Africa, between Dakar and Sierra Leone, also broke out in 1865 (McIntyre, 1967: 104–107). Diamonds were discovered in Orange Free State in southern Africa a year later, setting off decades of struggle for territory there.

Another turning point in Britain's shift to overseas empire was the 'Seven Weeks War' of 1866 between Prussia and Austria and the further establishment of a German great power, as more German states united with Prussia. This included the impact of the massive Prussian victory over Austria at Sadowa in July, a battle with armies in the hundreds of thousands and a front ten miles long. This shocked Britain profoundly, spreading the impression that she would likely never be a land power in Europe again (Harcourt, 1980). Bismarck's Prussia was a new power, but Bismarck was not an avid colonizer; nonetheless Germany was rising and the world was becoming a more competitive place. European pressures made other countries – Belgium, Italy, Britain, France – interested in colonial expansion and in playing the role of great power, which included having colonies.

The brief but decisive war brought profound shifts in political discourse regarding Britain's position in the world. A campaign speech by Disraeli days after Sadowa looked elsewhere for Britain's glories – "England has outgrown the continent of Europe" (Parry, 2006: 23). Disraeli also mused that Britain was now "more an Asiatic than a European power" (2006: 23). Elections produced a new Conservative Disraeli government in 1866, in power for two years and embracing new imperial adventures such as an invasion of Abyssinia in 1867. British politicians around this delicate time – dealing with expansion of the voting franchise domestically – were increasingly attracted to issues of national interest that united Britons, rather than class politics that divided them and demanded socioeconomic equality (Harcourt, 1980: 93–94). Indeed, "a new age had emerged by the later 1860s" as Disraeli initiated "a new phase of imperialism" (Harcourt, 1980: 88); "Cobden's vision of a golden age of peace and free trade had vanished by 1866" (p. 84). Instead it was commonly noted that "Britain's center of gravity had moved to Calcutta" (Harcourt, 1980: 97). Britain's self-image, global role, and old order project were changing. Free trade, if it had had any pacific impact, was abandoned in a few years, most fully after the depression of 1873.

Britain, meanwhile, also sought to shore up key parts of her existing empire. The British North American Act of 1867 created the Confederation of Canada, desired by Canadians and welcomed by Britain since it would "make the Canadians more able to resist the Americans" (Chamberlain,

1988: 131). British fear of French and Spanish expansionism had transferred to the US, now showing interest in acquiring Caribbean islands and prospecting in Central America with a view to constructing the inevitable isthmian canal (Smith, 1995: 255–257); naval and military facilities in Bermuda were massively upgraded to project power into the West Indies. Finally, the hegemony of Britain made a more resolute turn to imperialism in 1868, when in effect a lobby for colonialism and colonial interests was created, in the Royal Colonial Society (Beasley, 2005). Its motto was "United Empire" (James, 1977: 23), its purpose to work for integration of the colonies together into one giant, cohesive empire.

Global competitive tensions were ever more manifest. By 1867 Italy was already entering the nascent global colonial competition, in North and East Africa, beginning with territorial interests in Abyssinia/Eritrea (Ramm, 1944). Negotiations between Britain and Russia sought to arrange a neutral zone between the two powers in Central Asia (Mahajan, 2002: 24), but concluded in 1873 without success. Most consequentially, 1869 saw the opening of the Suez Canal (Mahajan, 2002: 25–29). Palmerston had said in the 1850s, when a French canal project was first mooted, that any such canal would lead to war with France over control of Egypt. Opening the Suez Canal changed everything. Within months the Gladstone government had set up an investigative committee to consider strategy and the availability of the Canal in the event of war. Finally, 1869 saw the publication of the highly successful book *Greater Britain*, by Sir Charles Dilke, basically a call for colonial expansion and a paean to the glorious future of the Anglo-Saxon race (James, 1977: 23).

Disraeli and his enthusiasm for empire during his premiership (1874–1880) were on the horizon. The British political right embraced imperial jingoism as a policy after 1868 (James, 1977: 23–26), and Liberals gradually leaned further in that direction. Britain was changing her attitudes to colonies and empire, catching up with the new competitive environment and abandoning, fitfully, her old laissez-faire hesitations about colonial-territorial expansion. The final climax of the new era was the Franco-Prussian War of 1870–1871, but also the rapacity of that quick and ferocious conflict was made possible by the right-nationalist developments of the previous decade. While the greatest colonial expansion was indeed after 1870, the crucial developments that made the route of territorial conquest and competitive imperialization possible took place in 1856–1869, when patterns were laid and alternatives abandoned.

The utility of a new narrative

Historical narratives are of paramount importance and powerfully shape the rest of the research agenda in many disciplines (Green, 1995), so we hope ours is similarly stimulating. While others have noticed key developments in the nineteenth century, our narrative for the century summarizes it more inclusively in global terms and hopefully will shape future scholarship. It extends our thinking about the 'modern' era of international relations into the nineteenth century, to the time in the 1860s when the world came together into one place, in the violent origins of a unified global system. This also problematizes the familiar simplifying dates of 1648 or 1945, providing an alternative to the old Westphalian state-system story and a different context for a *Pax Americana*. A new narrative raises new questions, about power and order, hegemony and hierarchy, and how they are founded and lost. One is also drawn to think of narratives generally, the different periods of the century, and possible periodizations in other subject areas. If the focus is geopolitical power competition, however, what we have come up with is the most appropriate.

We also re-ask the important questions of what the *Pax Britannica* was, when it happened, and how it evolved. After 1856 the *Pax Britannica* was increasingly challenged and geographically patchy. Some maintain it was primarily an effort to guarantee freedom of the seas (Gough, 2014), maintained by the British navy; it certainly also fought against slavery and the slave trade, especially in the years 1815–1848. This qualifies the extent of the Pax, to open seas but eventually ineffective limits on imperial expansion and the conquest of the non-West; a Pax more modest and limited in its impacts. It is also better to think of the Pax as having two eras, before and after the pivot period.[9] This sheds a different light on comparative hegemonies, their maintenance and failure, and should improve our comparative grasp of liberal projects, their features and fate.

We offer a new focus we argue warrants greater attention – the coming together of the world into one politico-military system – and provide a periodization argument to accompany it. This includes a founding set of years for the world as a single competitive political system, in which there was no hiding from that order, as had been possible before. The very possibility of a 'pivot period' also deserves attention. Others have weighed in on such periodization choices (e.g., Doyle, 1986). Osterhammel (2014: 58–59) highlights Koselleck's *Sattelzeit* of 1750–1830, when modernity is arguably born, but also claims that the 1880s and 1890s are so different that they are their own sub-era, and that indeed the era 1880–1945 could be seen as "the age of empires and imperialism" since the two world wars were essentially about empire (p. 58; citing Rosenberg 2012). Our findings support such a framing, but is IR ready to consider 1870–1945 as an age when empires are the predominant unit-type? How would this impact IR's historical narratives about sovereignty and the state-system?

Second, how do features of the two eras of the nineteenth century translate to other periods, and to the present, or do they at all? This is the continuity/discontinuity question. This raises the theme of cultures of rapacious international competition and how they are produced. Conversely, such eras may be historically specific and utterly time-bound. Realist systemic approaches have a weakness for common mechanisms and motivations across time, but have to eliminate context to do so. We should be able to see, however, that the New Imperialism and its aftermath into the 1920s and 1930s could only happen once in history – a special period, with unique features. As we now enter another era of multipolarity and rising great power hostility, what can be learnt from the past? What old norms and accepted practices made events in the nineteenth century possible but are no longer present? What controversies of the past are now resolved and no longer a source of friction and violence?

Finally, there is the wisdom of even worrying about grand historical narratives of a century or two in the first place. Is such an endeavor truly important, useful, and worthy of our academic efforts? I turn to that question in the concluding chapter.

Notes

1 Paul Schroeder (1986: 9) finds that Europe was not really the sight of a 'struggle for mastery' until 1890 or 1900; instead British hegemony globally lasts up to that point. Paul Kennedy (1989) dates British hegemony to 1885 at least.
2 Keal (2003) surveys historical and sociological treatments of European encounters with the Other, but finds that periodizations do not hold up well and that significant turning points are not in the nineteenth century (e.g., p. 66).
3 For some, this was a product of geopolitics: Russia and Britain basically declared themselves the global powers, and others were confined to Europe (Schroeder, 1992: 689; 1994). Morgenthau (1960) argues that the separateness of European stability was maintained by applying the principle of compensation globally, since there was 'so much space' for the taking.
4 Mearsheimer (2001: 88–97) discusses revisionism in Japan, Germany, and Italy and the 1860s, and has a case study of Prussia in the years 1862–1870 (though his purpose is to explain failures to balance against Prussia's rise). For Morgenthau also, 1866 is a turning point, at least for Europe (1960).
5 Though, interestingly, Adam Watson's grand English School account of the history of the international system (1992) does not take note of this turning point.
6 While we share key points, we do not address, contradict, or substantiate their argument about the details of the Global Transformation, nor engage with their 'new modernity' notion.
7 There was relatively little imperial territorial conquest in the years 1815–1856, with two exceptions: the US expansion into the interior of North America and the British East India Company's absorption of portions of India.
8 As Foreign Secretary Palmerston stated in 1847: "All we want is trade and land is not necessary for that…" (Porter, 2012: 252). How that formula would change in twenty years time!
9 This might imply that there are not two British Empires – before and after the Age of Revolution (Darwin, 1997) – but three, if the pivot period reconfigures its order principles and mission.

Bibliography

Anderson, Sheldon. (2007) Metternich, Bismarck, and the Myth of the 'Long Peace', 1815–1914. *Peace & Change* 32(3): 301–328.
Bayly, C.A. (2004) *The Birth of the Modern World, 1780–1914*. Malden: Blackwell Publishing.
Beales, Derek. (1961) *England and Italy, 1859–60*. London: Thomas Nelson and Sons.
Beasley, Edward. (2005) *Empire as the Triumph of Theory: Imperialism, Information, and the Colonial Society of 1868*. London: Routledge.

Bell, Duncan. (2014) Before the Democratic Peace: Racial Utopianism, Empire and the Abolition of War. *European Journal of International Relations* 20(3): 647–670.

Bowden, Brett. (2009) *The Empire of Civilization: The Evolution of an Imperial Idea*. Chicago: University of Chicago Press.

Bowden, Brett. (2014) To Rethink Standards of Civilization, Start with the End. *Millennium: Journal of International Studies* 42(3): 614–631.

Braithwaite, Roderick. (1996) *Palmerston and Africa*. London: British Academic Press.

Brantlinger, Patrick. (2011) *Taming Cannibals: Race and the Victorians*. Ithaca: Cornell University Press.

Bull, Hedley. (1984) The Emergence of a Universal International Society. In Hedley Bull and Adam Watson, eds., *The Expansion of International Society*. Oxford: Clarendon Press.

Buzan, Barry and George Lawson. (2013) The Global Transformation: The Nineteenth Century and the Making of Modern International Relations. *International Studies Quarterly* 57: 620–634.

Buzan, Barry and George Lawson. (2015) *The Global Transformation: History, Modernity and the Making of International Relations*. Cambridge: Cambridge University Press.

Buzan, Barry and Richard Little. (2000) *International Systems in World History: Remaking the Study of International Relations*. Oxford: Oxford University Press.

Buzan, Barry and Richard Little. (2014) The Historical Expansion of International Society. In Cornelia Navari and Daniel M. Green, eds., *Guide to the English School in International Studies*. Chichester: John Wiley & Sons.

Chamberlain, Muriel E. (1988) *Pax Britannica? British Foreign Policy, 1789–1914*. London: Longman Group.

Clark, Christopher. (2006) *Iron Kingdom: The Rise and Downfall of Prussia, 1600–1947*. Cambridge, MA: Harvard University Press.

Cox, Robert W. (1981) Social Forces, States and World Orders: Beyond International Relations Theory. *Millennium: Journal of International Studies* 10(2): 126–155.

Darwin, John. (1997) Imperialism and the Victorians: The Dynamics of Territorial Expansion. *English Historical Review* 112(447): 614–642.

Darwin, John. (2008) *After Tamerlane: The Global History of Empire since 1405*. New York: Bloomsbury Press.

Darwin, John. (2011) *The Empire Project: The Rise and Fall of the British World System, 1830–1970*. Cambridge: Cambridge University Press.

Doyle, Michael. (1986) *Empires*. Ithaca: Cornell University Press.

Echard, William E. (1983) *Napoleon III and the Concert of Europe*. Baton Rouge: Louisiana State University Press.

Fregosi, Paul. (1990) *Dreams of Empire: Napoleon and the First World War, 1792–1815*. New York: Birch Lane Press.

Gilpin, Robert. (1981) *War and Change in World Politics*. Cambridge: Cambridge University Press.

Gilpin, Robert. (1988) The Theory of Hegemonic War. *Journal of Interdisciplinary History* 18(4): 591–613.

Go, Julian. (2011) *Patterns of Empire: The British and American Empires, 1688 to the Present*. Cambridge: Cambridge University Press.

Goldstein, Joshua S. (1988) *Long Cycles: Prosperity and War in the Modern Age*. New Haven: Yale University Press.

Gough, Barry. (2014) *Pax Britannica: Ruling the Waves and Keeping the Peace before Armageddon*. Houndmills: Palgrave Macmillan.

Grainger, John D. (2008) *The First Pacific War: Britain and Russia, 1854–56*. Woodbridge: Boydell Press.
Green, William A. (1995) Periodizing World History. *History and Theory* 34(2): 99–111.
Hall, Rod. (1999) *National Collective Identity: Social Constructs and International Systems*. New York: Columbia University Press.
Hanna, Alfred J. and Kathryn A. Hanna. (1971) *Napoleon III and Mexico: American Triumph over Monarchy*. Chapel Hill: University of North Carolina Press.
Harcourt, Freda. (1980) Disraeli's Imperialism, 1866–1868: A Question of Timing. *Historical Journal* 23(1): 87–109.
Hauch, Charles C. (1947) Attitudes of Foreign Governments towards the Spanish Reoccupation of the Dominican Republic. *Hispanic American Historical Review* 27 (2): 247–268.
Hobsbawm, Eric. (1989) *The Age of Empire, 1875–1914*. New York: Vintage Books.
Hobson, John. (2004) *The Eastern Origins of Western Civilization*. Cambridge: Cambridge University Press.
Howe, Anthony. (2007) Free Trade and Global Order: The Rise and Fall of a Victorian Vision. In Duncan Bell, ed., *Victorian Visions of Global Order*. Cambridge: Cambridge University Press.
Husain, Mir Zohair. (1995) *Global Islamic Politics*. New York: HarperCollins.
Huzzey, Richard. (2012) *Freedom Burning: Anti-Slavery and Empire in Victorian Britain*. Ithaca: Cornell University Press.
Hyam, Ronald. (2002) *Britain's Imperial Century, 1815–1914: A Study of Empire and Expansion*. 3rd edition. Houndmills: Palgrave Macmillan.
James, Robert Rhodes. (1977) *The British Revolution, 1880–1939*. New York: Alfred A. Knopf.
Jenkins, T.A. (1994) *The Liberal Ascendancy, 1830–1886*. London: Macmillan.
Kagan, Robert. (2006) *Dangerous Nation: America and the World, 1600–1898*. London: Atlantic Books.
Keal, Paul. (2003) *European Conquest and the Rights of Indigenous Peoples*. Cambridge: Cambridge University Press.
Keefer, Scott Andrew. (2013) 'An Obstacle, Though Not a Barrier': The Role of International Law in Security Planning during the Pax Britannica. *International History Review* 35(5): 1031–1051.
Keene, Edward. (2002) *Beyond the Anarchical Society: Grotius, Colonialism and Order in World Politics*. Cambridge: Cambridge University Press.
Kennedy, Paul M. (1986) *The Rise and Fall of British Naval Mastery*. New York: Penguin.
Kennedy, Paul M. (1989) *The Rise and Fall of Great Powers*. New York: Random House.
Kindleberger, Charles P. (1973) *The World in Depression, 1929–1939*. Berkeley: University of California Press.
Lake, Marilyn and Henry Reynolds. (2008) *Drawing the Global Colour Line: White Men's Countries and the Question of Racial Equality*. Cambridge: Cambridge University Press.
Little, Richard. (2007) *The Balance of Power in International Relations*. Cambridge: Cambridge University Press.
Mahajan, Sneh. (2002) *British Foreign Policy, 1874–1914: The Role of India*. London: Routledge.
Mantena, Karuna. (2010) *Alibis of Empire: Henry Maine and the Ends of Liberal Imperialism*. Princeton: Princeton University Press.

Marsh, Peter T. (1999) *Bargaining on Europe: Britain and the First Common Market, 1860–1892*. New Haven: Yale University Press.
Matzke, Rebecca Berens. (2011) *Deterrence through Strength: British Naval Power and Foreign Policy under Pax Britannica*. Lincoln: University of Nebraska Press.
May, Robert E. (1973) *The Southern Dream of a Caribbean Empire*. Baton Rouge: Louisiana State University Press.
McIntyre, W. David. (1967) *The Imperial Frontier in the Tropics, 1865–75*. London: Macmillan.
Mearsheimer, John J. (2001) *The Tragedy of Great Power Politics*. New York: W.W. Norton.
Milza, Pierre. (2007) *Napoléon III*. Paris: Editions Perrin.
Mishra, Pankaj. (2013) *From the Ruins of Empire: The Revolt Against the West and the Remaking of Asia*. New York: Picador.
Mitzen, Jennifer. (2013) *Power in Concert: The Nineteenth Century Origins of Global Governance*. Chicago: University of Chicago Press.
Morgenthau, Hans J. (1960) *Politics among Nations*. 3rd edition. New York: Alfred A. Knopf.
Newbury, C.W. and A.S. Kanya-Forstner. (1969) French Policy and the Origins of the Scramble for West Africa. *Journal of African History* 10(2): 253–276.
O'Brien, Patrick K. (2002) The Pax Britannica and American Hegemony: Precedent, Antecedent or Just Another History? In Patrick K. O'Brien and Armand Clesse, eds., *Two Hegemonies: Britain 1846–1914 and the United States 1941–2001*. London and New York: Routledge.
O'Brien, Patrick K. and Geoffrey Allen Pigman. (1992) Free Trade, British Hegemony, and the International Economic Order in the Nineteenth Century. *Review of International Studies* 18(2): 89–113.
Osterhammel, Jürgen. (2014) *The Transformation of the World: A Global History of the Nineteenth Century*. Princeton: Princeton University Press.
Parry, Jonathan. (2006) *The Politics of Patriotism: English Liberalism, National Identity and Europe, 1830–1886*. Cambridge: Cambridge University Press.
Phillips, Andrew. (2011) *War, Religion and Empire: The Transformation of International Orders*. Cambridge: Cambridge University Press.
Pomeroy, Earl S. (1943) French Substitutes for American Cotton, 1861–1865. *Journal of Southern History* 9(4): 555–560.
Ramm, Agatha. (1944) Great Britain and the Planting of Italian Power in the Red Sea, 1868–1885. *English Historical Review* 59(234): 211–236.
Reus-Smit, Christian. (2016) Theory, History, and Great Transformations. *International Theory* 8(3): 422–435.
Ridley, Jasper Godwin. (1971) *Lord Palmerston*. London: Dutton.
Rosenberg, Emily S., ed. (2012) *A World Connecting: 1870–1945*. Cambridge, MA: Belknap Press.
Sabaratnam, Meera. (2011) IR in Dialogue … But Can We Change the Subjects? A Typology of Decolonising Strategies for the Study of World Politics. *Millennium: Journal of International Studies* 39(3): 781–803.
Schroeder, Paul W. (1986) The 19th-Century International System: Changes in the Structure. *World Politics* 39(1): 1–26.
Schroeder, Paul W. (1992) Did the Vienna Settlement Rest on a Balance of Power? *American Historical Review* 97(3): 683–706.
Schroeder, Paul W. (1994) *The Transformation of European Politics, 1763–1848*. Oxford: Oxford University Press.

Shannon, Richard. (1976) *The Crisis of Imperialism, 1865–1915*. London: Paladin.
Sheehan, Michael. (1996) *The Balance of Power: History and Theory*. London: Routledge.
Smith, James Patterson. (1995) Empire and Social Reform: British Liberals and the 'Civilizing Mission' in the Sugar Colonies, 1868–1874. *Albion* 27(2): 253–277.
Spiezio, K. Edward. (1990) British Hegemony and Major Power War, 1815–1939: An Empirical Test. *International Studies Quarterly* 34(2): 165–181.
Suzuki, Shogo. (2005) Japan's Socialization into Janus-Faced European International Society. *European Journal of International Relations* 11(1): 137–164.
Suzuki, Shogo. (2009) *Civilization and Empire: China and Japan's Encounter with European International Society*. London: Routledge.
Volodarsky, Mikhail. (1983) Persia and the Great Powers, 1856–1869. *Middle Eastern Studies* 19(1): 75–92.
Watson, Adam. (1992) *The Evolution of International Society*. London: Routledge.

2 Missionaries and the civilizing mission in British colonialism

Andrea Paras

Perhaps no person so completely symbolizes the fervor of the 19th-century missionary movement as the near-mythological figure of David Livingstone. In 1856, after Livingstone arrived back in Britain from his travels in southern and central Africa, his medical missionary work and his explorations had already gained him widespread celebrity. Within three days of arrival, he was fêted by the Royal Geographical Society in London, and by a welcome reception at the Freemasons Hall attended by numerous political and scientific luminaries (Ross, 2002: 110–111). Over the course of the following year, he published a bestselling book, *Missionary Travels and Researches in South Africa*, which sold more than 70,000 copies (Thorne, 1999: 64). He also embarked on a six-month speaking tour around the country, during the course of which thousands of people crowded into halls to hear him speak about his work. Even Charles Dickens, who was notoriously critical of foreign missions, wrote in his review of Livingstone's book that the missionary explorer was "as honest and courageous a man as ever lived" (Ross, 2002: 115).

Today, scholars typically view Livingstone as an icon of British imperialism. He is best known for his promotion of "commerce, Christianity, and civilization," a triad he believed could support each other in eliminating the slave trade (Nkomazana, 1998: 44–57). In December 1857, he charged a particularly enthusiastic gathering of students in Cambridge to take up missionary life, saying, "I go back to Africa to try to make an open path for commerce and Christianity; do you carry out the work which I have begun. I leave it with you" (Ross, 2002: 121). Throughout his lectures and writings, he made the classic "legitimate trade" argument current at the time, that trade for cotton produced by free African labourers would eliminate Britain's reliance on American slave-run plantations, and would, at the same time, pave the way for the introduction of Christianity into the region.

In her account of imperial culture in 19th-century England, Susan Thorne observes that David Livingstone returned to England at the apogee of the missionary movement's popularity (Thorne, 1999: 89). Indeed, the widespread interest in his missionary travels took place within a broader context of interest and involvement in foreign missions by different church denominations around the country. However, most contemporary scholarship overlooks the fact that the British missionary movement had a much quieter, gradual, and more controversial start, more than 50 years prior to Livingstone's boisterous welcome back to his home country. Furthermore, the popular mythology around Livingstone's civilizing mission belies the complex relationship between British empire-building and missionary endeavors. In the last decade of the 18th century, when the first missionary sending agencies were founded in England, they had to face much higher levels of skepticism about the need to send English men and women to faraway places in order to evangelize the non-Christian world. Nevertheless, by the time Livingstone delivered his address to the students at Cambridge, foreign missions had already become a commonplace and acceptable endeavor.

The purpose of this chapter is to explain how British foreign missions transformed from being a fringe activity amongst minority religious groups at the end of the 18th century, to becoming a feature of the laissez-faire order Britain propounded at the time – as well as one of the primary ways in which most ordinary Britons framed their understanding of and relationship with foreign places (Cox, 2004: 246). This significant shift took place relatively rapidly during the first half of the bifurcated century, and was a result of extended theological debates within Christian communities. In contrast to an assumption found in international relations scholarship that the missionary movement was driven by imperial interests, I argue that its success can be accounted for by the emergence of new theological beliefs about the obligations of Christians, as well as through contestation about religion's relationship to the civilizing mission. The seemingly irrefutable consensus about the link between "commerce and Christianity," which Livingstone so successfully advocated during his tour, had been forged through earlier debates within Christian communities about how best to implement their religious obligations to foreign peoples. The chapter argues that analyzing these debates within the religious communities of the time can help to both explain the emergence of the British missionary movement, and can provide a better understanding of how religious actors contributed to 19th-century British colonialism.

Although scholars acknowledge that missionaries played a significant role in spreading European ideas and values across the world, missionaries, as a subject of study by themselves, have largely been neglected in both historical and contemporary international relations scholarship. Hence, this chapter contributes new insights about a relatively understudied topic in IR. Furthermore, the chapter proposes that missionaries should be understood not only in religious terms, but also as political actors. I argue that understanding the origins of the missionary movement during the first half of the bifurcated century, as well as the debates and controversies within it, can provide a more complete understanding of the role of missionaries in later 19th-century colonial projects. This will require moving beyond the traditional confines of political science into an engagement with theology and missions history. I should note from the outset that this chapter's purpose is not to analyze the positive or negative impacts of the missionaries, as this has already been the subject of considerable debate (which I will review below). Rather, the more modest aim is to engage with a prior historical question: how did the missionary movement gain traction during the first half of the bifurcated 19th century, such that it was able to become an integral part of British colonial policy in the latter half?

The first part of the discussion below provides an overview of the limited attention paid to missionaries in existing international relations scholarship, and how these treatments do not account for how missionaries came to be associated with the civilizing mission. The second part provides a historical overview of the emergence of missionary agencies at the end of the 18th century, and explains the rise of the missionary movement during the opening decades of the 19th century. The third section then examines some of the controversies and divergences of opinion within the movement, with a view to explaining how the missionary and imperial agendas became increasingly integrated. The final part concludes with some reflections on the complex relationship between missionaries and colonialism in the age of the British Empire.

Missionaries and international relations

While few IR studies have focused on missionaries as the main subject of analysis, as Lankina and Getachew (2013) observe, it is "often taken for granted" that missionaries in the 19th century acted as agents of imperialism or colonial authority (104).[1] This is exemplified by Johan Galtung's (1971) comparison of the neo-imperial objectives of contemporary international organizations with the "old missionary command" to "make all peoples my disciples" in his structural analysis of center-periphery imperialism (97). More recently, Michael Doyle's (1986) sweeping study of empire identifies missionaries as simply one of the many different actors who played an integral role in 19th-century European colonial claims in Africa: "... [On] the African continent itself, explorers, officials, traders, and missionaries went about the slow business of making effective the paper annexations accredited in Berlin" (143). Doyle does little here to differentiate between these actors, even though their functions differed significantly. Accordingly, Doyle identifies three impacts of Christian missionaries in Africa: they converted, supported imperial conquests, and sustained imperial development (170). Although Doyle concedes that missionaries were not "straightforward agents of imperial expansion" (172), as some participated or supported local populations in resistance against European colonial advances, at the very least they helped popularize imperial conquest. Generally, Doyle concludes missionaries spearheaded the opening of non-Western territories by encouraging the dissemination of Christian teachings alongside the development of commerce.

In contrast to Doyle's negative assessment of missionary-led imperialism, other scholars have taken a more revisionist stance in their views. In particular, they question the assumption that the long-term effects of missionary activity were always harmful. Robert Woodberry (2006) provides an example of this line of thinking when he asserts, "[It] is time for a reevaluation of the glib assertions popular in intellectual circles today about the close connection between missionaries and colonialism, and the overwhelmingly deleterious impact of missions on nonwestern societies" (11). He goes on to assert that colonialism could have been far worse if missionaries had not been present and engaged in resistance against colonial administrations. Likewise, other scholars have analyzed the positive roles that missionaries played in promoting democratization (Lankina and Getachew, 2012), health care (Håkansson, 1998), or education (Lankina and Getachew, 2013), despite operating within a colonial context.

Related to missionaries' connections with imperialism, scholars commonly associate 19th-century missionaries with the "civilizing mission" or "white man's burden." In one of the only extended studies of missionary agencies by an IR scholar, Miwa Hirono (2008) investigates how such agencies promoted the Western civilizing mission in China during the early 20th century. Hirono defines the civilizing mission in terms of two key presuppositions: an asymmetrical image of the relationship between "civilized" and "uncivilized" peoples, and the self-proclaimed duty of the "civilized" to help the "uncivilized" (1). Although Hirono recognizes that missionaries' conceptions of civilization changed over time, with "civilization" increasingly associated with Western culture rather than Christianity in particularly, she does not explicitly interrogate the link between 19th-century missionaries and the civilizing mission (192). Likewise, Michael Barnett's (2011) exhaustive history of humanitarianism discusses how 19th-century missionaries viewed colonialism and capitalism as a means to bring civilization and Christianity to "backward" populations (although he also acknowledges how some missionaries fell out of favor with colonial administrators for their solidarity with indigenous peoples) (66–67).[2] Finally, it is particularly telling that in the index of Brett Bowden's (2009) historical analysis of the idea of civilization in international society, the entry "Missionaries" simply advises the reader, "See Civilizing missions" (298).

There are good reasons for associating missionaries with 19th-century imperialism and the civilizing mission. By the time of the Berlin Conference in 1884, European powers regarded missionaries as key actors in the civilizing process. Article 6 of the 1885 General Act of the Berlin Conference argued that European powers had the responsibility to bring the "blessings of civilization" to occupied territories, and recognized special protections for "Christian missionaries, scientists, and explorers" to this end. Nevertheless, we must remember that, by the time of the Berlin Conference, the height of the missionary movement was already in the past (Stanley, 1983), and missionaries had largely gained mainstream acceptance as Western agents for colonization. However, this was not always the case. Rather, what is missing from these accounts is an explanation of how missionaries came to be identified with the British civilizing mission in the first place. The literature reviewed above begins from the assumption that missionaries were always regarded as legitimate agents of the civilizing mission in the 19th century, and that imperialism was the driving force behind missions. Yet this assumption neglects the fact that in the last decade of the 18th century and the early decades of the 19th, most Britons regarded missionaries as radical or fringe groups, and certainly not representative of mainstream Christianity or Western civilization. Nevertheless, within approximately 50 years – and certainly by the time of Dr. Livingstone's 1857 speaking tour – missionaries had become one of the most important conduits of the civilizing mission, and one of the primary ways in which ordinary Britons gained information about the non-Western world. In other words, this shift reflects another dimension of the bifurcated century that is the subject of this volume. By the latter half of the century, missionary movements were fully integrated into British colonial policy, but during the first half they were disregarded as fringe religious radicals. None of the existing scholarship in international relations – or political science more broadly – accounts for this shift in missionaries' political identity, or for the fact that it took place relatively rapidly. The next section will turn to the first half of the bifurcated century, in order to show how theological evolution contributed to the emergence and growth of an evangelical missionary identity that became increasingly aligned with British imperial ambitions.

The rise of missionaries in Britain

In 1793, William Carey, a former shoemaker turned minister, arrived in Calcutta intent on setting up a missionary station. The year prior, he had published a widely read pamphlet (1792) about the obligation of Christians to "convert the heathens," as well as helped to found the Baptist Missionary Society, one of first agencies of its kind in Britain. If Carey expected an enthusiastic welcome, he must have been disappointed. The British East India Company banned him from their territory, and it was only years later, in 1799, that he was invited to settle in the Dutch colony of Serampore, just outside Calcutta. As Jeffrey Cox (2004) describes, the local British East India Company official – an evangelical himself – was mortified at the presence of Baptist missionaries in Company territory and viewed Carey as a "dangerous fanatic" (250). Back home, Carey and his associates were mocked by the editor of the *Edinburgh Review* for being a "little detachment of maniacs" (Twells, 2009: 144). In stark contrast with David Livingstone's enthusiastic reception in Britain not much more than a half-century later, the response to William Carey – who as early as 1887 was regarded as the father of modern missions (Brown Myers, 1887) – provides a good sense of the overall skepticism towards foreign missions in the early years of the movement. Moreover, there is no evidence that the political establishment of the time viewed missionaries as natural allies.

As Brian Stanley (1990) argues, the rise of the missionary movement – and Carey's efforts in this regard – cannot be understood without considering the theological shifts taking place during that time. Political scientists increasingly recognize the importance of accounting for religious beliefs and theology in their analyses (Fox and Sandler, 2004; Guilhot, 2010; Petito and Hatzopoulos, 2003), and this case should be no exception. Along similar lines, British colonial historian Alison Twells (2009) argues, scholars need "to understand the mission from the point of view of the missionary himself/herself and to take seriously the issue of religious faith" (19). It is to these theological issues that the discussion will now turn.

Missions historian Andrew Walls (1996) points out that the missionary movement that began to emerge in the 1790s was a child of the Evangelical Revival that had taken place in Britain and America 50 years earlier.[3] Prior to this Revival, there was, as church historian Brian Stanley (1990) similarly argues, "no consistent acceptance of the missionary obligation" by any Christian denomination (55–56). Up until this point, the main organization concerned with foreign ministry was the Society of the Propagation of the Gospel in Foreign Parts (SPG), which focused on British colonies in North America and India, and provided clergy for white colonial administrators rather than indigenous peoples (van der Veer, 2001: 35).

The rise of evangelicalism began in the 1730s with the enthusiastic outdoor revival meetings of George Whitefield and John Wesley, ministers who traveled around the English countryside and across the Atlantic to spread the gospel. These meetings were accessible to all, not only to those who had purchased a pew, and they encouraged active participation amongst congregants through popular hymn singing and watch-night services (Twells, 2009: 28). During this period of Evangelical Revival, large numbers of people turned away from the established Anglican Church towards different nonconformist denominations, including Methodist and Baptist. Part of the attraction of evangelicalism is that it developed as a reaction against the established Anglican Church, which evangelicals saw as perpetuating a superficial or stale version of religious belief. Instead, evangelicals argued for a return to a more authentic form of faith that was based on a direct knowledge of sin, a personal trust in Christ, and an emphasis on the individual's godly life (Twells, 2009: 79). Andrew Walls (1996) identifies what was unique about evangelicalism in contrast with the established tradition: "Evangelical faith is about inward religion as distinct from formal, *real* Christianity as distinct from nominal" (82).

Evangelical beliefs also entailed a rejection of the Calvinist notion of predestination, which assumed the entire course of history had already been determined by an omniscient God. Instead, evangelicals turned to the doctrine of justification by faith, which placed an emphasis on a specific conversion moment and the unfolding of personal faith in God (Porter, 2004: 32). Another important theological development was a fixation on the coming of the millennium, that is, the belief that Christ would rule the earth for a 1000-year reign. Although there was some debate about whether Christ would return before or after the millennium (most Evangelicals of the period believed the latter), all were certain that the millennium was imminent (Stanley, 1990: 74). They also believed there would be a moral and spiritual decline before it would take place, which contributed to the conviction that Christians needed to convert as many people as possible before it would occur (Stanley, 1990: 75).

Even though these shifts provided a theological basis for foreign missions, a robust missionary movement did not result immediately during the Evangelical revival. The SPG continued with its focus of providing colonial clergy, and missionary efforts were isolated to individual efforts, rather than a systematic and widespread movement. For his part, John Wesley's efforts were mostly confined to England and Scotland, although he spent a term as an SPG clergyman in Savannah, Georgia from 1736 to 1738 (Porter, 2004: 30). However, rather than inspire him to pursue missionary work abroad, his experience in North America impressed him with the hardship of trying to convert non-Western people. Several decades later, Wesley had not warmed up to the idea of foreign missions, as evident when he tried to discourage fellow Methodist Thomas Coke from pursuing an overseas mission in West Africa in 1778 (Porter, 2004: 31). In fact, the Wesleyan Methodists were latecomers to the missionary movement, as the first Methodist missionary society was not founded until 1813, approximately 20 years after the Baptists and other independent denominations had taken up the missionary cause (Twells, 2009: 30). What this demonstrates is that, as Andrew Porter (2004) observes, "the experience of religious revival and the evangelical promotion of missions are by no means necessarily connected" (28). In other words, although these theological evolutions were necessary building blocks for foreign missions, they were not sufficient in bringing about a more widespread, systematic endeavor. As Wardlaw Thompson and Arthur Johnson (1899) concluded over a century ago, the missionary enterprise for most of the 18th century, despite the evangelical revival, was a "feeble and limited" enterprise (5).

By the 1780s, however, three changes had occurred which made conditions more favourable for foreign missions. First, dedicated groups of evangelicals increasingly acknowledged that foreign missions were not likely to expand through existing institutions. The SPG, which had been founded through Parliamentary Charter and whose management was linked to the Church of England (Walls, 1996: 243), was simply too dependent on unreliable sources of state support for missions to have any major or lasting impact (Porter, 2004: 36–37). In 1784, the Northamptonshire Association of Baptist Churches issued a nation-wide call, appealing to Christians to unite in prayer to bring about the "revival of evangelical religion and the extension of the kingdom of God in the world" (Stanley, 1990: 60). One outcome of the Prayer Call was the institution of regular Monday night missionary prayer meetings in Baptist churches throughout the country. While assessing the efficacy of regular prayer is beyond the purview of this chapter, the meetings demonstrate how missionary work had become a point of focus for evangelical communities around the country.

Second, the growth of shipping and trade networks, particularly through the East India Company, as well as the well-publicized Pacific voyages of Captain James Cook, provided Britons with a greater sense of connection to foreign places and peoples (Stanley, 1990: 58; Twells, 2009: 185–186). As 19th-century missions historians Thompson and Johnson (1899) wrote, "[The] time had come when the evangelical spirit must find an outlet in the *newly-opened world abroad*' (9).[4] Alongside this, however, there was also growing criticism about Britain's place in the world, especially in relation to its overseas empire. Frequent reports of profiteering and despotism amongst British East India Company nabobs contributed to an overall impression that Britain's profits in India were founded on "corruption, greed, and tyranny" (Bowen, 2006: 15). Furthermore, the loss of the American colonies after the American Revolution led to crisis of identity, and a re-evaluation of the moral character of British overseas enterprise (Brown, 2006: 160). From the perspective of many evangelicals, the loss of the American colonies was the consequence of Britain's tyrannical rule (Thorne, 1999: 41). For evangelicals, the sense that Britain had become a nation "cold in religion," both at home and overseas, only fueled the notion that missions, both domestically and abroad, were necessary to reverse the moral decline (Hall, 2002: 87). Even further, they believed that missionary philanthropy could help to absolve the country of its wrongs (Thorne, 1999: 42).

Thirdly, underscoring the fear of spiritual decay at home and abroad was the growing popularity of the abolitionist movement. Starting in the 1760s, a number of high-profile court cases brought public scrutiny to Britain's involvement in the trans-Atlantic slave trade. Abolitionists pointed to Britain's complicity in slavery as further evidence of moral decay (Pybus, 2007: 111–112). Furthermore, many high-profile abolitionist leaders were well-known figures in evangelical circles, including Granville Sharp, a self-taught lawyer who had brought the first anti-slavery case to the courts in 1765, and William Wilberforce, the famous abolitionist MP (Porter, 2004: 40–41). In fact, Sharp was appointed honorary chair of the Society for Effecting the Abolition of the Slave Trade after its founding in 1787. Indeed, two failed attempts to set up colonies for freed slaves from Nova Scotia on the coast of West Africa (the first of which was arranged by Sharp) highlighted the importance of establishing institutions that were solely devoted to promoting the missionary cause, rather than assuming that missionary work could piggy-back on other initiatives (Porter, 2004: 45–48). In 1794, Melville Horne, one of the ministers involved in the second attempt in Sierra Leone, published a series of letters urging "liberal Churchman and conscientious Dissenters, pious Calvinists and pious Arminians" to found an interdenominational missionary society (Stanley, 1990: 56). Horne argued that missionary associations needed to be distinct from any commercial interests, and that they should keep their distance from the state (Porter, 2004: 48–49). In other words, what was needed to put evangelical theology into practice were new institutions suited to the purpose.

It was in this context that William Carey published his pamphlet in 1792, in which he argued that Christians had a religious obligation to spread the Gospel worldwide, and work towards the "conversion of the heathens" (Carey, 1792). Carey (1792) makes his case first by arguing that Jesus' command to "teach all nations" still applied to British Christians (7), second by implying that Carey's contemporaries were the direct missionary heirs of the original twelve apostles (14–37), and third by refuting several counter-arguments about potential "impediments" to the missionary enterprise (67–76). One of Carey's main argumentative strategies was to include more than 20 pages of data tables about the numbers of religious adherents worldwide. The aim of this quantitative data was to impress his readers with Christianity's successes in Europe (notwithstanding the worrying numbers of "papists" around the Mediterranean), and to highlight its absence in the rest of the world, signified by column after column of "Mahometans" and "Pagans" in Asia, Africa, and America (Carey, 1792: 39–61). The use of data tables in this manner puts a quasi-scientific spin on his argument by providing numbers as irrefutable evidence, as well as paints a stark image of a globe that remained mostly unevangelized. Carey (1792) concludes the pamphlet by drawing on the model of a trading company to suggest the formation of a Baptist Society of "serious Christians, ministers, and private persons," who would work together to identify and support potential foreign missionaries (82).

While the idea of a voluntary society does not seem radical by today's standards, Andrew Walls (1996) points out the novelty of the argument: the average 18th-century parishioner would only have experienced religious activities through the structure of regular parish churches. One might argue that Carey was simply imitating the newly founded abolitionist societies, and, indeed, political scientists often point to the abolitionist societies as early examples of organized activism (Crawford, 2002; Keck and Sikkink, 1998). However, at the time of Carey's call to action, the abolitionist movement was also in its infancy, so it was not necessarily available to would-be missionaries as a model for action. Even though Carey's argument in favor of forming voluntary missionary associations was unprecedented, his readers took up the call quickly, with the Baptist Missionary Society (BMS) founded later the same year in Kettering. A wave of new missionary societies followed through the remainder of the decade. The ecumenical founders of the London Missionary Society (LMS) in 1795 were particularly influenced by Melville Horne's argument in favor of a non-denominational missionary organization (Porter, 2004: 49), in contrast with Carey's emphasis on the society's need for denominational affiliation (Carey, 1792: 84). The Edinburgh and Glasgow Missionary Societies were founded in 1796 (Porter, 2004: 40), and a group of evangelical Anglicans broke away from the LMS to form the Society for Missions to Africa and the East in 1799 (known as the Church Missionary Society from 1812) (Thorne, 1999: 24).

While the theological foundations and institutional structures for supporting foreign missions were in place by the beginning of the 19th century, this did not mean that mainstream consensus existed in Britain about the need for foreign missions, or that foreign missions had become associated the British imperial enterprise. As has already been mentioned above, Carey's work in Bengal was the subject of criticism and ridicule for several years. Despite the rapid formation of the voluntary missionary agencies in the 1790s, the work got off to a slow start. The missionary societies' annual incomes for their first 20 years of existence were low; donations were inconsistent and unreliable

(Porter, 2004: 55–56). Furthermore, volunteers were equally as difficult to recruit, and many of the missionaries that took up foreign posts either abandoned the calling within a few years or succumbed to illness (Porter, 2004: 56–58; Thorne, 1999: 60–61; Twells, 2009: 36–37; Walls, 1996: 166–171).

Furthermore, there was disagreement about the appropriate scope of missionary activity. The original missionary societies were primarily motivated by a religious duty to convert, but they were subject to criticism about the extent to which they should be involved in other more earthly endeavors, such as promoting commerce or engaging in philanthropic activities in addition to conversion. The lack of consensus about the role of missionary agencies indicates that there was not necessarily a "natural and harmonious alliance" between commerce and Christianity, as has been suggested by Brian Stanley (1983: 72). Indeed, Porter refutes this suggestion by demonstrating how, at the time of their founding, the original missionary societies were a long way from identifying with the mantra of "commerce, Christianity, and civilization" that was so widely accepted by the time of Livingstone (1985: 601). The next section of the paper will turn to a discussion of the debates that took place in the first decades of the 19th century, with a view to understanding how Christianity and the civilizing mission became increasingly linked in the minds of both missionaries and colonial administrators.

Bringing together Christianity with the civilizing mission

> The object of our Redeemer's visit to our world was not to teach men the arts and sciences, not to instruct them in letters, not to introduce the reign of philosophy, not to break the yoke of civil tyranny, nor to promulgate the best theory of human government ... No, my brethren, there is but one object in the universe, which, according to all the ideas we can entertain, is sufficiently dignified to justify the humiliation of the Son of God, and that is, the salvation of the human soul.
>
> (Angell James, 1907: 86)

So spoke the Reverend John Angell James in a sermon given before the members of the London Missionary Society in 1819. The sermon contained a pointed reminder to its listeners that the primary purpose of foreign missions was not the spread of commerce, or bringing the so-called benefits of Western civilization: it was eternal salvation of the soul. The Reverend's sermon goes on to assert that the benefit of salvation was available to all people – even those in a so-called "savage state" – and, moreover, that Christianity was "strictly and essentially a civilizing process" (Angell James, 1907: 92). In other words, civilization could not be properly established without Christianity, but Christianity would undoubtedly lead to civilization. What is important to note for the purposes of the present discussion is how the spiritual goals of conversion were kept distinct from the more earthly goals of material progress, with emphasis placed on the former rather than the latter.

British imperial historian Susan Thorne (1999) identifies a general tendency of missionary discourse to dismiss the merits of the civilizing mission during its first quarter century (77). Part of the reason for this, as Thorne explains, is that the evangelical missionary movement was, in its formative years, a middle-class phenomenon, which enabled evangelicals to position themselves in relations to the Anglican establishment above and the laboring classes below (79). In rejecting civilization over conversion, the missionaries and their supporters also directed their opposition to the official classes who dominated the Church of England and the political establishment. Advocates of missions saw themselves as pursuing a more egalitarian approach, insofar as they believed that salvation of the soul was accessible to "the whole family of man," whereas civilization contained the trappings of a particular class or culture (Thorne, 1999: 75). Similarly, Porter argues that the missionary agencies viewed civilization as much broader than mere commerce, and that both were clearly distinguishable from Christianity (Porter, 1985: 601).

The Reverend James' firm convictions notwithstanding, there were nevertheless other Christians who believed that civilization and commerce should be prioritized over conversion. For instance, in 1817, Richard Watson, the bishop of Llandaff, expected that "India will be Christianized by the government of Great Britain" through science and commerce, rather than through the efforts of missionaries (Porter, 1985: 600). Similarly, the first Anglican Bishop in Calcutta, Thomas Middleton, argued that there was enough work to do "in school, barracks, hospitals and prisons ... without interfering with any species of superstition" (Cox, 2004: 249). The Quaker doctor Thomas Hodgkin, who would later found the Aborigines' Protection Society (APS), also criticized missionaries in his 1818 "Essay on the Promotion of Civilization" for their efforts to convert "uncivilized nations," since "illiterate, uneducated savages would not be able to appreciate the benefits of Christianity" (Laidlaw, 2007: 139). Instead, Hodgkin argued that material humanitarian concerns should prevail over spiritual ones – although he tried to sidestep any criticism of this position by admitting that both were religious duties.

Despite the initial separation between Christianity on the one side and the civilizing mission on the other, they began to merge as the missionary movement gained greater momentum. Partly this was due to foreign missions' expansion alongside the growth of the middle class, which pursued a strong program of moral reform both at home and abroad in the first half of the 19th century. As Alison Twells (2009) argues:

> [The] networks and technologies of the civilizing mission gave shape to middle-class identity and culture, enabling the emergence of a 'social' sphere of cultural intervention and facilitating middle-class claims to greater power and influence founded on leadership of a global civilizing project.
>
> (3)

The missionary societies provided the institutional infrastructure around which middle-class people could organize themselves into a national network (Thorne 1999: 72). In turn, support for foreign missions societies became a source of collective identity for the mostly middle-class people who made up evangelical congregations. In a similar vein, Thorne (1999) writes that the "missionary spirit" was regarded as the characteristic feature of religious piety with which the middle-class was widely associated (55). Furthermore, as Thorne writes, these evangelicals were able to re-cast the meaning of civilization in terms that were consistent with their own religious values, so that conversion and civilization became mutually supporting goals, although the former underpinned the latter, and any distinction between them became less apparent (Thorne, 1999: 76).[5] Because religious piety was a prerequisite of civilized habits, conversion would necessarily lead to the abolition of "savage" cultural practices, such as sati, idolatry, human sacrifice, or cannibalism (Twells, 2009: 49).

By the 1830s, missionaries had gone mainstream. In 1813, the British East India Company had agreed to allow missionaries to operate in India. By this time, however, even the Company had recognized the potential usefulness of collaboration with missionaries, as demonstrated by its appointment of William Carey as Professor of Oriental Languages in their college at Fort William in 1801 to help train imperial civil servants. Elsewhere, the revival of anti-slavery sentiment during the 1820s also led to enthusiasm for missions, particularly in the West Indies (Twells, 2009: 88, 310) as the shared abolitionist and missionary networks sought to engage in social reform projects amongst slaves and former slaves (Stanley, 1983: 77). Foreign missions increasingly became an important part of the collective imaginary, as missionaries returned home to speaking tours in churches and missionary pamphlets became a popular literary genre. As Catherine Hall (2002) writes, the "missionary public" was one of the main contributors to the British public sphere of the 19th century (292). Beyond this, the missionaries became the primary mediators between a growing middle-class British public and the foreign places to which they traveled.

Nevertheless, missionary societies remained wary of potential infringements or even cooptation of their activities by colonial administrators, as was demonstrated by the controversy that erupted within the LMS after the British government offered to fund the society's education efforts amongst former slaves (Rutz, 2006). Porter's (2004) revisionist history concludes that there was only ever a tenuous compatibility between missions and empire: "By and large most missionaries did not want to be imperial propagandists and colonial rulers, any more than they intended to be consistent or uncritical supporters of capitalist enterprise" (323). Porter goes on to insist that missionaries could not avoid empire, but they did try to keep it in its place (330).[6] While taking Porter's objections into account, it is impossible to avoid the fact that, at the very least, the missionary societies benefited indirectly from Britain's interest in promoting civilization in the first half of the century, as "the newly-opened world abroad" entered evermore into the consciousness of the British public.

The full acceptance of missionaries as legitimate agents of empire can be demonstrated by the Report submitted by the Parliamentary Select Committee on Aborigines for 1837, which was chaired by the abolitionist Thomas Fowell Buxton. The committee had been set up to determine what responsibility Great Britain held towards the

> NATIVE INHABITANTS of Countries where BRITISH SETTLEMENTS are made, and to the neighbouring Tribes, in order to secure to them the spread of Civilization among them, and to lead them to the peaceful and voluntary reception of the Christian Religion.
> (Select Committee on Aborigines, 1837: 2)

The opening pages of the Committee Report acknowledge that the policies of Britain had already "sacrificed the lives of many thousands" (3), and go on to consider what measures could be taken to reverse the negative consequences of European expansion. The secretaries of the three principal missionary societies, the CMS, the LMS, and the Wesleyan Methodist Missionary Society, appeared before the Committee to provide evidence. All three unanimously agreed that "the effect of European intercourse has been, upon the whole, a calamity on the heathen and savage nations," which has tended to "prevent the spread of civilization, education, commerce and Christianity" (Select Committee on Aborigines, 1837: 74). The Committee accepted the evidence of its missionary witnesses, and the Report concludes that the most effective way to reverse these negative consequences of imperial growth, and to "[make] such nations desirable neighbours, is the [sic] giving them Christian instruction" (74). Among the recommendations that the Committee made was to limit interactions between "uncivilized races" and their more "cultivated neighbours," with the exception of missionaries, who should be encouraged to pursue "moral and religious improvement" along with "social and political improvement of the tribes" (80–81).

Thus, in 1837, a mere 45 years after the founding of the BMS by Willian Carey, missionaries had gone from a minority group regarded as religious fanatics to full – albeit sometimes reluctant – partners in the British imperial enterprise. Even more remarkably, the missionaries' convictions that religious instruction and conversion should be a central aspect of the civilizing mission became widely accepted amongst the middle-class public and up to the highest levels of British Parliament. The salvation of souls was not only an imperative of individual religious faith, but by the middle of the century, Christianity had become an integral part of Britain's foreign policy of promoting the civilizing mission in its empire.

The irony is that, by the pivot period in the middle of the century, missionary organizations again made efforts to disassociate themselves from imperial trade policy and the promotion of commerce, particularly in the years after Livingstone's famous speaking tour in 1857. Livingstone's much-vaunted expedition up the Zambesi River to create new avenues for trade in Central Africa collapsed in failure and ignominy in 1864 (Porter, 1985: 618), and expanded trade in India and China through the 1860s failed to yield significant benefits for missionary organizations (Stanley, 1983: 91). In light of these developments, many missionary organizations increasingly thought it best to "conceive of the missionary task in terms of evangelism pure and simple" (Stanley, 1983: 92). Thus, even though many international relations scholars have identified the triad of "commerce, Christianity, and civilization" as one of the defining features of 19th-century colonialism, the reality is that the association between these three objectives was much more contentious and short-lived than is generally acknowledged. Nevertheless, even though many missionary organizations later attempted to retreat from their imperial affiliations, by the second half of the bifurcated century colonial ambitions had already acquired momentum and moral legitimacy through their associations with the missionary enterprise.

Missionaries and the age of empire

The international relations scholar who seeks to explain the importance of missionaries in the 19th century faces what Naeem Inayatullah and David Blaney have identified as the "condemnation imperative: an eagerness to condemn an act ... before one has tried to explain or understand them" (Inayatullah and Blaney, 2015: 889). In the case of the British Empire and missions, there is often a temptation to condemn the missionaries for their role in perpetuating British colonialism without trying to understand them as a political phenomenon. Without denying the problematic imperial legacy of missionaries or their ethnocentrism, one objective of this chapter has been to provide a more nuanced understanding of the politics behind the 19th-century missionary phenomenon, specifically by analyzing how missionaries emerged as legitimate political actors during the first half of the bifurcated century. Such a goal requires one to take theology seriously and to try to understand the missionaries in terms they would have understood themselves.

When sorting through the historiography of the British Empire and missions, one has the challenging task of mediating between two competing accounts. On the one side, missions historians tend to privilege theology over empire, and argue that missionaries were driven by the desire to bring spiritual liberation, rather than by any loyalty to British imperial interests. On the other side, even when imperial historians acknowledge the importance of taking theology seriously, they tend to emphasize the emergence of a national imperial identity and overseas colonial interests. The missions historians accuse the imperial historians of overplaying missionaries' commitment to empire, while the latter accuse the former of being missionary apologists (Stanley, 1990: 11–13). In order to focus on the task at hand, the present paper has attempted to avoid falling into either of these two positions. On the one hand, I have acknowledged the central role of theology in the formation of British imperial interests, while on the other, I have avoided attributing imperial ambitions to missionaries where they did not necessarily exist.

Existing accounts of missionaries in international relations scholarship have tended to follow the lead of imperial historians, in that they assume that there is a strong connection between foreign missions and the civilizing mission. This is not surprising considering the general neglect of religion in the discipline. Nevertheless, the result of the focus on imperial history (as opposed to missions history) is that international relations scholars have overlooked the theological changes that led missionaries to occupy such a central role in the first place. This is the equivalent to writing about the abolition of the slave trade without trying first to understand how advocacy networks could successfully argue that slavery was morally reprehensible (Keck and Sikkink, 1998), or the prohibition of chemical weapons without first looking to the long history that explains how they eventually became taboo (Price, 1997). In other words, looking at any end result only tells a part of the story, and therefore provides an incomplete understanding of the political process that led to the result. The consequence of this blind spot in international relations vis-à-vis missionaries is that scholars have assumed that British imperial interests drove the rise of missionaries, insofar as missionaries were an inevitable agent of the civilizing mission. Instead, this paper provides an alternative perspective, arguing that imperialism alone cannot account for the emergence of the missionary movement. Rather, I have shown that the missionary movement became possible only after theological changes conferred legitimacy on missionary agencies. Furthermore, for the most part, missionaries consistently viewed conversion as their primary goal, even if they admitted that civilization was an inevitable by-product. In other words, although religious conversion eventually came to be regarded as one of the objectives of British imperialism, imperialism by itself was not necessarily a goal of foreign missions.

In order to understand the emergence of what Catherine Hall (2002) calls the "missionary public" (292) during the first half of the bifurcated century, it is necessary to turn to the history of ideas. The 18th-century evangelical revival provided the theological foundations for the new missionary societies of the 1790, which believed that they had a religious obligation to work towards the global spread of Christianity. Missionaries, like their abolitionist contemporaries, only gained broader acceptance after their theological beliefs gained legitimacy through a process of contestation and activism. The growing strength of the missionary movement by the 1830s then helped to give content to the moral obligations of British imperialists. As such, this paper has also demonstrated that missionaries should be regarded – alongside the abolitionists – as early examples of transnational religious activists.

Missionaries' belief in the importance of conversion provided impetus to British imperialism, despite the fact that the missionary agencies were often wary of their connections to the colonial cause. In this regard, 19th-century missionary agencies have much in common with contemporary faith-based organizations that must navigate the ill-defined boundaries between religious missions and secular development.[7] This discussion demonstrates how the blurriness of such distinctions has been a feature of missionary work ever since its beginnings. Even the great missionary David Livingstone decided to renounce his affiliation with the LMS after he had gained support from the British government for his expedition up the Zambesi. Although the officers of the LMS were sorry to lose their popular figurehead, they were not willing to support any further "adventures," which they considered distractions from their primary mandate of conversion (Ross, 2002: 117). As for Livingstone, his friends advised him to play down his break with the LMS, as people might think he was giving up on missionary work (Ross, 2002: 120). Livingstone himself did not see any contradiction between his religious commitments and his objectives of furthering economic development. He wrote:

> My views of what is missionary duty are not so contracted as those whose ideal is a dumpy sort of man with a Bible under his arm. I have labored in bricks and mortar, at the forge and at the carpenter's bench, as well as in preaching and in medical practice … [Am] I to hide the light under a bushel, merely because some will consider it not sufficiently, or even at all, *missionary*?
> (Ross, 2002: 122–123)

In the end, the distinction did not matter so much, as both sides – the missionary agencies and his government backers – got to profit from their association with him. Likewise, as British imperialism proceeded during the second half of the bifurcated century, the missionary agencies benefited – protestations to the contrary – from the expansion of the Empire. At the same time, European colonialism (as exemplified by the 1885 Berlin Act) was given moral legitimacy through its association with the moral obligation to convert. Livingstone has entered the annals of history as the iconic missionary, but perhaps the reasons for this have been misplaced. He is exemplary not so much for his promotion of "commerce, Christianity, and civilization" as for the fact that even he had to negotiate the politics of what it meant to be a missionary in the age of Empire.

Notes

1 Similarly, Geraldine Forbes describes female missionaries in India as the "helpmates of the imperialists" (1986: WS8).
2 In contrast with Barnett's account, Peter Stamatov's (2013) more recent book on the origins of global humanitarianism does not contain any discussion of 19th-century missionaries, although the book contains extensive discussions of the role of religious reformers in pro-indigenous advocacy in the Iberian empire and the British abolitionist movement.
3 In America, this period of Evangelical Revival is known as the Great Awakening.
4 My emphasis.
5 Along similar lines, Peter van der Veer writes: "In mainstream evangelicalism, religious enthusiasm was channeled into public activity spreading middle-class values over the larger population" (van der Veer, 2001: 36).
6 Ibid., 330.
7 I have discussed the blurriness of these boundaries in the contemporary context elsewhere (Paras, 2012; Paras 2014).

References

Angell James, John. 1907. "The Attraction of the Cross." In *The Highway of Mission Thought: Eight of the Greatest Discourses on Missions*, edited by T.B. Ray. Nashville: Sunday School Board Southern Baptist Convention.

Barnett, Michael. 2011. *Empire of Humanity: A History of Humanitarianism*. Ithaca: Cornell University Press.

"General Act of the Berlin Conference on West Africa, 26 February 1885." http://africanhistory.about.com/od/eracolonialism/l/bl-BerlinAct1885.htm. ThoughtCo. Accessed on January 24, 2015.

Bowden, Brett. 2009. *The Empire of Civilization: The Evolution of an Imperial Idea*. Chicago: University of Chicago Press.

Bowen, H.V. 2006. *The Business of Empire: The East India Company and Imperial Britain, 1756–1833*. Cambridge: Cambridge University Press.

Brown, Christopher Leslie. 2006. *Moral Capital: Foundations of British Abolitionism*. Chapel Hill: University of North Carolina Press.

Brown Myers, John. 1887. *William Carey: The Shoemaker Who Became 'The Father and Founder of Modern Missions'*. New York: Revell.

Carey, William. 1792. *An Enquiry into the Obligations of Christians to Use Means for the Conversion of the Heathens*. Leicester.

Cox, Jeffrey. 2004. "Were Victorian Nonconformists the Worst Imperialists of All?" *Victorian Studies* 46(2): 243–255.

Crawford, Neta. 2002. *Argument and Change in World Politics: Ethics, Decolonization, and Humanitarian Intervention*. Cambridge: Cambridge University Press.

Doyle, Michael W. 1986. *Empires*. Ithaca and London: Cornell University Press.

Forbes, Geraldine. 1986. "In Search of the 'Pure Heathen': Missionary Women in Nineteenth Century India." *Economic and Political Weekly* 21(17): WS2–WS8.

Fox, Jonathan, and Shmuel Sandler. 2004. *Bringing Religion into International Relations*. New York: Palgrave Macmillan.

Galtung, Johan. 1971. "A Structural Theory of Imperialism." *Journal of Peace Research* 8(2): 81–117.

Guilhot, Nicolas. 2010. "American Katechon: When Political Theology Became International Relations Theory." *Constellations* 17(2): 224–253.

Håkansson, N. Thomas. 1998. "Pagan Practices and the Death of Children: German Colonial Missionaries and Child Health Care in South Pare, Tanzania." *World Development* 26(9): 1763–1772.

Hall, Catherine. 2002. *Civilising Subjects: Metropole and Colony in the English Imagination, 1830–1867*. Chicago: Chicago University Press.

Inayatullah, Naeem, and David Blaney. 2015. "A Problem with Levels: How to Engage a Diverse IPE." *Contexto Internacional* 37(3): 889–911.

Keck, Margaret, and Kathryn Sikkink. 1998. *Activists beyond Borders: Advocacy Networks in International Politics*. Ithaca: Cornell University Press.

Laidlaw, Zoë. 2007. "Heathens, Slaves and Aborigines: Thomas Hodgin's Critique of Missions and Antislavery." *History Workshop Journal* 64(1): 133–161.

Lankina, Tomila, and Lullit Getachew. 2012. "Mission or Empire, Word or Sword? The Human Capital Legacy in Postcolonial Democratic Development." *American Journal of Political Science* 56(2): 465–483.

Lankina, Tomila, and Lullit Getachew. 2013. "Competitive Religious Entrepreneurs: Christian Missionaries and Female Education in Colonial and Post-Colonial India." *British Journal of Political Science* 43(1): 103–131.

Nkomazana, Fidelis. 1998. "Livingstone's Ideas of Christianity, Commerce, and Civilization." *Pula: Botswana Journal of African Studies* 12(1&2): 44–57.

Paras, Andrea. 2012. "CIDA's secular fiction and Canadian faith-based organisations." *Canadian Journal of Development Studies* 33(2): 231–249.

Paras, Andrea. 2014. "Between Missions and Development: Christian NGOs in the Canadian Development Sector." *Canadian Journal of Development Studies* 35(3): 439–457.

Petito, Fabio, and Pavlos Hatzopoulos, eds. 2003. *Religion in International Relations: The Return from Exile.* New York: Palgrave Macmillan.

Porter, Andrew. 1985. "Commerce and Christianity: The Rise and Fall of a Nineteenth-Century Missionary Slogan." *The Historical Journal* 28(3): 597–621.

Porter, Andrew. 2004. *Religion versus Empire? British Protestant Missionaries and Overseas Expansion, 1700–1914.* Manchester: Manchester University Press.

Price, Richard M. 1997. *The Chemical Weapons Taboo.* Ithaca: Cornell University Press.

Pybus, Cassandra. 2007. "'A Less Favourable Specimen': The Abolitionist Response to Self-Emancipated Slaves in Sierra Leone, 1793–1808." In *The British Slave Trade: Abolition, Parliament and People*, edited by Stephen Farrell, Melanie Unwin, and James Walvin. Edinburgh: Edinburgh University Press.

Ross, Andrew. 2002. *David Livingstone: Mission and Empire.* London: Hambledon and London.

Rutz, Michael A. 2006. "The Problems of Church and State: Dissenting Politics and the London Missionary Society in Britain." *Journal of Church and State* 48(2): 379–398.

Select Committee on Aborigines. 1837. *Report from the Select Committee on Aborigines (British Settlements) With the Minutes of Evidence, Appendix, and Index.* [Report].

Stamatov, Peter. 2013. *The Origins of Global Humanitarianism: Religion, Empires, and Advocacy.* Cambridge: Cambridge University Press.

Stanley, Brian. 1983. "'Commerce and Christianity': Providence Theory, the Missionary Movement, and the Imperialism of Free Trade, 1842–1860." *The Historical Journal* 26(1): 71–94.

Stanley, Brian. 1990. *The Bible and the Flag: Protestant Missions and British Imperialism in the Nineteenth and Twentieth Centuries.* Leicester: Apollos.

Thompson, R. Wardlaw, and Arthur N. Johnson. 1899. *British Foreign Missions, 1837–1897.* London: Blackie & Son, Limited.

Thorne, Susan. 1999. *Congregational Missions and the Making of an Imperial Culture in Nineteenth-Century England.* Stanford: Stanford University Press.

Twells, Alison. 2009. *The Civilizing Mission and the English Middle Class, 1792–1850.* New York: Palgrave Macmillan.

van der Veer, Peter. 2001. *Imperial Encounters: Religion and Modernity in India and Britain.* Princeton and Oxford: Princeton University Press.

Walls, Andrew F. 1996. *The Missionary Movement in Christian History: Studies in the Transmission of Faith.* Maryknoll, NY: Orbis Books.

Woodberry, Robert D. 2006. "Re-claiming the M-Word: The Legacy of Missions in Nonwestern Societies." *The Review of Faith and International Affairs* 4(1): 3–12.

3 Republican privateering

Local networks and political order in the western Atlantic

Jeppe Mulich

Introduction

While colonial empires dominated the shaping of regional and global order in the nineteenth century, the western Atlantic witnessed an early move towards the fashioning of a postcolonial, albeit not a post-imperial, order (Buzan and Lawson, 2015: 127–170; Osterhammel, 2014: 392–467; Mulich, 2016). A few decades after a bloody civil war had disrupted the British Empire and the Thirteen Colonies had won their independence, a different kind of revolutionary movement swept through the region. These revolutionary currents hit both the Spanish and the Portuguese Americas and led to prolonged struggles for independence in the first decades of the nineteenth century. This was a particularly multifaceted struggle, however, and as it became clear that Lisbon and Madrid would not be able to win back their erstwhile colonies by military force alone, a different kind of battle played out over international recognition. The claims to sovereignty made by Latin American leaders would be key in shaping the new political order of the western hemisphere, and the success or failure of the various emerging polities had long-lasting legacies. No borders were set in stone in the revolutionary decades of the 1810s and 1820s and political skirmishes between individual postcolonial polities were frequent, such as those within the United Provinces of Río de la Plata (Benton and Mulich, 2015: 158–159; Prado, 2015). The theater in which claims to sovereignty were made and battles over independence fought was not just the European one, but also the greater Caribbean region. Here the revolutionary entrepreneurs of Latin America operated in a complex space of intercolonial politics and overlapping sovereignties, in which regional actors and networks were more than willing to engage with and profit from the continued struggles for recognition.

The present chapter is about a certain legal and political strategy, the issuing of letters of marque in order to seek interstate recognition, as employed by political entrepreneurs in the western Atlantic. It tells the story of how this particular strategy of recognition, one amongst many others used by early nineteenth-century revolutionary leaders, was co-opted by existing regional networks of opportunistic Caribbean and American traders and adventurers for their own ends, while nonetheless still serving its original purpose.

Privateering in the greater Caribbean presents a particularly interesting case of commerce, law, and international politics coming together. It also illuminates some of the ways in which illicit underground networks of the Caribbean became entangled with revolutionary movements of the Spanish and Portuguese Americas, and how interactions and strategies in one region spilled into another, altering their meaning and content in the process.

Following the end of the Napoleonic Wars, and alongside the growing strength of Latin American independence movements, the Caribbean region witnessed a widespread return of both piracy and privateering in the 1810s and 1820s. This new wave of maritime violence was in many ways different from earlier periods of sea robbery. Its practitioners operated in an increasingly connected world of cross-colonial networks. Sailing under the flags of Buenos Aires, Venezuela, and Gran Colombia, these new privateers used, and were in turn themselves used by, a new breed of political entrepreneurs and self-declared sovereign states. In order to analyze the dynamics of this relationship and document the transformation of these practices, the chapter focuses on a particularly revealing set of court cases from the late 1820s concerning the schooner *Las Damas Argentinas* and her unfortunate crew. When one crewmember, Jean Jayet de Beaupré, was arrested on the Danish island of St. Thomas a complicated web began to unravel, spanning from Latin American revolutionaries to shady Caribbean financiers and local European governors. While both captain and crew soon found themselves hanging from the gallows of St. Thomas and St. Christopher, most of their financial backers managed to escape in the midst of a heated war of words waged in the local newspapers. This is the story of a global struggle for recognition being swept up in very local political skirmishes, simultaneously emphasizing transcontinental connectivity and local specificity.

An age of Atlantic revolutions

The decades surrounding the turn of the nineteenth century were dominated by revolutionary upheavals on both sides of the Atlantic Ocean. This period, stretching roughly from the start of the American Revolution in the 1760s to the end of the Latin American Wars of Independence in the 1830s, saw four of the largest empires of the Atlantic world torn apart in violent internal and external confrontations (Hobsbawm, 1962; Klooster, 2009).[1] These conflicts were not just revolutions but a series of imperial civil wars, erupting in the colonies or metropoles of Britain, France, Spain, and Portugal (Rodríguez, 1998; O'Shaughnessy, 2000).[2]

The age of revolution was not directly driven by a domino effect, with straight links from one revolution to the next, but rather by a series of conflicts – interimperial and intra-imperial – cohering into half a century of violence and rupture. Political ideas circulated across the ocean and the economic and social ties between polities in the Atlantic world caused inevitable reverberations when one power was struck by internal tumult. The Revolutionary and Napoleonic

Wars, rippling through the Atlantic at the turn of the century, were particularly momentous in this regard. The fallout of the French Revolution and Napoleon's war in Europe in many ways created the opportunity for independence in the Iberian colonies, leaving the monarchies of Spain and Portugal without the capacity to govern their overseas territories (Adelman, 2006: 102–140).

While the period was rife with revolutions and political reforms, it was not a moment of complete transformation. Rather, what took place in terms of state building was to some degree a continuity of imperial politics in a distinctly New World register. The breakdown of Old World empires led to widespread political innovation in the western hemisphere, but none of these new polities looked particularly like the national-states of the twentieth century. Rather, they were a varied collection of city-states, federations, republics, and multicentered empires. The Americas were thus rife with experiments with the state form, from the loosely organized confederations of Spanish South America to the new constitutional monarchy in Brazil, but these political experiments were for the most part conducted within imperial frames of reference (Mulich, 2016). The new republics and confederacies continued to rely on many of the legal practices and bureaucratic institutions of the Iberian empires from which they had broken loose (Chiaramonte, 2004; Adelman, 2006; Benton and Ford, 2016). However radical and momentous the age of revolution was, it was not, as sometimes claimed, the birth of the modern nation-state.

Even after breaking free from Spanish and Portuguese direct control, numerous conflicts continued within and between the former American colonies. The political struggles were not just limited to those between loyalists and revolutionaries, but also fought between advocates of state unity and proponents of confederation; between different urban centers competing over economic and political hegemony; and between European, creole, and indigenous interests. Such conflicts resulted in both political maneuverings and more violent military clashes over control and territory, including outright wars such as the Cisplatine War over the Banda Oriental, erupting between the Empire of Brazil and the United Provinces of Río de la Plata in the 1820s. There were also more clandestine conflicts over political influence, several of which saw the direct involvement of North American agents, and attempts at coopting the former Iberian colonies, especially in Central America, with the United States acting every bit as imperial as the former European colonizers (Warren, 1943; Blaufarb, 2007). Central to the struggles in Latin America were attempts by revolutionary leaders to gain interstate recognition, not just in order to defend against the potential of European reconquest, but also to strengthen their own political legitimacy internally.

Britain's role in the Americas went through major changes during this period. Some historians have gone so far as to divide the British Empire into two distinct incarnations – a "first" empire, stretching from Elizabeth to American independence and a "second" empire encompassing the period after 1783 (Marshall, 1964 and 2005). Certainly the British Empire shifted much of its formal colonization efforts from the Atlantic world to the Pacific and Indian Oceans following the American Revolution, but this in itself is not a particularly compelling reason to argue for the rise of a "second" empire. Not only were there significant continuities in the imperial apparatus and its institutions, but British imperial involvement in the Atlantic world hardly stopped after the loss of the Thirteen Colonies. Beyond the numerous formal colonies the empire retained in the Caribbean and North America, the turmoil of the Latin American Wars of Independence allowed Britain to establish new commercial connections to the southern continent.[3] This new trade-based relationship across the Atlantic has often been characterized as an informal empire (e.g. Gallagher and Robinson, 1953), to some extent obfuscating the two-sided nature of the relationship. Britain, as well as other European imperial powers, certainly attempted to use the opening provided by the civil war within the Spanish Empire to gain political and economic influence on the continent, but revolutionary leaders also took an active role in inviting in outside European powers. Indeed, many Latin American elites saw the informal involvement of other European empires, and especially the British, in the affairs of the continent as a bulwark against potential Iberian recolonization.[4]

The period after the British abolition of the slave trade in 1807, and especially following the end of the Napoleonic Wars in 1815, in some ways heralded the beginning of what the late Victorians would come to call the Pax Britannica of the nineteenth century (Darwin, 2009: 1–5: Osterhammel, 2014: 452–461). This was a peace in only the most tentative of ways, however, as the globe continued to be rife with bloodshed and violence, especially outside the narrow confines of Europe. Britain did nevertheless enjoy an unparalleled dominance of the seas, as growing British naval power and the emerging treaty regime created by the abolition of the slave trade allowed the Royal Navy to patrol the coastal waters of both Atlantic and Indian oceans (Keene, 2007). In the Western Hemisphere such patrols were generally limited to the greater Caribbean region, where British naval patrols fought a persistent but losing battle against the local intercolonial networks of smugglers and slave traders, while reminding the colonial governors of other empires of Britain's regional dominance in the process. Further south it was British merchant ships, rather than man-of-wars, that peppered the Latin American coastline after 1815.

Part of what altered the European role in the Americas following the end of the Napoleonic Wars was the new hemispheric policy of the United States. The Monroe Doctrine, a set of policy propositions authored by American President James Monroe and Secretary of State John Quincy Adams in 1823, made it clear that the Western Hemisphere, or at least the Americas, was first and foremost a space of New World empires and would from now on be outside the reach of Old World colonialism. The doctrine was arguably more about demarcating spheres of influence than about rejecting the notion of imperialism, with the United States positioning itself as the new preeminent power in the Western Hemisphere (Murphy, 2009). It did not entirely eliminate European influence, however, and the considerable overlap between

British and US interests in keeping Iberian empires out of the Americas following 1815 contributed to securing continued autonomy in Latin America. Thus emerged a tentative postcolonial order in the western hemisphere. Before any new transatlantic relationships could be fully established, however, the young American polities had to stake out their claims to sovereignty and project these across the ocean.

Privateering as a strategy of recognition

Privateering was a well-established component of early modern European imperial warfare. It was a widely used military and political practice in a world of relatively weak state institutions, where the boundary between private and state violence was weak at best (Thomson, 1994: 22–26; Mabee, 2009; Colás and Mabee, 2010; Barkawi, 2010). Seeing privateering specifically as a practice is key, since it was as much a part of the geopolitical landscape as other repertoires of imperial power and interaction at the time, including diplomacy, treaty-making, and traditional land-based skirmishes.[5] Privateering was in this sense not merely a different form of organized sea robbery, but a way to include private vessels in the imperial military effort by hurting the supply lines, finances, and general maritime capacity of the enemy. The practice had its own established norms, legal coda, and political implications.

It is important here to note the legal differences between the practices of piracy and privateering. While privateers were operating under a letter of marque or a commission from a state or sovereign, stipulating the nationality of ships they could target, pirates generally had few if any qualms about the vessels they boarded (Benton, 2011: 225–240; Rubin, 1988: 29–30). Privateering was in this way limited to attacks on belligerent parties to an ongoing conflict and was one of several military practices making up seventeenth- and eighteenth-century inter-imperial maritime warfare. Of course, issues of neutrality and national belonging were usually more complicated than that, especially in a period where many vessels carried multiple different flags and registers for their own convenience, and the line between what was considered piracy and what was privateering was often blurry at best.

In this very ambiguity lay one of the key features of privateering – its ability to project claims of sovereignty abroad. In the words of Lauren Benton, "Distinguishing between piracy and privateering ultimately required a political act of choosing to recognize or to question the legitimacy of the polity sponsoring maritime violence" (Benton, 2010: 130). When faced with letters of marque and privateering commissions in prize courts, where legal disputes over the taking of vessels and cargo were settled, judges and magistrates had to evaluate not just the commission itself but also the legitimate authority of the signatory. In this way, being confronted with letters of marque coming from self-declared states or breakaway republics claiming sovereign authority could essentially force foreign governments to make a decision on the status of these claims of independence. At the very least, these acts of legal posturing added to the existing pressures for recognition coming through more conventional diplomatic channels.

With the growing unrest in the Western Atlantic stemming from the struggles for independence in the Americas came a host of opportunities for unaffiliated actors to make a profit. Newly independent Latin American republics such as Gran Colombia and the United Provinces of Río de la Plata issued a substantial number of letters of marque, allowing holders to conduct privateering in their name (Blaufarb, 2007; Perrone, 2008; Head, 2008). This was both a political and a military strategy. It led to numerous attacks on enemy ships, most prominently those of the Spanish Empire. At the same time, it forced other imperial actors to take Latin American claims of independence seriously when they were faced with such privateering commissions in courts, which had been issued by governments and presidents who forcefully claimed their own sovereignty and political legitimacy (McCarthy, 2011; Benton, 2012; Head, 2013). While some holders of such commissions were no doubt genuine patriots and ideological revolutionaries, many more were mercenaries and adventurers who needed little other incentive than that of profit. This went double for the owners and outfitters of the privateering vessels, men of wealth who were often based in countries and colonies well outside of Latin America.

While privateering and piracy had been mainstays of the Caribbean geopolitical landscape since the late sixteenth century, the republican privateering of the early nineteenth century marked an important endpoint. Privateering would be formally abolished in most western empires with the Paris Declaration Respecting Maritime Law, issued in 1856 (Bowles, 1900), but at that point the practice had already been all but abandoned in the Caribbean for close to three decades. As the campaigns off the Barbary Coast came to an end in the same period (Panzac, 2005; Colás, 2016), the Atlantic world more widely saw a steep decline in privateering following the 1820s. Meanwhile, piracy went from being framed primarily as the illegal activity of individual crews to a specific *state practice* in a different oceanic theatre entirely – maritime South East Asia and the Indian Ocean. Here Dutch and British imperial agents increasingly leveled accusations of piracy against indigenous polities as part of larger conflicts over colonization and imperial trade, arguably altering the political implications of the practice in the process (Warren, 2007: 251–253; Reid, 2010; Atsushi, 2010; Layton, 2013).

A networked order in the Caribbean

The regional setting in which this privateering took place is particularly interesting for what it reveals about the dynamics of early nineteenth-century international politics in general and the greater Caribbean in particular. Regional systems have long been of interest to historians and IR scholars alike, from the identification of oceanic or other spatial configurations as units of analysis (e.g. Braudel, 1972; Games, 2006; Horden and Purcell, 2006; Vink, 2007; Cañizares-Esguerra and Breen, 2013; Phillips and Sharman, 2015; Benton and Mulich, 2015) to comparisons between different regional orders (e.g. Lake and Morgan, 1997; Buzan and Wæver, 2003; Katzenstein,

2005; Lieberman, 2009). These regional systems are particularly important in historical periods prior to the global convergence of the mid-to-late nineteenth century, as early global flows and connections were often filtered through or emanating out from regionally anchored networks.

However, much like empires and other polities, regions were rarely discrete spaces. The claims to sovereignty made by Latin American revolutionaries took place in at least three distinct regional systems. These systems were not separate geographic spaces, but rather overlapping regional configurations – networks within networks, operating under different social and political logics and displaying increasing levels of density and integration, from the loose transoceanic networks of the Atlantic to the more tightly knit transnational and intercolonial networks of the Caribbean. The first of these systems was the Atlantic world, stretching from the coast of the Americas in the west to West Africa and Europe in the east. This was the primary theater for European colonial expansion in the seventeenth and eighteenth centuries, and imperial networks emanating out of the metropoles of Western Europe dominated the political order of the region for much of the later part of that period. The main initial audience for Latin American claims-making were agents of these European empires including those of Britain, which, as mentioned above, was quickly rising to dominance following the end of the Napoleonic Wars.

The second regional system was the western hemisphere, the rise of which heralded the transformation of the existing Atlantic order. With the gradual independence of the new Latin American republics and the announcement of the Monroe Doctrine, the western hemisphere emerged as a political region in its own right, governed by certain sets of New World imperial repertoires as described earlier (Mulich, 2016; Murphy, 2009). It still saw significant involvement from European imperial powers, both formally in the Caribbean and more informally in the Americas, but this involvement was supplemented and sometimes overtaken by the influence of regional powers acting on their own imperial ambitions. Indeed, some European powers, namely Britain, at times worked directly or indirectly towards supporting such intra-regional autonomy, primarily for financial reasons. In this way connections within the region became as important for revolutionary leaders as those crossing the Atlantic Ocean.

The third and most important region for this chapter was the greater Caribbean, the space in which the majority of republican privateering took place and from which many of the crews and vessels were recruited. Characterized first and foremost by colonial rule and the institution of slavery, with the only successful anticolonial revolution in the region being that of Haiti at the turn of the century, the Caribbean was in many ways a different political domain than the Americas. While formally colonized by various European empires, most early nineteenth-century Caribbean islands experienced a surprising degree of autonomy and intercolonial networks were key in shaping the trans-imperial institutions of the region, including political, social, and commercial ones.

Beyond these three regions, the Latin American republics' strategies of recognition were arguably caught up in an emerging global order as well, one placing an imperial mode of power at the center of inter-polity relations and dividing the world into colonized and non-colonized spheres (Bell, 2007; Keene, 2012; Buzan and Lawson, 2015: 171–196). This global order was not yet fully formed in the 1820s, however, and the establishment of a new alignment of autonomous republics in the western hemisphere would be key for subsequent global developments in the latter part of the century.

The Caribbean region and its intercolonial networks are at the center of this chapter. The region was at once tied to the wider imperial politics of the Atlantic world and a distinct space within it, operating under its own peculiar political logic and displaying a great degree of intercolonial entanglement. A maritime borderland with its own institutions and a significant degree of autonomy granted to individual governors and councils, the Caribbean often saw inter-imperial or indeed intra-imperial conflicts spill over into the regional sphere, but more often than not such conflicts were filtered through the particular dynamics of local politics and practices. While the old notion of "no peace beyond the line" was more a faded memory than reality in the realm of European imperial rivalry, the Caribbean nonetheless retained its own peculiar forces of competition and cooperation. But in the wake of the violent upheavals of the age of revolution, this autonomy gradually began to change and wider, even global, shifts in power and practice came to influence and alter the regional order of the colonial Caribbean.

In the Caribbean British, Danish, Dutch, French, Spanish, and Swedish colonies formed an exceptionally pluralistic region. Cross-colonial practices such as contraband trade, slavery, and opportunistic privateering came together to shape and define much of the region as a politically polyglot zone of thin sovereignty and local integration, characterized more by the interests of transnational networks than by those of individual nations or empires (Mulich, 2013: 72–94).

The small but busy Caribbean island of St. Thomas, at the time a Danish colony, was known as a place frequented by both smugglers and privateers. The entrepreneurial traders, sailors, and moneylenders of St. Thomas participated in privateering activities as, at various times, perpetrators, backers, or victims. Local officials, in contrast, found themselves in a political tight spot. Denmark's membership in the Holy Alliance and its general support of absolutism against democratic revolutionaries meant that the government preferred not to take sides in the Latin American struggles directly. Instead they largely left the daily diplomatic decisions to local governors. These then had to try to maintain good relations with their Spanish counterparts in the neighboring colony of Puerto Rico, an important regional actor, while also favoring the private commercial interests of St. Thomas, which profited substantially off the continued wars in the Spanish Americas. The solution was to stay neutral for the most part, while purposefully ignoring most local involvement with the independence movements.[6]

The case of *Las Damas Argentinas*

In 1828, a case began to unravel which could not so easily be ignored. In that year a Caribbean sailor named Jean Jayet de Beaupré was arrested in the port of Charlotte Amalie on Danish St. Thomas, after having flaunted a spectacular collection of gold and silver jewelry and other seemingly ill-gotten goods, including a number of remarkable wedding dresses. He quickly confessed to having been a crewmember of the schooner *Las Damas Argentinas*, a privateering vessel sailing under the flag of the Republic of Buenos Aires and operating in and around the Caribbean Sea. Over the next few days, local colonial authorities rounded up and arrested a number of his former shipmates who were also lying low in the Danish port. This turned out to be a motley crew of men, mostly of British, French, and Creole origin.[7] While *Las Damas* had ostensibly been sailing under the flag of Buenos Aires and carried a privateering commission from that young nation, the ship had never actually been to the Latin American country, nor did its crew seem to have shown much discrimination in their choice of vessels to board.

While contemplating what to do with their prisoners, the Danish magistrates received news that British authorities on nearby St. Christopher currently held in custody both *Las Damas*, her captain, and the remainder of her crew, who had been arrested after similar indiscretions on the Dutch island of St. Eustatius.[8] In the eyes of the British Empire, the line between politically questionable privateering and outright piracy was crossed when, two hundred miles off the Canary Islands, the privateers had boarded and plundered a British brig from Liverpool named the *Carraboo*. Despite warnings from some crewmembers that targeting British vessels was not a sound strategy, the brazen captain Joseph Buysan could not resist the temptation of claiming the ship, which carried a cargo worth close to 28,000 pound sterling. Despite the stipulations of his commission to only attack the vessels of countries at war with Buenos Aires, Buysan had never restricted himself to Spanish ships, but had also boarded both French and Brazilian vessels.

It is worth briefly considering the market for such privateering commissions. Not only were these letters of marque relatively easy to obtain, with representatives of Latin American polities sometimes selling them as far away as Baltimore and New Orleans; the number of different republics also created a thriving market, with the commissions of different governments competing against one another. Thus while a commission from Buenos Aires only nominally allowed attacks upon Spanish ships, a commission from José Artigas' smaller Provincia Oriental allowed the targeting of vessels sailing under both Spanish and Portuguese flags. On the other hand, the prize court of Buenos Aires stopped accepting Artigas' commissions following the conflict between the two polities in the early 1820s, making it potentially more difficult for privateers to offload prizes legally in the region.

What complicated the case of *Las Damas Argentinas* further, and illustrates the complex web of formal and informal networks across the region, were the accusations made in the Leeward Islands newspaper *The St. Kitts Advertiser*.

Articles in this publication argued strongly that *Las Damas*, while she might have sailed under the flag of Buenos Aires, was in actuality backed by influential moneymen on St. Thomas, namely the merchant house of Cabot, Bailey, & Co. This group of traders had alleged ties to local Danish officials, including, according to some sources, to the Governor General himself – Peter von Scholten.[9] The commentators in the *Advertiser* claimed that financial support of such shady and illicit activities was neither surprising nor uncommon in the Danish colony, which was a veritable smugglers' den.

The Danes were hardly alone in their involvement with unsavory regional networks. The foreman of the grand jury on St. Christopher, M.R. Burke, subsequently raised similar allegations against Dutch colonial authorities, claiming that "various acts of piracy" had been committed "not only with encouragement from private individuals in the islands of Saint Thomas and Saint Eustatius, but under the sanction of the Public Authorities on the latter island."[10] The same note mentioned the merchant house of Cabot on St. Thomas as a private entity involved in the affair, and one Mr. Shaw, a partner in the house, was apparently even on board *Las Damas* at one point. Officials further alleged that Governor Willem Albert van Spengler of Dutch Saba received a bribe for letting piratical goods from the vessel be transshipped via his harbor and giving the vessel a Dutch register. Parenthetically, the governor's price seems to have been "500 dollars and some coffee and sugar" – a detail reinforcing van Spengler's reputation for being both corrupt and cheap to buy off. For the privateer's second cruise, Cabot paid between 1200 and 1500 dollars to finance the crew, but since St. Thomas authorities did not allow crews to openly board privateering vessels in their harbor, the crew was hidden on a smaller sloop that followed *Las Damas* out of the port. On this second cruise the vessel allegedly raided five Portuguese vessels, one Spanish brig, an English schooner, and a French brig. Finally the *Carraboo* was taken, an act that ultimately proved the downfall of the pirates.[11]

While a court of law never tested the validity of the accusations of corruption made against the colonial authorities on St. Thomas or St. Eustatius, the allegations illustrate the way in which such issues were caught up in local intercolonial politics, as sensational news stories and criminal cases became new fodder for long-standing inter-island rivalries, such as the one between the British Leewards and the Danish Virgin Islands. British magistrates in the Leewards had had their eyes on the Danish islands since at least the early eighteenth century, and although cooperation was ubiquitous at the level of intercolonial commerce and security, imperial officials were prone to competition over territorial and jurisdictional control.

Privateering, smuggling, and other such informal trade in the Caribbean region took place within trans-imperial networks that ranged from tightly knit communities to loose and flexible webs of familiarity. As the case of *Las Damas Argentinas* illustrates, the Caribbean was an inherently multicultural and multilingual space. Not only were the colonies of various empires porous in regard to territorial sovereignty, but they also exhibited a peculiar sense of imperial transience. Many of the smaller islands shifted from one European empire to another, and their populations often comprised diverse peoples with a number of different cultural, linguistic, and political affiliations. Indeed, most actors in these maritime borderlands were so integrated into the region's intercolonial networks that they cared little about which empire claimed which island for their own. This environment was perfect for the opportunistic privateers, and the polyglot nature of the region was reflected in the diversity of many of the privateering crews operating there. The merchant house of Cabot, Bailey, & Co. was a striking example of the expansiveness of illicit commercial networks within the region. Not only had the company sponsored other privateering vessels sailing under various Latin American flags, it also had an extensive history of involvement in the illegal slave trade to Cuba and Puerto Rico. The company owners claimed both English and Danish subjecthood, depending on the needs of the situation, and they financed smuggling vessels sailing under Dutch, French, and Danish colors. While any personal connections between the merchant house and von Scholten, the Danish governor, are unproven, the merchants no doubt did have links to local magistrates on both the Danish and British Virgin Islands, and they were under investigation by imperial authorities on more than one occasion.

The web of connections surrounding *Las Damas Argentinas* was not confined to the Caribbean, however. While Cabot, Bailey, & Co. had been involved in the financing of the ship, the original owner was one John D. Quincy of Baltimore. In the United States Quincy had bought and outfitted the schooner, at that time called *Bolivar*, acquiring the commission of privateering from Latin American agents in the process, and had then sent her to the West Indies. Here she arrived at St. Thomas, where the captain sought out willing financiers who could provide arms and a crew with the proper experience. This seems to be the point at which contact was made with Cabot and Bailey, who had extensive experience with the dark underbelly of maritime commerce and access to a wide network of contacts in the Caribbean underworld.[12] The original commission was passed on twice, first to one Mr. Stiles and then to the unfortunate Captain Buysan.[13] As it happened, St. Thomas, together with Dutch St. Eustatius, also proved to be convenient ports in which to offload the cargoes and valuables acquired in the course of privateering.

While most of the men arrested and accused of piracy on St. Eustatius and St. Thomas were sentenced and hanged in the winter of 1828–1829, the financial backers of the enterprise fared better.[14] The owners of Cabot, Bailey, & Co. had left the island in the midst of the affair's unraveling and were now nowhere to be found. Their history of illicit activities and their prior run-ins with British imperial magistrates indicate that they might have fled for greener, and safer, pastures. Their partners in Baltimore were less adept at avoiding the consequences of their questionable entrepreneurship. US authorities arrested Quincy, accusing him of illegally arming and outfitting a vessel to participate in piratical activities. Since the schooner had specifically targeted at least one Brazilian ship, an ally of the United States at the time, this act was deemed a serious criminal offense. The legal ambiguity of the terms "arming and fitting out" made the case go all the way to the Supreme Court, which in 1834 ruled in favor of the state.[15] As for the schooner herself, her history continued, as the Royal Navy confiscated her, renamed her *Kangaroo*, and used her in the Caribbean for the next several years (Colledge and Warlow, 2010: 211).[16] Both names were curious, since the vessel visited neither Argentina nor Australia in its lifetime. A similar fate awaited the three youngest members of her crew who were pardoned and made to serve in the Navy for a period of ten years.[17]

Conclusion

The case of *Las Damas Argentinas* is revealing on a number of levels, related to the fashioning of a new republican order in the western Atlantic, to the practice of privateering itself, and to the view of the Caribbean as a zone of dense networks and porous sovereignty. Three points in particular are worth highlighting.

First, as already mentioned, the relationship between opportunistic pirates and politically motivated revolutionaries in Latin America was one of mutual convenience, but it went beyond the classic principal–agent dynamic. By selling commissions, Latin American polities could act as sovereign or quasi-sovereign states, even when they did not have the institutional infrastructure of proper states. Claims to political recognition were pushed in front of judges and magistrates with every case of privateering that made it to court, and revolutionary governments had very little to lose in practice when selling commissions to foreigners. Even in a case like this, where the privateers were captured, tried, and found guilty of piracy, the validity of their commission itself was never in question. The actions of Captain Buysan did not reflect badly on Buenos Aires as a polity directly, but rather showed him to be an agent with neither loyalty nor restraint. For their part, the carriers of such commissions had to pay close attention to regional and imperial politics. When they went beyond the scope of their letter of marque, it had potentially devastating consequences, and their best attempts at legal posturing would only work if they had not overstepped their bounds.

This leads to the second point. The line between the practices of piracy and privateering was a thin one, and which side a given case came down on depended on both political and legal factors. While the privateering commission held by the captain was one potential point of contention, the vessels targeted by his ship was another. For the United States court, it was the confirmed attack on a specifically Brazilian ship that made the difference between wartime privateering and illegal sea robbery. For the Danish governor on St. Thomas it was less the attack on a British brig itself that was at issue, than it was the British reaction to this attack. That is, once British authorities on St. Christopher had taken action, the Danish colonial authorities had to react in a similar manner in order to retain their regional relationship. Britain was at this point the dominant power in the Caribbean, and few small colonies could afford to blatantly disregard the actions of the de facto hegemon. The case of the *Carraboo* and *Las Damas Argentinas* coincided with the end of an era for privateering in the wider Caribbean as the Latin American strategy of issuing commissions was effectively abandoned, not because it had been a failure but because recognition had already been achieved. While there were later cases of piracy in the region, none captured the imagination and attention of contemporaries quite to the same degree, and in a way that so distinctly cast the deed as a case of piracy. Following the trial of Captain Buysan and his crew, privateering all but disappeared from the wider Atlantic region. This trend, combined with the French conquest of Algiers in 1830, which effectively put an end to privateering off the Barbary Coast, signaled a significant decline in the scale of privateering activities, well before the signing of the Paris Declaration.

Third, then, this case illustrates the way in which all such activities in the early nineteenth-century Caribbean took place within a thoroughly transnational regional order. They involved profit-seekers and political entrepreneurs across the Americas, operating within the dense intercolonial networks of the region. Not only were crews transnational in composition, but the entire process of securing letters of marque, financing cruises, outfitting privateering vessels, and ultimately offloading prizes took place within a context of transnational and intercolonial connections and underground markets. *Las Damas Argentinas* was a ship from Baltimore; financed by moneyed interests in the United States and the Danish West Indies; manned by a ragtag band of Spanish, French, Irish, and Creole sailors; and carrying a privateering commission issued by the government of Buenos Aires. She boarded ships of numerous origins, including Spain, France, Brazil, and Britain, and operated as far away as the Canary Islands. And when her crew became too boisterous about their exploits, flaunting obviously stolen goods, she was met with an equally intercolonial response from multiple empires at once.

Actors in the region operated under its own particular logics and norms, but they were not immune to wider international shifts. As the global imperial order began to harden in the middle decades of the nineteenth century, even the polyglot landscape of the Caribbean saw a tightening of boundaries and a resettling of practices, narrowing, although never outright erasing, the role and influence of local politics.

Notes

1 It is worth noting that the age of revolution was not restricted to the greater Atlantic region alone. The turn of the century saw significant and often violent challenges to the reigning social and political order across Asia and the Pacific as well, mirroring in some respects the global crisis experienced during the seventeenth century (Armitage and Subrahmanyam, 2009; Parker, 2013).
2 Indeed, contemporary historians and commentators often described the American Revolution in terms of a civil war (e.g. Ramsay, 1785: 280–281). The label is important in part because it reminds us of the large numbers of loyalists in the colonies, fighting against independence.

3 The immediate aftermath of the American Revolution had seen several British attempts to gain a more formal foothold in South America, which were ultimately unsuccessful (Bassi, 2012: 107–125).
4 Such a view was, of course, not uncontested, especially in the early years of Latin American independence, with arguments ranging from the ambivalent rejection of European powers by José Artigas to the very direct embrace of imperial intervention by Carlos de Alvear (Benton and Ford, 2016).
5 The concept of practice used here mainly follows the theoretical framework of Bourdieu (1977) and the recent practice turn in International Relations (e.g. Adler and Pouliot, 2010; Adler-Nissen and Pouliot 2014; Kustermans, 2016; McCourt, forthcoming). For more on imperial repertoires, see the approach put forth in the work of Burbank and Cooper (2010: 3–22).
6 A few examples of criminal investigations into piracy by local inhabitants can be found in Rigsarkivet, Copenhagen (henceforth RA), Sheriff of St. Thomas, 13.6.3, Proceedings of criminal cases, 1823–1826.
7 RA, Government-General, 2.42, The case against Jean Jayet de Beaupre and others concerning piracy, 1828–1829, court papers, St. Thomas.
8 *The Annual Register, or a View of the History, Politics, and Literature of the Year 1828* (T.S. Hansard: London, 1829), 355–359.
9 Newspaper cutouts from *The St. Kitts Advertiser* found in RA, Government-General, 2.42, The case against Jean Jayet de Beaupre.
10 "Reports on the Piracy of the Carraboo," August–September 1828, The National Archives of Britain (henceforth TNA), Colonial Office (CO) 239/18, 7–20.
11 Ibid.
12 On their alleged involvement in the illegal slave trade to Cuba by the Dutch schooner *Zee Bloem*, see "Mr. Secretary George Canning to The Right Hon. Frederick Lamb, Foreign Office, April 4, 1825, including 15 enclosures," in *British and Foreign State Papers vol. 12* (London: H.M.S.O., 1846), 242–251.
13 *The Annual Register, 1828*, 358; "The United States v. John D. Quincy," in *Report of Cases Argued and Adjudged in the Supreme Court of the United States, January Term 1832* (D.B. Canfield & Co.: Philadelphia, 1853), 445–469.
14 Letter from Governor Maxwell to President Rawlins, March 26, 1829, TNA, CO 239/20, 7. De Beaupré and his accomplices arrested on St. Thomas were hanged on February 6, 1829. Records contained in "Court Cases, 1806–1907," in the Caribbean Collection: Virgin Islands Documents, the Florence Williams Library, Christiansted, St. Croix.
15 "The United States v. John D. Quincy (see n. 13)," 465–469.
16 Such a fate was common for both smuggling and pirate vessels seized by the Royal Navy in this period, greatly increasing the number of fast and maneuverable vessels in British hands.
17 *The Annual Register, 1828* (see n. 13), 359.

Bibliography

Adelman, Jeremy. (2006) *Sovereignty and Revolution in the Iberian Atlantic*. Princeton: Princeton University Press.
Adler, Emanuel and Vincent Pouliot. (eds.) (2010) *International Practices*. Cambridge: Cambridge University Press.
Adler-Nissen, Rebecca and Vincent Pouliot. (2014) Power in Practice: Negotiating the International Intervention in Libya. *European Journal of International Relations* 20 (4): 889–911.
Armitage, David and Sanjay Subrahmanyam. (eds.) (2009) *The Age of Revolutions in Global Context, c. 1760–1840*. New York: Palgrave Macmillan.

Atsushi, Ota. (2010) The Business of Violence: Piracy around Riau, Lingga, and Singapore, 1820–1840. In Robert J. Antony, ed., *Elusive Pirates, Pervasive Smugglers: Violence and Clandestine Trade in the Greater China Seas*. Hong Kong: Hong Kong University Press.

Barkawi, Tarak. (2010) State and Armed Force in International Context. In Alejandro Colás and Bryan Mabee, eds., *Mercenaries, Pirates, Bandits and Empire: Private Violence in Historical Context*. New York: Columbia University Press.

Bassi, Ernesto. (2012) Turning South before Swinging East: Geopolitics and Geopolitical Imagination in the Southwestern Caribbean after the American Revolution. *Itinerario* 36(3): 107–132.

Bell, Duncan. (ed.) (2007) *Victorian Visions of Global Order: Empire and International Relations in Nineteenth-Century Political Thought*. Cambridge: Cambridge University Press.

Benton, Lauren. (2010) *A Search for Sovereignty: Law and Geography in European Empires, 1400–1900*. New York: Cambridge University Press.

Benton, Lauren. (2011) Toward a New Legal History of Piracy: Maritime Legalities and the Myth of Universal Jurisdiction. *International Journal of Maritime History* 23(1): 225–240.

Benton, Lauren. (2012) Una Soberanía Extraña: La Provincia Oriental en el Mundo Atlántico. *20/10 Historia: El Mundo Atlantico y la Modernidad Iberoamericana*. Mexico: GM Ediciones.

Benton, Lauren and Jeppe Mulich. (2015) The Space between Empires: Coastal and Insular Microregions in the Early Nineteenth-Century World. In Paul Stock, ed., *The Uses of Space in Early Modern History*. New York: Palgrave Macmillan.

Benton, Lauren and Lisa Ford (2016) *Rage for Order: The British Empire and the Origins of International Law, 1800–1850*. Cambridge, MA: Harvard University Press.

Blaufarb, Rafe. (2007) The Western Question: The Geopolitics of Latin American Independence. *American Historical Review* 112(3): 742–763.

Bourdieu, Pierre. (1977) *Outline of a Theory of Practice*. New York: Cambridge University Press.

Bowles, Thomas G. (1900) *The Declaration of Paris of 1856*. London: Sampson Low, Marston and Co.

Braudel, Fernand. (1972) *The Mediterranean and Mediterranean World in the Age of Philip II*. New York: Harper and Row.

Burbank, Jane and Frederick Cooper. (2010) *Empires in World History: Power and the Politics of Difference*. Princeton: Princeton University Press.

Buzan, Barry and George Lawson. (2015) *The Global Transformation: History, Modernity and the Making of International Relations*. Cambridge: Cambridge University Press.

Buzan, Barry and Ole Wæver. (2003) *Regions and Power: The Structure of International Security*. Cambridge: Cambridge University Press.

Cañizares-Esguerra, Jorge and Benjamin Breen. (2013) Hybrid Atlantics: Future Directions for the History of the Atlantic World. *History Compass* 11(8): 597–609.

Chiaramonte, J.C. (2004) *Nación y Estado en Iberoamérica: El Lenguaje Político en Tiempos de les Independencias*. Buenos Aires: Editorial Sudamericana.

Colás, Alejandro. (2016) Barbary Coast in the Expansion of International Society: Piracy, Privateering and Corsairing as Primary Institutions. *Review of International Studies* 42(5): 840–857.

Colás, Alejandro and Bryan Mabee. (2010) The Flow and Ebb of Privatised Seaborne Violence in Global Politics: Lessons from the Atlantic World, 1689–1815. In Alejandro Colás and Bryan Mabee, eds., *Mercenaries, Pirates, Bandits and Empire: Private Violence in Historical Context*. New York: Columbia University Press.

Colledge, J.J. and Ben Warlow. (2010) *Ships of the Royal Navy: A Complete Record of All Fighting Ships of the Royal Navy from the 15th Century to the Present*. Havertown: Casemate.
Darwin, John. (2009) *The Empire Project: The Rise and Fall of the British World-System 1830–1970*. Cambridge: Cambridge University Press.
Gallagher, John and Ronald Robinson. (1953) The Imperialism of Free Trade. *Economic History Review* 6(1): 1–15.
Games, Alison. (2006) Atlantic History: Definitions, Challenges, Opportunities. *American Historical Review* 111(3): 741–757.
Head, David. (2008) A Different Kind of Maritime Predation: South American Privateering from Baltimore, 1816–1820. *International Journal of Naval History* 7(2).
Head, David. (2013) New Nations, New Connections: Spanish American Privateering from the United States and the Development of Atlantic Relations. *Early American Studies* 11(1): 161–175.
Hobsbawm, E.J. (1962) *The Age of Revolution: Europe, 1789–1848*. London: Weidenfeld & Nicholson.
Horden, Peregrine and Nicholas Purcell. (2006) The Mediterranean and 'the New Thalassology'. *American Historical Review* 111(3): 722–740.
Katzenstein, Peter J. (2005) *A World of Regions: Asia and Europe in the American Imperium*. Ithaca: Cornell University Press.
Keene, Edward. (2007) A Case Study of the Construction of International Hierarchy: British Treaty-making Against the Slave Trade in the Early Nineteenth Century. *International Organization* 61(2): 311–339.
Keene, Edward. (2012) The Treaty-making Revolution of the Nineteenth Century. *International History Review* 34(3): 475–500.
Klooster, Wim. (2009) *Revolutions in the Atlantic World: A Comparative History*. New York: New York University Press.
Kustermans, Jorg. (2016) Parsing the Practice Turn: Practice, Practical Knowledge, Practices. *Millennium* 44(2): 175–196.
Lake, David A. and Patrick M. Morgan. (eds.) (1997) *Regional Orders: Building Security in a New World*. University Park: Penn State University Press.
Layton, Simon H. (2013) Hydras and Leviathans in the Indian Ocean World. *International Journal of Maritime History* 15(2): 213–225.
Lieberman, Victor. (2009) *Strange Parallels, Southeast Asia in Global Context, c. 800–1830, vol. 2: Mainland Mirrors: Europe, Japan, China, South Asia, and the Islands*. Cambridge: Cambridge University Press.
Mabee, Bryan. (2009) Pirates, Privateers and the Political Economy of Private Violence. *Global Change, Peace & Security* 21(2): 139–152.
Marshall, Peter J. (1964) The First and Second British Empires: A Question of Demarcation. *History* 49(165): 13–23.
Marshall, Peter J. (2005) *The Making and Unmaking of Empires: Britain, India, and America c. 1750–1783*. Oxford: Oxford University Press.
McCarthy, Matthew. (2011) 'A Delicate Question of a Political Nature': The Corso Insurgente and British Commercial Policy during the Spanish-American Wars of Independence, 1810–1824. *International Journal of Maritime History* 23(1): 277–292.
McCourt, David. (2016) Practice Theory and Relationalism as the New Constructivism. *International Studies Quarterly* 60(4): 475–485.
Mulich, Jeppe. (2013) Microregionalism and Intercolonial Relations: The Case of the Danish West Indies, 1730–1830. *Journal of Global History* 8(1): 72–94.

Mulich, Jeppe. (2016) Empire and Violence: Continuity in the Age of Revolution. *Political Power and Social Theory* 32: 181–204.

Murphy, Gretchen. (2009) *Hemispheric Imaginings: The Monroe Doctrine and Narratives of U.S. Empire.* Durham: Duke University Press.

O'Shaughnessy, Andrew Jackson. (2000) *An Empire Divided: The American Revolution and the British Caribbean.* Philadelphia: University of Pennsylvania Press.

Osterhammel, Jürgen. (2014) *The Transformation of the World: A Global History of the Nineteenth Century.* Princeton: Princeton University Press.

Panzac, Daniel. (2005) *Barbary Corsairs: The End of a Legend 1800–1820.* Leiden: Brill.

Parker, Geoffrey. (2013) *Global Crisis: War, Climate Change and Catastrophe in the Seventeenth Century.* New Haven: Yale University Press.

Perrone, Sean T. (2008) John Stoughton and the *Divina Pastora* Prize Case, 1816–1819. *Journal of the Early Republic* 28(2): 215–241.

Phillips, Andrew and J.C. Sharman. (2015) *International Order in Diversity: War, Trade and Rule in the Indian Ocean.* Cambridge: Cambridge University Press.

Prado, Fabrício. (2015) *Edge of Empire: Atlantic Networks in Bourbon Río de la Plata.* Oakland: University of California Press.

Ramsay, David. (1785) *The History of the Revolution of South Carolina, from a British Province to an Independent State, vol. II.* Trenton: Isaac Collins.

Reid, Anthony. (2010) Violence at Sea: Unpacking "Piracy" in the Claims of States over Asian Seas. In Robert J. Antony, ed., *Elusive Pirates, Pervasive Smugglers: Violence and Clandestine Trade in the Greater China Seas.* Hong Kong: Hong Kong University Press.

Rodríguez, Jaime E. (1998) *The Independence of Spanish America.* Cambridge: Cambridge University Press.

Rubin, Alfred P. (1988) *The Law of Piracy.* Newport: Naval War College Press.

Thomson, Janice E. (1994) *Mercenaries, Pirates, and Sovereigns: State-Building and Extraterritorial Violence in Early Modern Europe.* Princeton: Princeton University Press.

Vink, Markus P.M. (2007) Indian Ocean Studies and the 'New Thalassology'. *Journal of Global History* 2(1): 41–62.

Warren, H.G. (1943) *The Sword Was Their Passport: A History of American Filibustering in the Mexican Revolution.* Baton Rouge: Louisiana State University Press.

Warren, James F. (2007) *The Sulu Zone 1768–1898: The Dynamics of External Trade, Slavery, and Ethnicity in the Transformation of a Southeast Asian Maritime State.* 2nd edition. Singapore: NUS Press.

4 Limits of cooperation

The German Confederation and Austro-Prussian rivalry after 1815

Tobias Lemke

Introduction

The French Revolution marked a decisive break in the development of the European state-system. Between 1792 and 1815, the forces it unleashed introduced a new and more devastating type of war across the continent. Entire societies were mobilized to fight each other – uprooting and displacing a generation of peoples in one of the deadliest and most destructive episodes in the history of European warfare. In France alone, one in five people born between 1790 and 1795 perished during this conflict (Evans, 2016: 3). Moreover, French armies brought with them revolutionary notions of representative government, juridical equality, and national identity. These doctrines posed a direct challenge to Europe's traditional social order based on divine rule, ascribed social status, and corporate membership and accelerated a process of political, social, and economic transformation that had boiled beneath the surface of European public life for almost a century (Fehrenbach, 2008).

Perhaps nowhere were the effects of these shocks felt as much as in the German territories of the Holy Roman Empire. For almost a millennium this motley collection of tiny principalities, church estates, and mid-sized fiefdoms was governed by a complex web of imperial duties and special privileges dating back to the Ottonian dynasty of the tenth century. While few contemporaries anticipated that the empire would go the way of the Bourbon monarchy, their optimism quickly proved misplaced. By 1804, a series of military defeats and the wholesale annexation of imperial territory by France brought the empire to the brink of collapse. In August 1806, Emperor Francis II formally dissolved his realm and with it the hierarchical governance structures that had stabilized much of central European life for centuries. Resultantly, many of the smaller political units that belonged to the empire disappeared completely, while those that survived underwent significant processes of state consolidation, bureaucratization, and political reform.

Against this backdrop representatives of the victorious anti-Napoleonic coalition met in Vienna in 1814 to negotiate the restoration of European social and political life. The reorganization of those German territories was crucial to this endeavor. The empire's destruction left few of Europe's pre-revolutionary institutions intact and suspended the region in a state of incomplete transformation. Moreover, Napoleon's so-called "clean sweep" created an acute geopolitical power vacuum in the region while making a return to the old order impossible. Too many of the traditional imperial estates had vanished and those that remained now vehemently defended their newfound independence.

The delegates eventually compromised on the formation of the German Confederation, the *Deutscher Bund* – a loose federation of 41 sovereign states including the two German great powers, Austria and Prussia. The *Bund* was meant to provide for the internal and external security of the German states and serve as a stable foundation for the wider European balance of power (Schroeder, 1986: 19). More importantly, it sought to create an institutional framework to stabilize German affairs by neutralizing the power-political aspirations of its two key members, Austria and Prussia, while simultaneously placating demands for sovereign equality and independence voiced by the *Mittelstaaten* – a group of recalcitrant middle-rank powers that emerged from the Napoleonic wars as a potential counterweight to Austrian and Prussian designs in German central Europe. This twin function was a key element of the Vienna order: the operation of the entire continental system depended on an intra-German balance of power.

The *Bund* was the institutional mechanism designed to achieve this balance, and managed to do so for a while. But soon after its conception, the limits of the arrangement became apparent. Much to the chagrin of the *Mittelstaaten*, the *Bund* offered few avenues for advancing a federal reform program, and the reactionary views of Vienna and Berlin dominated German affairs from the start. The upside of this balance of interest between Vienna and Berlin was that while the two conservative powers cooperated, the stability of the region was ensured. However, as I will argue below, the structural realities of the post-1815 settlement also meant that Austria, Prussia and the *Mittelstaaten* developed along distinct paths of political and economic development that made the convergence of their interests less likely over time. Finally, the revolutions of 1848 shattered the institutional guardrails of the *Bund* and set Austria and Prussia on a collision course that resulted in the war of 1866, whereby the question of German leadership was permanently settled in favor of Prussia.

Given its obvious importance for the development of international politics in the post-Vienna period, it is surprising that the *Bund* attracts little interest from students and scholars of International Relations (IR). While historians have focused extensively on its role in the reorganization of Europe after 1814 (e.g. Mosse, 1958; Kraehe, 1983; Doering-Manteuffel, 1991), it receives scant attention from a discipline that tends to study the post-Napoleonic era through the macro-lens of great power diplomacy (Ikenberry, 2001; Kupchan, 2010; Mitzen, 2013). This chapter offers an alternative reading of the period which challenges accounts that portray it exclusively as a time of great power cooperation and their 'legal hegemony' over the lesser powers (Simpson, 2004; Clark, 2011). While the story of the 'Pentarchy' and the Concert undoubtedly captures an important aspect of international politics after

1815 – namely the avoidance of great power war – it tends to obscure the role played by smaller states and regional actors in shaping the pathways of intrastate cooperation and conflict during this time. In contrast, I argue that by reexamining the politics of the *Bund* we gain insight into the multitude of challenges the architects of the Concert system faced in constructing a lasting regional security system.

To unpack this point further, this chapter proceeds as follows: first, I survey the territorial and political transformation of Germany resulting from the collapse of the old empire and briefly discuss how the *Bund* was designed to address this. Next, I focus on three related but analytically separable themes that complicated the operation of the *Bund* from its inception in 1815 to its final collapse in 1866. The first addresses Austria's decision to withdraw from her dynastic possessions along the Rhine in exchange for territorial compensation in northern Italy. This southward shift weakened her geographical position vis-à-vis Prussia and raised questions about leadership and influence among the German states. The second theme turns to Prussia's role as the champion of economic integration in the *Bund*, through the creation of a customs union that excluded Austria and tipped the intra-German balance of power further in the direction of Berlin. The third theme discusses the formation of an independent and constitutionally "third Germany" and the extent to which the policies of the *Mittelstaaten* contributed to the paralysis of German politics in the post-Vienna order. I contend that over time these dynamics hamstrung the operation of Europe's regional system and contributed to its eventual collapse in the middle of the century. To provide evidence, I review several key developments in German politics between the revolutions of 1848 and the war of 1866. The final section concludes with a discussion of how this argument fits into the overall theme of this volume: the two worlds of the nineteenth century.

Germany between the old empire and the Congress of Vienna

By declaring war on Austria on April, 20 1792, France began the process of revolutionizing European affairs. Just five years later, French armies had conquered large parts of western and southern Europe and a reeling Prussia and Austria were forced to cede significant territories to France. These were the first in a series of steps that would fatally undermine the territorial and political integrity of the Holy Roman Empire and challenge the classical balance of power system that had managed European affairs for much of the previous century. The following sections briefly discuss the most important of these changes before turning to the creation of the *Bund* in 1815.

The territorial transformation of Germany

The inability of the imperial authorities to spearhead a cohesive military response to French expansionism meant that the German states had little choice but to accept the new realities imposed by their conquerors. Following separate treaties with Prussia (1795) and Austria (1797), France marshalled the representatives of the imperial estates together for a special congress at Rastatt to negotiate a permanent peace between France and the empire. The French began negotiations from a position of strength since the strategic withdrawal of the two German great powers gave the lesser princes few options but to turn to France for guidance and protection. French delegates quickly coaxed and cajoled the imperials to cede the left bank of the Rhine to the French Republic permanently. In April 1798, the delegates also agreed to the principle of secularizing the ecclesiastical estates to compensate the secular princes (themselves) for the territories lost to France as part of this annexation (Blanning, 1986: 178).

The events at Rastatt kickstarted the systematic divestiture of the smaller, politically weak dominions of the empire. The disappearance of the clergy's power also precipitated the political neutralization of the smaller secular estates, which historically depended on church support in imperial affairs (Gruner, 1993: 95–97). In February 1803, the secularization process culminated in the complete dissolution of all ecclesiastical territories, as agreed by an imperial deputation negotiating with France. Over these years, 41 of the existing 47 imperial cities were absorbed by their larger neighbors, roughly 122 polities ceased to exist and, by 1808, 60 percent of the German population had changed rulers at least once. On the right bank of the Rhine alone, 3 electorates, 19 bishoprics, and 44 abbeys – totaling some 10,000 square kilometers and approximately three million subjects – disappeared from the European map forever (Sheehan, 1989: 243–244; Wilson, 2016: 652–660).

In August 1804, the Holy Roman Emperor Francis II declared himself Emperor Francis I of Austria – a move to preserve his own imperial credentials in the face of the empire's likely collapse and Napoleon's own coronation as Emperor of the French earlier that year (Schroeder, 1994: 252). The ultimate collapse of the Empire became a reality following another devastating Austrian defeat at the hands of the French army at Austerlitz in December 1805. As part of the ensuing peace negotiations, Vienna was forced to cede even more territory to its neighbors. The year 1805–1806 also witnessed the mediatization of the last 350 imperial knightly orders (*Reichsritterschaften*) and many of the smaller imperial estates that were spared before. Of the old order, fewer than 50 political units remained in 1806.

Finally, on August 1, 1806, sixteen German principalities, including Bavaria and Württemberg, left the imperial fold permanently and joined the *Rheinbund* – a confederation of states designed to consolidate French military, diplomatic, and economic control over central Europe (Weiss, 1973, 1984). Membership in Napoléon's security-system increased a state's chances of political survival but also proved lucrative for its members. The Duchy of Baden, for example, became a Grand Duchy and both Bavaria and Württemberg assumed the titles of Kingdom (Schroeder, 1994: 282–283; Kaiser, 2009: 100). Five days later, Francis II abdicated the Imperial German crown, making the Holy Roman Empire a part of history. Germany was now separated into three distinct parts: a Prussian sphere in the north and east, an Austrian sphere in the southeast, and a third sphere of *Mittelstaaten* allied to France.

The political transformation of Germany

The transformation of Germany's territorial map brought with it a host of political issues. Traditionally, political authority in the old Reich was grounded in the multilayered and fragmented notion of *Herrschaft* – a form of rule that fused economic with political power and located it in the person of the *Herr*, usually an individual (male) lord or master (Brunner, 1965; Sheehan, 1989: 32). As part of this arrangement, individuals and social groups sought recognition for their particular identities by obtaining legally recognized positions of autonomy within the constitutional framework of the empire (Wilson, 2016: 235). Thus, status, influence, and power chiefly rested on the acquisition of shared rights and privileges that, once codified in charters, clarified the actor's position within the imperial hierarchy. Imperial subjects could also obtain status recognition from those superior to their own immediate lords. Cities often appealed directly to the emperor for status recognition and rights, forgoing the authority of their local lords and princes (Wilson, 2016: 242). Practically, this meant that while the Emperor was formally sovereign, his powers were shared with a multitude of local intermediaries including the imperial estates (*Reichstände*) and many smaller actors that nonetheless enjoyed significant liberties, privileges, and protections under the aegis of the emperor.

By 1806, however, the collapse of imperial authority raised questions regarding the necessary reorganization of the system. For the conquerors, the issue was straightforward: those states now within the French sphere of influence were to adopt the essential tenets of Napoleonic governance, including a unified administrative state apparatus that neutralized local power arrangements and a homogenizing national culture to sweep aside feudal particularisms. Full French-style legal and administrative reforms were limited to France's immediate satellites such as Berg, Westphalia, and the annexed Rhineland; elsewhere, change was largely driven by earlier forms of rationalization and codification and aimed at the consolidation of state control over newly annexed territories and peoples (Berding and Ullmann, 1981). As mentioned above, states such as Württemberg, Baden, Bavaria, Hessen-Darmstadt, and Nassau all gained significant territories following Napoleon's clean sweep, and substantial increases in population. German state elites welcomed and actively pursued these reforms to shore up their independent status while simultaneously managing the fiscal and military demands their treaty obligations with France required.

But centralization and bureaucratic reform was only the first step to guarantee political survival. The security and prosperity of regimes also depended on their ability to mobilize sufficient support for their state-building projects among the populace, including those subjects recently acquired via territorial gains. Again, the French model was illustrative by demonstrating the immensity of national power that could be harnessed through the political integration of the population – abrogating seigneurial privileges and granting juridical equality and political representation to propertied males (Fehrenbach, 1974; Sheehan,

1989: 253–274). Building on this template, the *Mittelstaaten* opted to introduce basic constitutional guarantees to bargain for the allegiance of their new subjects. This 'demythologized' the rule of the sovereign and placed him in a clear and constitutionally defined position in relation to the state and the rest of society (Aretin, 1980: 118–182; Langewiesche, 2007: 62–64). In this way, the revolution and the extension of the French empire was indeed the harbinger of the modern nation-state in central Europe (Woloch, 1994), bringing tighter government control over society and serving as the springboard for major change in Western Europe in the nineteenth century. Simultaneously, constitutional reforms among the *Mittelstaaten* contributed to creating a regional particularism in which liberal and constitutional sentiment would continue to incubate, setting the tone for the eventual introduction of representative governance and full-fledged constitutionalism – largely at odds with the reactionary policy preferences of Austria and Prussia.

Here, the domestic situation was demonstrably different. What separated the Prussian reform experience from that of the *Rheinbund*, for example, was that the former's relatively homogenous and obedient population precluded the need to mobilize addition public support through constitutional reform and political liberalization. Instead, reformers in Berlin focused on state centralization and economic recovery (e.g. Aretin, 1980: 138). Prussia's primary reform goal was to strengthen and perfect her bureaucratic-monarchical and military institutions, not diminish them. At stake was not simply the question of whether and when to strike against the French, but also the nature of the war that Prussia would ultimately wage against Napoleon. The reformers envisaged a new insurrectionary mode of warfare involving armed masses of citizen-soldiers inflamed by love of their fatherland.

The culmination of this project was the famous 'to my people' address by King Frederick Wilhelm III in March 1813, in which he justified the government's cautious policy hitherto and called upon his people to rise, province by province, against France (Clark, 2006). The address steered a careful middle path between the insurrectionary rhetoric of the patriot radicals and the hierarchical order of traditional absolutism, highlighting the efforts made to embed current events within a tradition of Hohenzollern dynastic leadership. The subsequent edict of April 1813 established the *Landsturm* (home army) and was perhaps the most radical official utterance of these weeks – stating that officers were to be elected, although eligibility for officer rank was still restricted to certain social and professional groups.

Despite their limited character, the long-term effects of these initiatives should not be underestimated. The reform of the educational system, the liberation of the peasantry, trade liberalization, and the rollback of the nobility's tax privileges laid the foundation for the economic awakening and prosperity that Prussia would experience throughout the second half of the nineteenth century. The result was a type of partial modernization – largely administrative and economic – that would assist Prussia to become the champion of reform and progress in the eyes of the wider German public.

In contrast, Austria's reform movement was comparatively limited, with minor advancements made in the codification of criminal and civil law and military reform. Plans to bureaucratize the state through the creation of a modern ministry-system failed and the national debt of the Habsburg Empire more than tripled between 1793 and 1810 (Hippel and Stier 2012: 153). In some respects, Austria not only failed to capitalize on the general pro-reform sentiment that existed among the German principalities at the beginning of the nineteenth century but actively rolled back some of the progress made under the Josephinian reforms of the previous century. Many in the Austrian elite believed that the solution to their woes was less centralization and a return to the traditional model of fragmented representation, whereby local elites enjoyed relative political and economic autonomy (Aretin, 1980: 134–135). The multiethnic makeup of the Austrian Empire also made modernization a potentially hazardous undertaking. Political and economic liberalization threatened to rouse nationalist sentiments among the empire's culturally and ethnically heterogenous population. Its stability depended on the neutralization of this threat (Kraehe, 1971: 232; Sheehan 1989, 280–286). Considering these circumstances, the Austrian reform projects often failed to materialize in the face of significant political resistance and structural deficits. More importantly, Austria's stunted reformism fueled the political fragmentation of Germany after 1815 and created a growing north–south modernization gradient that would obstruct intra-German cooperation throughout much of the nineteenth century.

The German Confederation as political compromise

Given the tumultuous territorial and political shifts resulting from the French Revolutionary and Napoleonic Wars, the primary goal of the Congress of Vienna was the creation of a political equilibrium that would guarantee the peaceful resolution of future conflicts in Europe (Schroeder, 1992: 692–694). Naturally, the reorganization of the German territories constituted an important puzzle piece of this challenge. The experience of the previous decades demonstrated the risk of a divided Germany for the long-term stability of the continent (Gruner, 1993: 102–106; Schroeder, 1994: 538). The power vacuum that now existed at the heart of Europe had to be filled.

This proved difficult, however. The newly consolidated *Mittelstaaten* were keen to retain their newly found independence. Moreover, these states had obtained legal guarantees for sovereign equality in exchange for defection from the *Rheinbund* in 1813. This meant that their interests as active participants during the negotiations at Vienna could not be ignored by the great powers. The separation of the German territories into three distinct poles had become a political reality. The critical question was how the relationship between these parts was to be organized – particularly considering the demonstrably different stages of economic and political development among them (Haldén, 2011: 7). Article Six of the Peace of Paris (1814) provided little guidance on this matter and simply stated that the German states should be organized in the form of a federation.

The onus for resolving the issue was placed on a German committee – a plenum of representatives from most of the empire's former members that met as part of the congress. In the committee, three projects vied for dominance. The first proposition favored a quasi-return to the imperial order and a partial restoration of the hierarchical structures of the estates-system (Aretin, 1980: 156–160). However, without the balancing function of the petty nobility and German clergy, a complete return to the status quo ante bellum would be impractical. A second project sought to establish an Austrian and Prussian co-dominium over the German territories. This type of dual hegemony was based on a plan developed by the Prussian minister Hardenberg and enjoyed the initial support of Austria's foreign minister Metternich. For Austria, the elevation of Prussia to parity with Austria was palatable because it fit into his plans for creating a strong central European system with Austria's position secured at its center (Kraehe, 1983; Schroeder, 1994: 540–542; Gruner, 2014: 86). It also granted both powers strong executive control over German affairs and isolated the influence of the *Mittelstaaten*, which strongly opposed the option. Instead, the third Germany proposed the creation of a decentralized federal-system that protected the middle-rank powers from the ambitions of Austria and Prussia while simultaneously diluting the political weight of the smaller German states (Gruner, 1993: 101).

When the crisis over the fate of Poland and Saxony erupted in the winter of 1814–1815, support for co-dominium faded as Austria and Prussia found themselves on opposing sides of the conflict. With the Austro-Prussian break in relations, the federal solution became the only viable option for reorganizing Germany. Here, Metternich's skill proved critical for marshalling enough political support for a German states-federation (Schroeder, 1994: 546). By exaggerating the hegemonic designs of Prussia, he gained the tacit support of the smaller states in backing the plan. In addition, Napoleon's return from Elba gave him the context to pressure both Prussia and the *Mittelstaaten* to enter a tentative agreement that would see the future of Germany designed along federal lines (Aretin, 1980: 162). Forced into a common denominator by both design and circumstance, the German representatives began deliberations on the specific shape and form of the future German confederation in the spring of 1815.

The final product of these negotiations, the *Bund*, is generally viewed as a compromise between the maximalist position of an Austro-Prussian co-dominium, with strong executive powers concentrated toward the top, and the minimalist position of a loose federation of states (Gruner, 2012: 23). Despite significant disagreements over the exact contours of the confederation, the Federal Act was signed into European international law through its incorporation into the Vienna Final Act on June, 9 1815. The *Bund* included 41 members and, by extension, the King of England via Hannover, the King of Denmark via Holstein and Lauenburg, and the King of the Netherlands via Luxembourg. Its central administrative organ – the Federal Assembly (*Bundesversammlung*) in Frankfurt – boasted only limited executive powers and was separated into an inner council (17 votes) and a larger plenum (69 votes). In neither chamber did the two great powers nor the *Mittelstaaten* possess an automatic majority (Aretin, 1980, 163). Influence in the assembly had to be won through argumentation and political coalition-building (Haldén, 2011: 13). Moreover, the *Bund* was to function under the de jure chairmanship of Austria, while its members were recognized as independent states under the control of both sovereign princes and free cities, effectively creating a "moderate and limited" Austrian hegemony in Germany (Schroeder, 1994: 548).

Overall, the *Bund* was meant to fulfill three basic functions. First, it guaranteed the political existence of the smaller German states. Second, it was to neutralize the intra-German rivalry between Austria and Prussia by forcing the two states to work together within its institutional framework (Schroeder, 1986: 19). Third, it served as the keystone of the European security-order, as a defensive central state that neutralized hegemonic aspirations from the European periphery (i.e., France and Russia). Here, we clearly see the European-international dimension in the forming of the *Bund* – a stable *European* balance of power had to be anchored to a stable *German* balance of power that protected central Europe from again becoming the stage for the political designs of a revisionist state (Gruner, 2012: 27). As Peter Haldén has pointed out (2011: 9), the *Bund* rested on a triad of interconnected elements: the European balance, the territorial shape of Germany, and the political constitution of the German lands. Without a modicum of harmony among the German states, the general European order was not sustainable.

The limits of the *Bund*: managing the Austro-Prussian antagonism

The operation of the *Bund* rested primarily on the mitigation of the Austro-Prussian rivalry and its ability to induce cooperation between the two in German and European affairs. This was the case throughout the 1820s, as both powers followed only limited power-political imperatives. But signs of the structural weakness of the *Bund* and its mounting inability to effectively manage the diverging interests of its member states appeared soon thereafter. Here I draw attention to three interrelated themes of contention that ran through the political landscape of the *Bund* from its inception in 1815 to its dismemberment in 1866. I argue that while the regional order devised at Vienna localized and contained the conflict potential among the German states for some time, its basic framework limited the ability of the assembly to find political solutions to the most pressing problems of the time.

Territorial shifts within Germany: Austria loses and Prussia gains

As part of the negotiations at Vienna, the Austrian presence in western Germany was scaled back significantly. In exchange Austria received Salzburg, Galicia, Illyria, and additional territory in Italy. This meant that Vienna emerged from the Congress as a consolidated and geographically more integrated territory, while her political center was relocated outside of the German heartlands. For the historian Wolf Gruner, this southward shift – designed to check French aggression in the south – hampered both Austria's ability to influence intra-German politics and her overall diplomatic maneuverability (1993: 108). Specifically, Vienna's hegemonic position in the Apennine peninsula meant that she had to constantly contend with insurrections and revolts in the Italian lands, exhausting the monarchy's already-weakened fiscal and military posture. Moreover, this diminished position contrasted with her nominal position as the *Bund*'s presidential power (*Präsidialmacht*). Per the Federal Act, Austria was meant to fulfill a leadership role in Germany. Instead, she was pushed to the periphery of the German political system with much of her attention and resources diverted elsewhere.

Austria's geographical and political dislocation stood in stark contrast with Prussia's significant territorial expansion in central and western Germany following the Congress of Vienna. Resultantly, Berlin's geopolitical focus and interests shifted from eastern to western central Europe (Gruner, 1993: 109). Through the absorption of the provinces of the Rhineland and Westphalia, Prussia became the strongest German power geographically speaking. Her predominant position along the Rhine also made her the first line of defense against potential French aggression. The resulting security dilemma forced the Hohenzollern dynasty to balance both internally and externally against the perceived threat of French expansionism, and some historians have gone as far as to argue that Prussia's role as the "watchman on the Rhine" made the eventual pursuit of regional hegemony a geopolitical necessity (Nipperdey, 1983: 91).

Moreover, Prussia's territorial gains proved extremely valuable in the long term. The incorporation of the industrially advanced territories of the Rhine provinces and northern Saxony, as well as the resource-rich Ruhr valley, boosted Prussia's developing economy immensely during the nineteenth century. This fueled Prussia's gradual transformation from an agrarian to an industrial society and enabled her to remain tied to the national and liberal movement across Germany. Prussia's relatively modern sociopolitical system appeared simply more attractive to many of the smaller German states compared to Austria's (Hippel and Stier, 2012: 168). In the process, Prussia increased its political capital among the German states considerably vis-à-vis Austria, whose increasing isolation would have long-term effects on the trajectory of federal politics.

At first glance, the geopolitical division of labor between Prussia in the north and Austria in the south made sense. The experiences of the wars had shown that French imperialism had to be checked in both places, since the fragmented political landscape of both regions lent itself easily to outside interference. Still, the decision to shift Austrian power southwards and Prussia's westwards put both states in a bind. Vienna's political flexibility decreased measurably as her financial recovery slowed and she became preoccupied with Italian affairs while Prussia was incentivized to pursue an aggressive balancing strategy to fulfill her hegemonic role in the north of Germany (Gruner, 2012: 27). This territorial organization also had direct legal and military consequences for Austria. The

Federal Act offered military protection only to those German territories that were officially part of the *Bund*. Austria – with significant extra-German lands in Italy and the Balkans – did not enjoy the kind of military support Prussia marshalled in the Rhineland. This put Vienna at a significant disadvantage both during the Crimean War and the Austro-Italian War of 1859 (Kraehe, 1990: 274), effectively isolating her from potential German allies while opening the door for Berlin to take the lead in central Europe.

Prussian economic hegemony and the Zollverein

The above-mentioned modernization advantage that Prussia enjoyed vis-à-vis Austria was not the result of territorial gains alone. In the years following her defeats at Jena and Auerstedt, Prussia's political elite began the arduous project of reforming the state's administrative, military, educational, and economic sectors. A flourishing bureaucratic class became the transmission belt for a centralizing state apparatus and a rapidly developing economy, despite political pushback from the more traditional segments of society (Sheehan, 1989: 300). Thus, the first half of the nineteenth century saw Prussia's dominance in the German economic sphere grow steadily, in hand with her perceived leadership role in the *Bund*.

Another factor that contributed to Prussia's rising stock was her effort to create an integrated free-trade zone in northern Germany in the form of a customs union, the *Zollverein* (e.g. Hahn, 1984). In the 1820s, voices started clamoring for the economic integration of the German territories to accelerate the economic recovery of the region and shield developing industries from the competition of advanced British manufactures (Hahn, 1990: 189). Many looked to Frankfurt to take up the initiative and begin coordinating the economic relations between the *Bund* members. But the assembly struggled in vain to provide a clear direction on the matter. A central obstacle in the way of a general framework for economic integration was the uneven economic development in Germany. Not all sectors of the economy were categorically interested in the creation of a free trade zone. Particularly the expanding preindustrial centers in the Rhineland, Westphalia, Saxony, and Silesia, as well as the more specialized small-scale agricultural centers in the south, insisted on internal tariffs to shield them from intra-German competition (Hahn, 1990: 191). Resultantly, deliberations on the economic integration of the German territories gridlocked in Frankfurt. Moreover, Metternich and the Austrian Court were suspicious of the potential spill-over effect economic-liberalization could have on similar demands for political change and national unification, complicating matters even further (Lutz, 1985: 72).

In contrast, Prussia was not only interested in broadening her economic influence throughout Germany but had the fiscal means and resources to do so. Her modernization advantage and size enabled her to provide the administrative and bureaucratic infrastructure necessary for the economic integration of the region. Berlin was willing to shoulder these costs in exchange for the strategic realignment of the smaller states. The gradual expansion of the Prussian tariff-system into northern and southern Germany streamlined the tariff administration and allowed many of the smaller states to save resources they would otherwise have to spend on managing their own trade policies (Hahn, 1990: 196). Between 1821 and 1828 several smaller German states joined the Prussian customs system, which began to look like an attractive alternative to the more inefficient and status-quo oriented politics of the *Bund* (and Austria). This allowed Prussia to pursue her economic and power-political interests simultaneously. On January 1, 1834, the *Zollverein* treaties officially entered into force and established a trans-German customs union throughout much of northern Germany. Membership increased steadily throughout the decade and held a population of over 26 million by 1836, a clear majority in the *Bund* (Schroeder, 1994: 712–713).

This had wide-ranging consequences for the future development of the *Bund*. Initially, the general economic benefits incurred from trade liberalization helped to stabilize the political situation in Germany because increased income levels and burgeoning revenue surpluses allowed many member states to forgo unpopular tax increases (Hahn, 1990: 196). This effectively lowered the protest potential across the German states and strengthened the authority of the monarchical bureaucracy vis-à-vis the regional assemblies. At the same time, it became obvious that economic integration would inadvertently lead to an increase in societal demands for political liberalization and national unification. Even though the *Zollverein* movement was driven by and sustained a diverse set of interests, it gradually fueled the formation of a unified German national state under Prussian leadership, and a growing segment of the liberal opposition saw in the *Zollverein* a political instrument to hasten the road to unification (Hahn, 1984: 129; Schroeder, 1994: 714).

The constitutional crisis

A third point of contention in the politics of the *Bund* was the interpretation of the elusive Article Thirteen of the Federal Act, which dealt with the question of constitutionalism and representative government in the German lands. Metternich – since 1821 State Chancellor at the Austrian court – was well aware of the general enthusiasm for constitutional guarantees throughout the *Bund*. At the same time, he feared that political reform could lead Austria's ethnic minority groups to demand political representation or even independence. To neutralize this problem Metternich began to shop his own, rather limited, constitutional model at Frankfurt. Per his plans, the assembly would suggest a generic constitutional template to be adopted by the individual German states, whereby a central state council (*Staatsrat*) would replace the legislative function of national assemblies and serve in an advisory role to the prince. Actual representational assemblies, Metternich argued, should be confined to the provincial and local level (Aretin, 1980: 168–169).

His plans were vigorously opposed by a group of South German states that regarded Vienna's alternative as an unabashed attempt to interfere in their domestic affairs. Instead, this group favored a more thorough constitutionalism at both the local and state level that would allow them to continue the process of political integration started during the *Rheinbund* ear. A strong legislature, they argued, would also serve as a necessary counterweight to the professional bureaucracy which had become enormously powerful following the administrative reforms of the past decade (Aretin, 1980: 176). A popular model for constitutional reform was France's Charte Constitutionelle introduced by Louis XVIII in 1814. It provided a modicum of individual political and civil rights including freedom of conscience, opinion, and speech, as well as judicial equality. It also sported a bicameral legislature which included both aristocratic and non-aristocratic representation (Hippel and Stier, 2012: 174–175).

Metternich, concerned about the trajectory of these developments, began to mobilize the reactionary forces across the *Bund*. His campaign was assisted by developments that seemed to underscore the urgency of Metternich's concerns. Following the Congress, a wave of constitutional and nationalist activism quickly spread across Germany, of which the student organizations (*Burschenschaften*) constituted the most radical element. The first of these formed at Jena University in June 1815 and soon included over 650 members. Within a few months affiliated groups had formed at other major universities. The student movement was also a principal organizer of the October 1817 Wartburg festival to celebrate the allied victory over Napoleon at Leipzig and the tricentenary of the Reformation – both redolent symbols of the nation's freedom from foreign domination and the freedom of thought from doctrinaire restraints (Sheehan, 1989: 406).

The situation intensified with the 1819 assassination of the Russian consul and author August von Kotzebue by the radical student Karl Ludwig Sand. The event helped to legitimate Metternich's social-conservative claims and gave resonance to his warning that all forms of liberal, national, and revolutionary sentiment posed a fundamental threat to the internal and external security of the German states (Kraehe, 1990: 276). In a meeting with the Prussian King Frederick William III at Teplitz in August 1819, Metternich managed to convince the Prussian leadership to jettison plans for the creation of a representative national assembly in Berlin (Sheehan, 1989: 423). After securing Prussian support, Metternich set out to convince the rest of the German states to follow suit.

His efforts reached a crescendo with the so-called "Carlsbad Decrees", which limited freedom of the press and of universities and enabled the authorities to investigate and pursue "rebellious movements" (Müller, 2006: 8–9). Metternich managed to swiftly ratify the decrees at the Federal Assembly and secured support for the establishment of a federal bureau of investigation to handle the "revolutionary agitation discovered in several states" (Sheehan, 1989: 408) as part of the Vienna Final Act. These measures stripped the *Bund* of the potentially progressive impulses that had been part of its original charter, such as the provision aimed at the emancipation of Germany's Jews. Furthermore, Article 57 of the Act legitimated the *Bund*'s coordinated, anti-revolutionary intervention in the domestic affairs of member states, while Article 58 explicitly prohibited states from establishing constitutions aimed at curtailing princely authority.

Still, the constitutional camp continued to resist Austria's reactionary program, often through the skillful interpretation of their legal rights and autonomy granted in the German Federal Act (Gruner, 2012: 42–43). No less than 29 of the *Bund*'s 41 members adopted constitutions between 1814 and 1824. The increasing politicization of public life also contributed to the development of cross-regional ties between the liberal opposition movements across Germany. Slowly and often at considerable cost, people created the intellectual systems and associational networks on which participatory politics could be based. In turn, the authorities could do little to stop the flood of liberal books, periodicals, and even newspapers that spread across German Europe as social clubs and cultural organizations became the forums for political discussions (e.g. Engelsing, 1969; Habermas, 1984; Sperber, 2005: 60–63).

The result was a broiling constitutional conflict that hamstrung the political efficiency of the *Bund* in the long run and permanently damaged Austria's reputation in the eyes of the broader German public (Schulze, 1985: 58). As the next section points out, the increasing political polarization between the forces of movement and reaction paralyzed the *Bund* and prevented it from developing viable policy solutions to some of the most pressing questions of its time. Moreover, debates surrounding the political and economic modernization of the federation also began to change the relationship between Austria, Prussia, and the *Mittelstaaten*. Although Prussia fell in line with Austria's position in the 1820s, Vienna was generally regarded as the catalyst behind the social-conservative turn in Germany. Conversely – and perhaps undeservingly – Berlin managed to retain a more positive image in Frankfurt. After all, Prussia had been the birthplace of the sixth and final war against Napoleon and in some ways symbolized a strong and united Germany. Lastly, her support for economic liberalization made her an attractive reference point for the other German states, many of which saw the future of German central Europe more likely to coincide with the political impulses coming out of Berlin than Vienna (Aretin, 1980: 171–172). The revolutions of 1848 and their aftermath would partly prove this assumption to be correct.

Conflict over cooperation: from the revolutions of 1848 to the war of 1866

In many ways, the revolutionary wave of 1848 was a culmination of these themes, fusing constitutional and economic grievances into a powerful political force that overwhelmed the *Bund*'s conservative bias (e.g. Sperber, 2005). While the revolutionaries fell short of their goal to create a unified and constitutional nation-state, their defeat in 1849–1850 by the forces of reaction did not precipitate a return to the status quo. Instead, the revolutions destroyed what little Austro-Prussian cooperation and goodwill had remained at the eve of 1848 and set both great powers on a more direct collision course. From this point forward until the Austro-Prussian War of 1866, the politics of the *Bund* were primarily driven by the open competition between Vienna and Berlin over political, economic, and military leadership in Germany.

The first step in this conflict came in the spring of 1849 with the decision of the popularly elected national assembly in Frankfurt to offer the imperial crown of a united German nation-state to King Frederick William IV of Prussia. The move underscored Prussia's growing status and prestige in the public's eye, and although the king refused to accept the title, it did not stop him from following his own unification plan at the expense of Austria. Over the next 12 months, Prussia pushed for a unified German state under Prussian leadership with the so-called "Erfurt Union" plans. While Austria was able to sabotage this plan, the issue would bring the two former allies to the brink of war – making it the first time Austria and Prussia had exchanged shots since 1778 (Taylor, 1954: 41). In the end, both sides failed to reach a satisfactory formula for redistributing political authority between them and only significant pressure by the other great powers prevented the escalation of the conflict. By 1851, still at odds but exhausted, the German states agreed to return to the *Bund* as the only practical option to organize German affairs for the time being.

In turn, Frankfurt became the battleground for the Austro-Prussian antagonism over the next decade and a half. Much of this struggle centered around the question of how to shape the economic integration of the confederation. Until 1848, Austria had accepted Prussia's leading economic role precisely because the latter did not outwardly abuse it for political purposes. This changed in the 1850s, when Prussia repeatedly used her economic leverage over the smaller states to economically and politically isolate Austria (Hahn, 1990: 201). Several times Prussia cajoled the smaller states to block Austria from entering the *Zollverein*, while the latter failed to marshal support for the creation of a separate South German custom union. The protectionist interests of her own industries posed another problem for Vienna. By the middle of the century, the development gap between the Hapsburg monarchy – especially the Bohemian crownlands – and the *Zollverein* had become too large to allow a seamless integration of Austria into the customs union (Katzenstein, 1976: 76; Komlos, 1983: 25). In contrast, the serendipitous proximity of coalfields and iron ore deposits in the Ruhr area spurred Prussia's economic development. Accordingly, the 1853 trade and customs treaty between Austria and Prussia was little more than an armistice in the contest for economic leadership in Germany (Austensen, 1983: 54). Theoretically, it gave Austria time to reform her economy and become more competitive vis-à-vis her northern neighbors, but the opportunity was squandered as Vienna became once again occupied with renewed insurrection in the Italian provinces.

The crisis that erupted in northern Italy in 1859 also highlights the extent to which questions of both political and economic leadership were closely intertwined. When Austria declared war against Piedmont in April of that year, she expected military assistance from the German confederation including Prussia. To the surprise of the diplomats in Vienna, however, the help was not forthcoming. Instead, the Prussian deputy in Frankfurt argued forcefully that the war in Italy was an extra-German affair that ought to be isolated. At first, this move provoked strong condemnation from Germany's nationalist movement, portraying it as a betrayal of German solidarity (Schulze, 1985: 83). But as Austrian loses began to pile up and it became clear that she would lose the war, the tone changed. Nationalists across Germany now argued that perhaps it was time to jettison the Hapsburg ballast and refocus political energy on the creation of a German nation-state under Prussian leadership.

The 1862 free-trade treaty between Prussia and France was another step in this direction (Sheehan, 1989: 876). Prussia secured the tacit approval from the smaller German states for this ostensibly anti-Austrian policy by threatening to resolve the *Zollverein*. Faced with the choice between continued cooperation with Prussia or economic self-reliance, most states followed Berlin's lead. Fears of losing the *Zollverein*'s collective benefits and the dividends of the free-trade policies also explain why Prussia – despite her increasingly revisionist position – retained a largely positive image among the German public. In the eyes of many, the *Zollverein* was simply the more popular and efficient vehicle for German reform and unification (Hamerow, 1969: 84). Prussian threats and vote intimidation at Frankfurt were equally effective in defeating Austria's constitutional reform project of 1862–1863 (Kraehe, 1951: 284–294; Sheehan, 1989: 881).

Within the back-and-forth of the constitutional crisis and the struggle over economic reform, we can observe the now-familiar dynamics of contention that plagued the operation of the *Bund* since its inception. First, Vienna's de jure leadership role and her de facto inability to fulfill it due to a general level of political, financial, and economic impotence was a thorn in the side of the *Bund* from the start. While Carlsbad marked the high point of Austrian influence in Germany, the Habsburg monarchy found it increasingly difficult to legitimize her policies using the rhetoric of conservative solidarity after 1820 (Gruner, 2012: 100). Perhaps more importantly, Austria had little choice but to let things unfold and hope for the best. An aggressive policy like Prussia's would jeopardize her credibility as the defender of legality and tradition, which – from the traditional Metternichean perspective – was Austria's greatest asset and the foundation for the influence she had (Austensen, 1980: 224). If Austria really wanted to compete for the allegiance of the *Mittelstaaten*, she was required to take a much more flexible attitude toward the demands of liberals and nationalists and offer a viable alternative to the Prussian *Zollverein*. Austria's identity as a dynastic, multinational state with a protectionist economy prevented her from making such concessions and by the 1860s, attempts to reform the Austrian administration and economy came too late.

The *Mittelstaaten* played their part in the obstruction of the national assembly as well. Concerned primarily with the protection of their sovereignty and political maneuverability, they were disinclined to follow Austria's conservative, anti-national policies or pay undue deference to Prussian reform plans. Whenever they pushed for their own reform projects, as they did in 1859 and 1861, it quickly became obvious that Bavarian, Saxon, and Badenese plans were as different from each other as they were opposed to the idea of Prussian or Austrian hegemony (Schulze, 1985: 91). The lack of a clear and substantive reform program on behalf of the third Germany and the political will to see it through left few alternatives but to eventually choose sides between Prussia's hegemonic-unitarian project or the traditional federal solution espoused by Austria. Consequently, when Prussia chose to force the issue militarily in 1866, some states found themselves bandwagoning with Prussia in 1866 while others stumbled into a faltering alliance with Austria. The *Bund* had failed to manage the interests of its member states through institutional and legislative means.

Discussion

Why should IR scholars care about the politics and policies of German regionalism in the nineteenth century? In this chapter I argued that the dynamics of intra-German politics are an important puzzle piece for understanding the trajectory of international relations and order during this period. The Congress of Vienna imposed an imperfect peace on central Europe, freezing relations between the leftover states of the Holy Roman Empire in an uneasy balance of interest and power, while also setting them on diverging trajectories of political and economic development that made long-term cooperation difficult. With the breaking of the revolutionary dam in 1848, the stage was set for a political transformation of central Europe that would reflect the ongoing modernization of political, economic, and cultural life. Instead, intra-German politics remained handcuffed; torn between the opposing interests of Austria and Prussia and the particularism of the *Mittelstaaten*. Given the political paralysis of the *Bund* and the increasingly diverging interests of the members states, it is perhaps not at all surprising that Bismarck chose a relatively minor dispute over the administration of two north German provinces as the pretext for leaving the *Bund* and declaring war on Austria in 1866.

This is not to say that the conflicts over German unification during the period 1866–1871 were inevitable, nor that the *kleindeutsche* solution (i.e. a unified German state under Prussian leadership) was desirable or even expedient. Instead, this chapter has sought to highlight the abundance of alternative political projects competing for prominence during much of the post-Vienna period. More importantly, it challenges IR scholars to transcend the narrow focus on great power relations that has characterized much of the literature by taking a closer look at the political, economic, institutional, and constitutional complexity of the period.

With this, the chapter connects directly with the overall theme of the volume: to view nineteenth-century international politics as chronologically separated into two worlds – one of localized cooperation and order, the other distinguished by global conflict and imperial competition. Through the recovery of the specific power configurations, institutional arrangements, and political processes of the *Bund*, this chapter draws attention to the political dynamics of one such regional order – the Concert of Europe. At the same time, by moving the analytical focus from the level of great power diplomacy to that of intra-German politics, we gain a more nuanced understanding of how this localized system functioned and – perhaps more importantly – why it collapsed. Accordingly, I argue that the precarious balance created in 1815 was set in a field of tension between various political, economic, and constitutional impulses that can be likened to a permanent stress test on the federal structure of the *Bund*. It was the resulting political paralysis of the system, coupled with the increasingly revisionist designs of Prussia, that eventually toppled this system. In this sense, the story of the *Bund* is the connecting tissue between the regional system of the first half of the nineteenth century and the globalized system that took shape throughout the second half and adds an important puzzle piece to our understanding of European politics at the time.

Bibliography

Aretin, Karl Otmar von. (1980) *Vom Deutschen Reich zum Deutschen Bund*. Göttingen: Vandenhoeck & Ruprecht Verlag.
Austensen, R.A. (1980) Austria and the 'Struggle for Supremacy in Germany', 1848–1864. *Journal of Modern History* 52(2): 196–225.
Austensen, R.A. (1983) Einheit oder Einigkeit: Another Look at Metternich's View of the German Dilemma. *German Studies Review* 6(1): 41–57.
Berding, Helmut and Hans-Peter Ullmann. (1981) *Deutschland zwischen Revolution und Restauration*. Düsseldorf: Droste.
Blanning, Tim. (1986) *The Origins of the French Revolutionary Wars*. Harlow: Pearson Education Limited.
Brunner, Otto. (1965) *Land und Herrschaft: Grundfragen der territorialen Verfassungsgeschichte Österreichs im Mittelalter*. Vienna: R.M. Rohrer.
Clark, Christopher. (2006) *Iron Kingdom: The Rise and Downfall of Prussia, 1600–1947*. New York: Penguin.
Clark, Ian. (2011) *Hegemony in International Society*. New York: Oxford University Press.
Doering-Manteuffel, Anselm. (1991) *Vom Wiener Kongress zur Pariser Konferenz*. Göttingen: Vandenhoeck & Ruprecht Verlag.
Engelsing, Rolf. (1969) Die Perioden der Lesergeschichte in der Neuzeit: Das statische Ausmass und die soziokulturelle Bedeutung der Lektüre. *Archiv für Geschichte des Buchwesens* 10: 944–1002.
Evans, Richard. (2016) *The Pursuit of Power: Europe 1815–1914*. New York: Penguin Books.
Fehrenbach, Elisabeth. (1974) *Traditionelle Gesellschaft und Revolutionäres Recht. Die Einführung des Cote Napoléon in den Rheinbundstaaten*. Göttingen: Vandenhoeck & Ruprecht Verlag.

Fehrenbach, Elisabeth. (2008) *Vom Ancien Regime zum Wiener Kongress.* München: Oldenbourg Verlag.
Gruner, Wolf D. (1993) *Die Deutsche Frage in Europa 1800–1990.* München: Piper Verlag.
Gruner, Wolf D. (2012) *Der Deutsche Bund 1815–1866.* München: C.H. Beck.
Gruner, Wolf D. (2014) *Der Wiener Kongress 1814/15.* Stuttgart: Reclam Verlag.
Habermas, Juergen. (1984) *The Structural Transformation of the Public Sphere: An Inquiry into a Category of Bourgeois Society.* Cambridge, MA: MIT Press.
Hahn, Hans-Werner. (1984) *Geschichte des Deutschen Zollvereins.* Göttingen: Vandenhoeck & Ruprecht Verlag.
Hahn, Hans-Werner. (1990) Mitteleuropäische oder kleindeutsche Wirtschaftsordung in der Epoche des Deutschen Bundes. In Helmut Rumpler, ed., *Deutscher Bund und Deutsche Frage 1815–1866.* München: Oldenbourg.
Haldén, Peter. (2011) Republican Continuities in the Vienna Order and the German Confederation (1815–1866). *European Journal of International Relations* 19(2): 1–24.
Hamerow, Theodore S. (1969) *The Social Foundations of German Unification 1851–1871, Vol. 1.* Princeton: Princeton University Press.
Hippel, Wolfgang von and Bernhard Stier. (2012) *Europa zwischen Reform und Revolution, 1800–1850.* Stuttgart: Eugen Ulmer Verlag.
Ikenberry, G. John. (2001) *After Victory: Institutions, Strategic Restraint, and the Rebuilding of Order after Major Wars.* Princeton: Princeton University Press.
Kaiser, Michael. (2009) A Matter of Survival: Bavaria becomes a Kingdom. In Alan Forrest and Peter Wilson, eds., *The Bee and the Eagle: Napoleonic France and the End of the Holy Roman Empire.* Houndmills: Palgrave Macmillan.
Katzenstein, Peter. (1976) *Disjointed Partners: Austria and Germany since 1815.* Berkeley: University of California Press.
Komlos, John. (1983) *The Habsburg Monarchy as a Customs Union. Economic Development in Austria-Hungary in the Nineteenth Century.* Princeton: Princeton University Press.
Kraehe, Enno E. (1951) Austria and the Problem of Reform in the German Confederation, 1851–1863. *American Historical Review* 56(2): 276–294.
Kraehe, Enno E. (1971) *The Metternich Controversy.* New York: Krieger Publishing Co.
Kraehe, Enno E. (1983) *Metternich's German Policy, Volume 2: The Congress of Vienna, 1814–1815.* Princeton: Princeton University Press.
Kraehe, Enno E. (1990) Austria, Russia and the German Confederation, 1813–1820. In Helmut Rumpler, ed., *Deutscher Bund und Deutsche Frage 1815–1866.* München: Oldenbourg.
Kupchan, Charles. (2010) *How Enemies Become Friends: The Sources of a Stable Peace.* Princeton: Princeton University Press.
Langewiesche, Dieter. (2007) *Europa zwischen Restauration und Revolution 1815–1849.* München: Oldenbourg Verlag.
Lutz, Heinrich. (1985) *Zwischen Habsburg und Preussen: Deutschland 1815–1866.* Berlin: Siedler.
Mitzen, Jennifer. (2013) *Power in Concert.* Chicago: University of Chicago Press.
Mosse, William E. (1958) *The European Powers and the German Question, 1848–71.* Cambridge: Cambridge University Press.
Müller, J. (2006) *Der Deutsche Bund 1815–1866.* München: Oldenburg.
Nipperdey, Thomas. (1983) *Deutsche Geschichte 1800–1866: Bürgerwelt und starker Staat.* München: C.H. Beck.

Schroeder, Paul. (1986) The 19th-century International System: Changes in the Structure. *World Politics* 39(1): 1–26.
Schroeder, Paul. (1992) Did the Vienna Settlement Rest on a Balance of Power? *American Historical Review* 97(3): 683–706.
Schroeder, Paul. (1994) *The Transformation of European Politics, 1763–1848*. Oxford: Clarendon Press.
Schulze, Hagen. (1985) *The Course of German Nationalism: From Frederick the Great to Bismarck, 1763–1867*. Cambridge: Cambridge University Press.
Sheehan, James. (1989) *German History 1770–1866*. Oxford: Clarendon Press.
Simpson, Gerry. (2004) *Great Powers and Outlaw States*. Cambridge: Cambridge University Press.
Sperber, Jonathan. (2005) *The European Revolutions, 1848–1851*. Cambridge: Cambridge University Press.
Weiss, Eberhard. (1973) Der Einfluss der Französischen Revolution und des Empire auf die Reformen in den süddeutschen Staaten. *Francia* 1: 569–583.
Weiss, Eberhard. (1984) *Reformen im rheinbündischen Deutschland*. München: Oldenbourg.
Wilson, Peter. (2016) *Heart of Europe: A History of the Holy Roman Empire*. Cambridge, MA: Harvard University Press.
Woloch, Isser. (1994) *The New Regime: Transformations of the French Civic Order, 1789–1820s*. New York: W.W. Norton.

5 Rejecting Westphalia

Maintaining the Sinocentric system, to the end

David Banks

The rapid and sudden expansion of European influence in the 19th century had more than political and economic effects for the wider world. It also often interfered with the underlying manner in which political units interacted in these regions. The export of European ordering-concepts such as sovereignty, territoriality, and international law were often alien "interaction processes" (Buzan and Little, 2000) to other regions, and were not easily incorporated by the actors that populated them. This chapter investigates how this struggle to adapt manifested itself in the Sinocentric system of East Asia. Although Europeans had been traveling to and trading with Imperial China since the 1600s, it was only in the late 1700s that European governments, beginning with Britain, reached out to make formal diplomatic arrangements with the Qing regime. Yet, this proved far more difficult than Europeans had anticipated, not simply due to an underlying conflict of strategic interests but also due to the conflict between the diplomatic practices of both international systems.

By the late 1700s European states were used to engaging in what I call 'Westphalian Diplomatic Practice': a diplomatic system in which socially equal states were entitled to ceremonial equality and the exchange of resident ministers. Some diplomatic practices of this system conflicted with those of the Sinocentric system in East Asia, in which China was accepted by Korea, Vietnam, Japan (sometimes), and other actors in the region to be the social superior of all other entities. This social (not political) dominance was expressed in a set of elaborate ceremonial practices – most notably the *koutou* ritual performed in front of the emperor. The Qing regime, already sensitive to the political and developmental issues it was having relative to Europeans, now found its entire cultural system under attack. As a consequence, it decided to reject Westphalian diplomatic practice entirely.

This decision to self-isolate had serious consequences as it created tensions, inhibited cooperation, and poisoned relations with increasingly aggressive European powers. Ultimately, it led to the destruction of the Chinese cultural system in East Asia in a way that not only altered and re-ordered the domestic politics of China but also in the other states in the Sinosphere. Had China simply agreed to engage in the diplomatic practice demanded by Britain and other European states many of these problems could have been avoided. This seemingly self-destructive behavior on the part of Qing China requires explanation.

In providing this explanation, this chapter proceeds as follows. First, I describe the 19th-century diplomatic practices of both European international society and those of China and its neighbors. Second, I outline in detail what occurred when these two systems came into direct diplomatic contact as European power expanded into Asia in the late 18th century. In particular, I focus on China's response to three official embassies sent by Britain between 1793 and 1861. Third, I argue that the reason the Qing regime guarded its diplomatic practices so closely was because they were a source of considerable domestic power. As a result, they could not be easily jettisoned. Instead, they were so jealously guarded that they ended up being utterly destroyed by increasingly outraged Europeans.

Competing diplomatic practices in 19th-century Europe and East Asia

The modern diplomatic system grew out of particular historical circumstances that began in 15th-century Europe. Many elements of modern diplomatic practice – such as resident embassies, ceremonial and protocol, and ranking and titles – are by-products of limited information technology, social and religious norms, and monarchical systems of government. They are anachronistic artifacts as much as they are functional institutions. Indeed, Zbigniew Brzezinski has stated that if foreign ministries and embassies "did not already exist, they surely would not have been invented" (quoted in Hamilton and Langhorne, 2011: 258). The idiosyncratic nature of modern diplomatic practice is somewhat obscure to us – or at least uncontroversial – largely because it is the only game in town. But the homogenization of diplomatic practice was not an accidental or efficiency-driven process. The elimination of alternative systems of diplomatic practice was the direct result of the sudden and massive expansion of European political power in the 19th century. Ironically, although some associate the European mode of diplomacy – what I call Westphalian diplomatic practice – with peace and managing conflict, this presupposes its use by all states in an interaction. As I show in this chapter, when diplomatic practices conflict, the resolution of this conflict can be quite violent. In order to understand such conflicts it is necessary to show how Westphalian diplomatic practice differed from the Sinocentric tributary system of East Asia.

Westphalian diplomatic practice

While 1648 was not the complete revolution of international order that some IR scholars consider it to be, the Peace of Westphalia nonetheless reaffirmed the system of international governance that was first laid down at the Peace of Augsburg in 1555 (Croxton, 1999; Osiander, 2001). These treaties saw the scales finally tipped against an international society that had been dominated by norms of Christian universalism and royal dynasticism. Westphalia reaffirmed that the sovereign nation-state, an entity first recognized at the 1415

Council of Constance, was the only authority in the international realm (Mann, 2012a). This political transformation required a new and more consciously state-centric form of diplomacy. By the 19th century this Westphalian diplomatic practice was fully in place. Composed of a bundle of overlapping material objects, institutions, and actions, it regulated diplomacy between European states. A few prominent elements were at the center of this practice.

First, Westphalian diplomatic practice entitled states to exchange resident missions. The resident mission was an Italian creation that first appeared in Renaissance Italy and was soon adopted by other powerful states in Europe. In 1432, the duke of Milan had a resident ambassador at the court of the Holy Roman Emperor. By the 1470s, Florence had representatives in Paris, and by 1500 England hosted numerous Italian resident diplomats in London. By the Westphalian era, the network of embassies had expanded considerably. By 1685, France had embassies in Rome, Venice, Constantinople, Vienna, the Hague, London, Madrid, Lisbon, Munich, Copenhagen, and Bern, as well as host of special missions and resident ministries in several other places (Nicolson, 1954). By the time of the Congress of Vienna in 1815, diplomatic missions had taken the form of either full embassies (or high commissions) that housed ambassadors, or legations that house lower-ranked diplomats. These types of missions were (and are) traditionally located in the capital cities of the hosting states.[1]

Second, embassies and chanceries (and their representatives) were entitled to the rights of immunity and inviolability. Originally, this simply meant that an envoy was to be free from molestation in any way that might impede his office. The adoption of resident embassies expanded the rights of immunity in both their degree and physical scope. The duration of residencies meant that being hounded by creditors or being subject to local laws could impede an ambassador's duties. Thus, with time, immunity came to also imply exemption from many laws. Furthermore, immunity was expanded to apply not only to the person of the ambassador or other accredited representatives, but also to the physical space of the embassy and to the diplomatic pouch (Hamilton and Langhorne, 2011).

Third, diplomatic representatives were obliged to engage in and to receive specific ceremonial rights governed by specific protocols. This included ceremonial displays put on by a hosting state, such as escorts that accompanied a visiting envoy, flags, displays, ritual reviews of troops, and so forth. Depending on rank, visiting envoys could expect to be met with ceremonial entries into a city, the public display of an envoy's entourage, the presentation and receipt of gifts, and specific ritual or symbolic behaviors. As such, diplomatic ceremonial was something that was engaged in by both representative and hosts. These ceremonies were (and remain) dictated by protocol: specific rules that codify and determine which ceremony a representative is entitled to at any particular time, how such a ceremony should be staged, and exactly how all participants in this ceremony should behave (Woods and Serres, 1970). In practice, these protocols are often highly specific and detailed, and can prescribe on issues as narrow as the procedure in which people enter the room, how one should be attired, the manner in which people should be addressed, where flags and national symbols should be placed, what form (if any) gift-giving should take, and so on (McCaffree and Innis, 1989).

As these elements indicate, Westphalian diplomatic practice has always been more than just a functional medium of interstate communication, but also a system loaded with social meaning. For instance, although the expansion of the resident-system had a proximately functional cause, a state's ability to send and receive embassies was soon seen as a mark of its power and prestige. By the 1700s being able to send an embassy (or markedly refusing to send full embassies, as the US did for much of the 19th century) sent a signal about a state's position in international society and its opinion of other members. As the 18th-century diplomat Abraham de Wicquefort (1716: 6) put it, "There is not a more illustrious Mark of Sovereignty than the Right of sending and receiving Ambassadors." Indeed, throughout the 18th and 19th century great powers usually only sent full embassies to the capitals of other great powers. Smaller states and non-European states were frequently host to nothing larger than legations or consular missions.[2] Similarly, representatives were initially expected to receive diplomatic inviolability and ritual care because as diplomats they were assumed to be acting in the cause of peace, and this made them akin to angels.[3] Later this same practice was upheld on the grounds that in a system of sovereign and equal states no state had the right to interfere with another's property or symbols (Berridge, 2001). Further, these functional and social properties of diplomacy could overlap in unexpected ways. For instance, although a state might wish to send an embassy for practical reasons, it might treat another state's refusal to house the embassy as an insult.

Thus, even though many of the earliest elements of Westphalian diplomatic practice – such as immunity, privileges, and ceremonial and protocol – all predated Westphalia, by the 19th century participating in diplomatic practice had become associated with being a full member of international society. To engage in Westphalian diplomatic practice was to participate in the maintenance of an international society in which independent and estranged sovereigns were (and are) continuously constituted and sustained by one another, and in which diplomats were expected to uphold amicable relations between one another in order to maintain this system (Der Derian, 1987). Westphalian diplomatic practice helped to recreate the "relations of separateness" necessary for the European state system to exist (Sharp, 2009: 10). Westphalian diplomatic practice helped to reaffirm and recreate the practice that 'anchored' European international society: that there existed a thing called international society, and that this was populated by juridically equal states. By extension, rejection of this practice – intentional or otherwise – indicated a rejection of this principle of equality and could only be treated as an insult.

Diplomatic practice and the Sinocentric system

Unlike Westphalian Europe – which had begun to think of domestic and foreign realms as distinct arenas – the Sinocentric system blurred the lines between the international and domestic. This blurring extended into every element of political practice, not least diplomacy. At the center of *both* Chinese domestic politics *and* East Asian international politics was the person of the emperor, whose rule was divinely sanctioned by a 'Mandate from Heaven'. Since the time of the Zhou dynasty in the 11th century BCE, the Chinese state had maintained that the emperor was the most important spiritual figure in the world: the Son of Heaven. This sacred personage was the link between the cosmos and the material plane. He was both a secular and a religious ruler, heir to millennia of tradition and custom, responsible for all events in his realm, and the center of political, social, cosmic, and moral order (Kang, 2012). This system dominated political activity in East Asia from at least the time of the Ming (1368–1644). Indeed, even though the Manchu Qing were technically foreign invaders when they toppled the Ming, they adopted almost wholesale the domestic narratives and symbolic practices that had been used by their predecessors.

While in many ways far more symbolically and functionally powerful than European absolute monarchs, the emperor's right to rule did not imply a right to unrestrained behavior. On the contrary, "the emperor was obliged to respect the norms and forms imposed on him" (Gernet, 1987: xxii). The emperor had an obligation to rule, rather than a right, and was heavily circumscribed in the actions he could legitimately take. All behavior, right down to the emperor's edicts, residences, calligraphy, seals, and rituals were carefully regulated. The stress on cosmic relationships was central to a Chinese political philosophy that saw man as part of nature, not in conflict with it, and that saw all nature as linked to heaven through the person of the emperor. This philosophy provided the ethical basis for the emperor's place in the social and political hierarchy of China. As the Son of Heaven, it was the emperor's function to maintain the harmony between earth and the celestial realm. Failure to do so indicated that the emperor was unfit to lead. Indeed, the Qing justified their deposition of the Ming on the grounds that the Ming had allowed an imbalance in the natural order (Spence, 1990: 58–64).

The most significant of all the symbolic practices associated with Qing imperial power was the ritual *koutou* that took place at Beijing. Because the emperor was the supreme lord (*huang di*) of the material world, Chinese protocol demanded that all petitioners to his court ritually acknowledge this by engaging in various public rituals and ceremonies. At the center of this ritual system was the *koutou,* which involved kneeling three times and knocking one's head on the floor. Visiting envoys who conducted this ceremony often did not even get to meet the emperor, and were expected to simply be thankful for the "extension of imperial grace" (Hevia, 1989: 84).

The Middle Kingdom narrative and the *koutou* ritual also informed China's relations with foreign powers. China was the center of what is commonly known as the 'tributary system'. The East Asian tributary system shared the same political myths as the Chinese domestic system. All states participating in the tributary system understood and accepted the superior hierarchical position of the Chinese emperor over all other monarchs and states. According to the norms of this system the emperor's demesne did not end at the borders of the Chinese state but was understood to extend across the entire world. While this system recognized the existence of de facto independent states beyond its direct command, these states were still socially regarded as dependent on the emperor for cosmological harmony and, therefore, as obliged to recognize the emperor's superiority as his own domestic subjects did. States on the periphery of the Chinese empire were expected to periodically send representatives to publicly pay tribute to the emperor and recognize his overlordship of the world.

For the states bearing tribute this practice was the main medium through which all other diplomatic intercourse was conducted, such as alliances, negotiations, and threats of force. It also allowed for the trade of luxury goods, which were transported duty-free as part of an envoy's baggage trains and then sold at special markets which lasted from three to five days at the Residence for Tributary Envoys (Fairbank, 1942). Thus the tributary system was symbiotic: the Chinese valued the moral element of tribute; the tributaries valued the material benefit of security and/or trade. Although tributary states were free to pursue their own particular interests, their behavior was understood to take place inside an international society in which all actors ostensibly recognized the power of the Imperial throne (Kang, 2012).

The norms of this system directly contradicted those of European international society. Unlike European international society, the Qing tributary system did not recognize the existence of legally and socially equal sovereign entities, nor did it recognize any need or obligation to engage in permanent resident diplomacy. Yet while the potential for friction between these two systems was obvious, there is no a priori reason that these incompatible social and political claims needed to necessarily lead to meaningful political conflict. For instance, many of the strict regulations regarding tributary visits – the limited the size of retinues, the route they would take to the capital, the locations where legations were to stay, the supplies they were to receive, when they were to pay homage to the emperor, banqueting, and when and how they were to leave – could all be accommodated to Westphalian diplomacy. However, as the first British ambassador to China and his successors would soon realize, there were some elements of Westphalian diplomatic practice that the Qing would reject entirely. In the next section, I will outline in detail how this rejection manifested itself.

Westphalia rejected: Chinese resistance to European diplomacy

Until the late 18th century China's only real European political relationship was with Russia. Conscious of its importance for the security of China's northern frontiers, Russia was granted a certain amount of special treatment by the Qing. Russia maintained treaty relations, sent missions, and was allowed special privileges in Beijing, including a permanent mission although, as is explained below, this was not an official diplomatic mission (Hsü, 1964). Aside from this interaction, China had not really encountered European international society at an official level. However, once it did it struggled to accommodate Westphalian diplomatic practice before finally deciding to reject it – and interaction with Europe – entirely.

China and European international society

With the exception of Russia, since the 1600s European states mediated their relationship with imperial China through private merchants and charter companies (Marshall, 1993). Due to a number of cultural and institutional roadblocks, these European merchants had a difficult time conducting trade with a Chinese state that had very little domestic demand for anything that European traders were selling, at least until the East India Company (EIC) decided to start smuggling opium in from India. Officially, European "barbarians" were subject to heavy regulations and restrictions. These inefficiencies had strategic consequences for European states in the 18th century, most notably for Britain, which was becoming increasingly dependent on the tea trade (Hillemann, 2009). In order to acquire an edict from the Qing emperor permitting trade, and to preempt any future problems, Britain decided to finally draw China formally into the European system of international relations by stationing an official diplomatic representative in Beijing. Following a failed attempt in 1788,[4] an official diplomatic mission left from England in 1792. As I show in the remainder of this article, China rejected the standards of Westphalian diplomatic practice from the time of the first British embassy's arrival in 1793 until the occupation of Beijing in 1861. Two prominent elements of Westphalian diplomatic practice in particular were rejected by the Chinese government: the diplomatic ceremonial and protocol in which the equality of European states was recognized; and the establishment of permanent resident embassies at Beijing.

The Macartney mission of 1793

China's first rejection of Westphalian diplomatic practice occurred with the arrival of the British Macartney mission in 1793. A career diplomat, George Macartney had been tasked with getting the Qing to sign a commerce treaty, open new ports, grant new land to the EIC, abolish the abuses of the Canton system, and allow the opening of new markets. Macartney arrived at the port of Taku, located on the Peiho (modern: Hai) River in July 1793. Here he was met by two "chief Mandarins" before sailing up the Great Canal to Beijing in August. At various points along the journey, Macartney's mission observed thousands of people assembled along its banks. In one instance, "both sides of the river were lined for nearly a mile in length with the troops of the garrison, all in uniform, accompanied by innumerable flags, standards, and pennants" (Macartney, 1963: 78). For most of their journey upriver the Chinese refused to discuss anything substantive with Macartney. As the retinue approached the capital, the Chinese representatives, "with the appearance of more formality than usual," first brought up the issue of the *koutou*, an issue which Macartney attempted to deflect on (Macartney, 1963: 84). For the next six days, Qing representatives refused to discuss any other issue. When Macartney finally arrived at the capital, he proposed a modification to the ceremony that might satisfy both parties: instead of performing the traditional *koutou*, he would bend down on one knee and kiss the emperor's hand. Macartney had explained that this was similar to the ceremony that he performed for the English king. The Chinese agreed to this rite, but warned Macartney not to touch the emperor in any way.

On September 14, Macartney was roused early and directed to a large and highly decorated tent containing over 600 attendees. Manchu princes and bannermen, tributary princes, envoys from other states, Chinese regional viceroys, and ministers from the court were all lined up according to rank (Singer, 1992). Macartney writes that when the emperor passed, he made a last-minute decision to violate his agreement with Qing officials and placed his credentials into the hands of the emperor (Macartney, 1963: 122). The day when he finally met the emperor, Macartney asked him for some consideration of the issues of the British mission but this request was ignored. Instead Macartney was given some gifts and was sent away. Thus he left Beijing with only an Imperial edict that offered no trade concessions and "a broad hint to leave as soon as possible" (Rockhill, 1897 633).

Macartney considered his mission a failure. He had failed to meet any of the substantive goals regarding trade. What puzzled Macartney even more was the degree to which the dispute over the *koutou* had come to dominate all of his interactions with Chinese representatives. What had begun as a minor issue when Macartney was in Taku had in Beijing expanded to become the *only* issue which Chinese representatives talked to Macartney about.

The Amherst mission of 1816

Qing rejection of Westphalian diplomacy was even more pronounced when, after winning the Napoleonic wars, Britain sent another embassy in 1816. Lord William Amherst was given the same mission as Macartney: to promote commerce and to establish formal diplomatic relations. Unlike Macartney – who had been taken by surprise when the *koutou* issue was raised – Amherst fully expected that "the Tartar Court Ceremony [was] likely to form part of

[his] earliest disruptions with the Chinese government."[5] He was right. At Tianjin, Amherst met some officials from the Qing court who immediately brought up the issue of the *koutou*, asking whether or not Amherst would be willing to practice it. Amherst tried to distract Qing officials from the issue, promising that he "should be prepared to meet with the Emperor in the most respectful manner."[6] Yet any attempts to change the topic of discussion or ignore it until reaching Beijing, as Macartney had done, was not possible. Adopting one of Macartney's solutions, Amherst offered to perform the ritual if a mandarin of equal rank performed it in front of a picture of the English Regent, Prince George. He was informed by one of the representatives "that the established usage of the Chinese Court could not be dispensed with and he added, after some high and haughty language, that as there was only one Sun in the firmament, so there was only one Sovereign in the Universe, the Emperor of the Heavenly Empire."[7]

Upon arrival at Beijing, Amherst was treated with little of the courtesy Macartney had received. Rather than entering the main gate, the entourage was brought through a dangerous side entrance at night. Instead of the plush apartments which had been offered to Macartney, Amherst was brought to a "mean and dirty dwelling." In short, the Chinese representatives refused to engage in Westphalian diplomatic practice. Amherst found the treatment of his mission humiliating and intimidating, and felt that his embassy had been subjected to "transactions of an extraordinary nature, so little to be accounted for by the usages of European Courts."[8] Most significantly, immediately upon arrival in the early hours of the morning, Amherst was ordered to meet with the emperor. When Amherst refused this order, arguing that he was not prepared, he was summarily ordered to immediately leave Beijing.

Even more than it had during Macartney's mission the *koutou* issue had plagued negotiations between Amherst and the Qing. Indeed the conflict led to a shift in Qing policy. When Amherst returned to his ship he found a note waiting for him from the Chinese emperor ordering the British to send no more embassies. In a letter to the British regent the emperor explained that there was no reason for future embassies, as it was clear that foreigners struggled to perform the ceremony of the *koutou*. This, combined with the fact that the "Empire does not value things brought from a distance ... all the extraordinary and ingenious productions of your country," meant that the British monarch need not suffer the burden of sending any more ambassadors.[9] Thus, not only had Amherst failed in his diplomatic mission, but his refusal to *koutou* had *worsened* diplomatic relations between the two states. Due to disputes over diplomatic practice, China had effectively isolated itself from European international society.

From Amherst to the Arrow War of 1856–1860

The Qing rejection of Westphalian diplomatic practice and its turn towards isolationism was not without consequence for China. In the first place, repeated Chinese demands for the public recognition of the emperor's putative superior position had poisoned European public opinion toward China. Whereas the imperial system of China had been held up as the exemplar of good governance in intellectual circles in Europe for much of the 17th and 18th centuries, from the late 18th century onward China was increasingly viewed as a despotic and decaying state, with – as the repeated disputes over the *koutou* indicated – ideas above its station.[10] In light of China's repeated "bad" behavior, popular opinion about the Chinese empire had considerably declined throughout Europe. At the official level, Britain thought that China's behavior was generally indicative of a hostile attitude toward British trade and interests in the region. Amherst thought that China's demands were incredible, writing that "it would have been a humiliation to accept an audience on the terms proposed."[11] While it might be considered acceptable for Japan or Siam to allow their envoys to *koutou*, Amherst would refuse "any comparison to be drawn between the King of Great Britain and the feeble states which surrounded the Chinese Empire."[12] This sentiment was shared by the British public who, already offended by the treatment of the first embassy, turned decisively against China following Amherst's return (Graham, 1978). This shift in British opinion regarding China was compounded by a second issue: the unresolved state of diplomatic affairs between the two states. At the exact time that British elite and mass opinion was shifting decisively toward treating China in a more aggressive manner, China had isolated itself.

In addition to the collapse of official diplomacy, the central conflict of interest between Britain and China – trade – was no closer to being resolved. Having given up on resolving this issue through negotiation, Britain finally declared war on China in 1839. Although the scholarly consensus is that the Opium War (1839–1842) was triggered by the British desire to alleviate its trade problems, it is worth noting how central the *koutou* dispute had become in framing the conflict. Observing events from afar, former US diplomat, Secretary of State, and President John Quincy Adams considered the Chinese demands for the *koutou* to have been "insulting and degrading" and the sole cause of the war (quoted in Hevia, 1993: 61). The war was a decidedly one-sided affair and ended in 1842 with the Treaty of Nanking. China was forced to open five ports for British trade, cede Hong Kong, pay indemnities, guarantee Most-Favored-Nation (MFN) status for Britain, and grant consular jurisdiction over all British subjects in China.

While the war settled the Sino-British conflict over trade, tensions remained between both states, and issues such as the status of the opium trade and the right of diplomatic representation remained unresolved. Although the Treaty of Nanking allowed Britain (and other European states) to post representatives, these representatives only operated at the periphery of the Chinese empire, and were unable to communicate directly with the central executive. This resulted in an international relationship between China and other powers that was mediated by local regional governors.

The inadequacy of this arrangement became apparent on October, 5 1856 when the *Arrow*, a ship crewed by Chinese sailors but flying under a British flag, was stopped and impounded by the Chinese navy. This local dispute triggered a sequence of events which escalated into the *Arrow* War (sometimes called the Second Opium War). After destroying the bulk of the Chinese navy, Britain sent James Bruce, Earl of Elgin, to end the war and find a settlement. Just before Lord Elgin attempted to force entry into Beijing, China surrendered, signing the Treaty of Tianjin in June 1858. This was the first treaty in which China conceded to allow a permanent resident ambassador in China. However, the Qing representatives with whom Elgin negotiated pleaded that the ambassador reside at Shanghai instead.[13] Although Elgin saw this concession as an important one, he nonetheless decided to allow it.

The incoming ambassador – Elgin's brother Frederick Bruce – was not as flexible. His first task was to ratify the treaty in Beijing, meet with the Chinese emperor, and then return to Shanghai (Graham, 1978). When he arrived at Shanghai in May 1859 he was met by the same Qing commissioners who had ratified the Treaty of Tianjin. They requested that the ratification ceremony be moved from Beijing to another port. When Bruce refused this request, he was asked if the mission could make its way to Beijing along a land route that twisted around the city and came from the north, as opposed to the southern entrance through the main gate on the Peiho. They also asked that the mission enter without banners or any escort which might "illustrate the power and prestige of Western arms" (Graham, 1978: 367).

Bruce ignored these requests as he had been given clear instructions that he was to head to Beijing and that he was not to engage in "any ceremony, or any form of reception, which might be construed into an admission of inferiority on the part of Her Majesty in regard to the Emperor of China" (Banno, quoted in Graham, 1978: 367). When Bruce reached the Peiho he found its mouth blocked and its forts occupied. An attempt to storm the position was unsuccessful and the British forces lost over 500 men dead and 400 wounded.

The Qing decision to bar entry into Beijing was to have terrible consequences for the regime. When news of the battle reached the British parliament and press there was universal outrage. Lord Elgin returned to China and stormed Tianjin. Yet even with the British approaching the gates of Beijing, the Qing defended their ritual system. When Elgin declared that a Qing refusal to allow him to hand the Queen's terms directly to the emperor would be treated as a *casus belli* the negotiations broke down. British representatives were kidnapped and murdered by Qing forces (Wang, 1971). In response, a combined Anglo-French force stormed Beijing and in retaliation destroyed the famous summer palaces in Beijing.[14] The Qing emperor fled Beijing and died in exile shortly thereafter. In command of the capital city, Britain and other European states now claimed full diplomatic rights. Resident embassies were established in Beijing, and European diplomats refused to engage in any ritual practices that suggested anything other than full sovereign equality. Chinese rejection of Westphalian diplomatic practice on the seemingly trivial issues of ceremonial and protocol and resident embassies had directly contributed to its own diplomatic isolation, to the escalation of the *Arrow* war, and ultimately to the deposing of the Qing emperor.

Explaining Qing behavior: legitimacy, practice, and power

Why did China reject Westphalian diplomatic practice for so long, even in the face of considerable aggression? In particular, what was it about the issues of the *koutou* and resident embassies that led the Qing regime to contest them so violently? This behavior is extremely puzzling once we consider that the Qing regime was willing to concede on issues that seem much more valuable, such as land concessions in the form of treaty ports, or accepting the importation of opium. Furthermore, Qing intransigence did not occur in a political vacuum. China's rejection of Westphalian diplomatic practice inflamed the mass and elite opinion of European international society at the exact time that policies of aggressive racist imperialism were becoming adopted by Europe. China's rejection of traditional diplomacy made Europe more hostile, while simultaneously making it harder for China to interact with it. What explains China's puzzling behavior at this time?

An obvious explanation for Qing rejection of Westphalian diplomatic practice is that it was done to somehow improve China's strategic situation. For instance, by jeopardizing a negotiation on symbolic issues regarding diplomatic practice, the Qing regime could had created the impression that they had little at stake in the negotiation, and thus had a better outside option (Lake and Powell, 1999). In the same vein it seems plausible that the Qing decided to adopt a confrontational stance in order to bolster their international reputation (Mercer, 2005).

Yet there is little evidence to support such interpretations. At the time of the Macartney mission the Qing had little interest in international trade and thus little interest in improving relations with trading states (Spence, 1990). Furthermore, the Qing did not really understand the concept of diplomatic missions in the same way that Europeans did (Zhang, 1993). Although Macartney thought that meeting with the emperor would be a precursor to negotiations, the Chinese mandarins leading Macartney to Beijing treated him as they would any other foreign envoy, and thus focused on the ceremonial obligations Macartney would be expected to fulfill. In this sense, the Qing regime was not 'bargaining' with the British as it saw nothing to bargain over. Qing officials were not negotiating with British officials or trying to send signals to a wider world that they knew very little about. Furthermore, such a strategic account completely fails to explain the persistent rejection of Westphalian diplomatic practice by China in later periods. Following Amherst's expulsion from Beijing in 1816, China forbade any more European embassies from coming to the capital. Even after the huge defeats of the Opium and *Arrow* wars, the Qing regime still refused to budge on issues regarding diplomatic practice. From a strategic perspective this is puzzling.

Because of the failure of strategic explanations, it is tempting to reduce the conflict over diplomatic practices to one of clashing civilizations and identity issues. From this perspective the Qing may have seen Westphalian diplomatic practice as threatening to their own sense of 'self' (Wendt 1999; Mitzen 2006). Such an explanation could certainly account for the fastidious way that the

Qing adhered to rituals and practice in Beijing. However, it cannot account for the flexible attitude the Qing exhibited regarding their ritual system in other areas. For instance, in the non-Chinese territories of Mongolia the Qing emperors appeared as great khans; to Tibetans as "turners of the wheel of time" (Waley-Cohen, 2006: 2). Indeed, the Qing regime was even flexible on the issue of resident ministers, and had allowed the *E-lo-ssu kuan* (Russian Hostel) to house a permanent minister since 1720. However, while this building de facto operated as a Russian mission, it was *officially* recognized as a religious building (Ssu-ming, 1960–1961). Similarly, the Qing regime was willing to compromise with Russia on issues of ceremonial and protocol. When Leon Izamailov appeared in 1721 he agreed to *koutou* to the emperor only if a Qing representative agreed to do the same to the Tsar when visiting Russia (Pritchard, 1943).

In other words, the Qing regime was willing to basically accept some of the functional elements of Westphalian diplomatic practice (such as resident missions) provided these elements were repackaged so as not to appear as official embassies. And although the Qing regime was immovable on issues of practice inside its borders, it could be very flexible on such issues when abroad. In short, the evidence suggests that the Qing relationship to practice seems calculating, although not in a way most strategic accounts would be familiar with.

Legitimacy, practice, and power in Qing China

In order to fully explain Qing China's puzzling behavior we must appreciate the political power the Qing maintained by faithfully engaging in its diplomatic practice. As mentioned earlier, the Qing dynasty legitimated its right to rule on the grounds that the emperor held the millennia-old Mandate from Heaven. Yet this was more than a simple rhetorical trope. Being a 'good' emperor meant not just implementing policies that supported this position, but also demonstrating – in practice – that he was observing and upholding all the traditions that this narrative of legitimation mandated. Failure to engage in the practices associated with this narrative could reduce imperial authority. This meant there were real incentives for the regime not to deviate from practices imbued with political significance.

The precarious nature of Qing rule

Since its founding in 1644 one of the most pressing concerns for the Qing dynasty was what Mark Elliot (2001: 3) calls the "minority-rule question." Even after migrating into China in the hundreds of thousands, the Manchu ruling class was outnumbered by ethnic Han Chinese by approximately 350 to 1. The Qing regime was conscious of the danger this represented and worried about the possibility of collective action against it (Wakeman, 1998). Initially, the Qing regime attempted to deter potential challengers by placing military garrisons of Manchu bannermen (nobles) throughout China. As time went on, the military effectiveness of the garrison system deteriorated due to a weakening of ethnic apartheid, the shirking of martial training by the bannermen, and (most significantly) the impoverishment of a class that was reliant on an increasingly devalued currency (Elliot, 2001). As the banners weakened, the Qing regime increasingly shared power with the Han elite. In the provinces (*zhou*) and counties (*xian*) the official imperial administration existed next to local networks of former Han officials and power-holders (Schwartz, 1987). These power-holders often had influence in the largest military force in China – the Green Standard Army – which was drawn from the Han populace and was about three times the size of the Manchu armies.

At exactly the time that European states were taking a formal interest in China, the cracks in Qing rule were beginning to show. From the second half of the 18th century onward rebellions and uprisings became more common. These rebellions took a number of forms and included secret societies, peasant revolts, urban workers' riots, garrison mutinies, and full-scale uprisings. Regardless of the type, most were led by Han Chinese literati such as monks and disaffected bureaucrats. Although these uprisings had many varied underlying causes, most were at least rhetorically justified in terms of reaction against illegitimate Qing rule (Wakeman 1997). In 1786, the millenarian Eight Trigams sect mobilized against the Qing province of Zhili and expressly condemned the Qing as illegitimate (Naquin, 1982). In 1813, the Eight Trigrams actually attempted to storm the palace in Beijing. By 1852 the situation was even more perilous when the Qing regime was wracked by the most severe rebellion of its history: the Taiping Rebellion. This erosion of material power and fear of uprisings had the effect of making the Qing regime unstable. With material power eroding over the course of the first half of the 19th century, the Qing became even more sensitive to public challenges to their authority.

The power of practice

By taking the Qing authority crisis and its weakening material position into consideration, we can better understand the growing importance of the ritual system the Qing relied on. Engaging in symbolic practices as a means of generating authority was at the heart of Qing authority from the outset of their rule. Shortly after the invasion of China, the Manchu regent ordered that Manchu dress and hairstyles – which included the distinctive shaved forehead and braided knot – were to be adopted by ethnically Han people who wished to obtain or retain government positions. This hugely unpopular edict was strictly enforced, as testified by the popular contemporary phrase, "lose your hair and keep your head." The topknot not only allowed the Manchu to erode the spirit of the newly conquered Chinese, but also served as a signal of obedience, and a common-knowledge generator of the power of the Manchu.[15] Qing emperors also projected their power by occasionally embarking on royal tours of the provinces, most notably under the rule of the Qianlong Emperor.[16] According to Chang (2007: 95), these tours allowed the Qing court to demonstrate its majesty to the far-flung populace and "to police the boundary between the realms of credible elite opinion and incredible popular rumors." Thus, ostentatious and imposing tours helped to reinforce the perception of a powerful and all-reaching imperial court. Imperial displays of power did not end with grand tours. The Qing also engaged in large-scale military rituals and grand hunts (Waley-Cohen 2006; Elliot 2001).

A fixation on public practices is not uncommon in repressive systems. By faithfully engaging in mandated symbolic practices, a regime can show potential challengers that it is in command of the public square, and that it is not worth collectively acting against. This is especially true in autocratic systems of rule where there are few institutionalized avenues of dissent. In states such as these, regimes have an incentive to display their power and generate common knowledge of their scope and supremacy. For instance, during the medieval era it was common for monarchs to engage in a sequence of grand tours around their territory. By traveling from town to town the majesty, but also the political reach, of the monarch could be observed by all potential dissenters (Anglo, 1969; see also Geertz, 1973). Similarly, Wedeen (1999) argues that the exaggerated and absurd cult-like worship of Assad's regime in Syria was over-the-top precisely to demonstrate the power of the state and the futility of resistance.

Second, symbols can also be important for mobilization. Symbolic displays can privilege one set of cultural norms over another, and make a certain set of values the hegemonic ones, to which all others are subordinated (Greenwald, 1973). Consequently, elites have an incentive to engage in symbolic practices that are highly valued by domestic constituents (Edelman, 1964). Associating with such symbols can trigger "value-rationality" in observers. This effect of symbols can also be instrumental to generating mass support by legitimizing or de-legitimizing particular forms of action (Swidler, 1986), for mobilizing groups (Kaufman, 2001), or forming and reforming coalitions (Goddard, 2006).

The most important element of the Qing ritual system was the *koutou* that took place in Beijing. Throughout this entire ceremony, the superiority of the emperor was maintained. Envoys were always to be seen as representing the orbit of all things around the emperor. Petitioners and envoys came annually, usually arriving at times when many other petitioners would also be present, such as new year celebrations. At these audiences the Qing bureaucracy, Manchu noble bannermen, regional viceroys, tributary envoys, and hundreds of officials from the empire publicly demonstrated their ritual subordination to the emperor. This practice thus had important coordinative and coercive effects. First, petitioners who *koutou*ed publicly legitimized the emperor's authority. Second, by participating, they generated common knowledge regarding the scope and permanence of the Qing regime's dominion. If the most powerful people in the empire and beyond were seen to subordinate themselves to the emperor, then this acted as an effective means of suppressing any potential collective action, especially as all highly ranked civil and military officials were obliged to have an audience with the emperor (Elliot, 2001: 163). This reliance on symbolic politics was not lost on visitors; it astonished Laurence Oliphaunt (1970: 276) who, when accompanying Lord Elgin to China in 1859, observed:

> Any person who has attentively observed the working of the anomalous and altogether unique system under which the vast Empire of China is governed will have perceived that, though ruling under altogether different conditions, supported, not by a physical force, but by a moral prestige unrivaled in power and extent, the Emperor of China can say with no less truth than Napoleon, "L'Empire c'est moi" ... Backed by no standing army ... he exercises a rule more absolute than any European despot.

Unsurprisingly, this made both the *koutou* ritual *and* the location in Beijing politically important to the Qing. It also made the regime dependent on these practices, and made it very difficult to abandon them.

Reassessing the evidence

Understanding the important political role of symbolic practices to a weak Qing regime can help to explain the unusual character of Chinese intransigence regarding diplomatic practices. While flexible on many political issues – such as treaty ports – the Qing regime was highly protective of the *koutou* ceremony, and of the location of Beijing. Indeed, not only did the Qing regime protect these elements of its domestic authority, it actively bargained to be allowed to keep them.

Regarding the *koutou,* the only time that the Qing regime showed any flexibility on this issue was during its encounter with Macartney in 1793. The Qing regime was initially excited at the prospect of his mission, as a tribute from such a faraway state would enhance the prestige of the throne. For instance, the evidence suggests that the many thousands of well-organized subjects that crowded the banks of the Peiho River as Macartney passed by were not assembled to solely impress Macartney. The banners that bedecked his boat – which read "The English Ambassador bringing tribute to the Emperor of China" – also created common knowledge of the emperor's prestige and power (Macartney 1963: 78). Macartney, like any other foreign envoy, was to be used as a prop by the Qing regime for its audience ceremonies and had been expected to simply pay tribute, banquet, and leave.

The Qing regime only became hostile to Macartney's mission once it became clear that (a) Macartney was unwilling to *koutou,* and later (b) when he actually violated the ritual. In an internal letter from the Grand Council, Macartney and his retinue were accused of being "ignorant barbarians" who had become "unwarrantably haughty" (Cranmer-Byng, 1963: 33). In fact, it appears that Macartney only got as far as Beijing without first agreeing to practice the *koutou* because of communication failures within the Qing administration (Singer, 1992). However, when the Amherst mission arrived in 1816, the Qing regime took no chances, and insisted that the *koutou* issue be resolved in advance. When Amherst refused to make assurances that he would practice it, his mission was expelled from China. Even more significantly, the Qing regime forbade any Europeans to visit Beijing from this date until 1860, when the city was occupied by European forces.

The Qing regime was equally defensive about the physical location of Beijing itself. As has been discussed, Beijing was the ritual heart of China and the place where governors, generals, and dignitaries came to seek an audience with the emperor. The location in which these embassies were housed was very public which meant that – like the *koutou* – the treatment and behavior of missions was open for all other elites to see. Any changes to the manner in which diplomacy in this city operated would conflict with the Qing narrative of legitimation. This can help us understand why the Qing refused to allow official embassies to be placed there, as such an act would be an unprecedented (and illegitimate) change in diplomatic practice.[17] Understanding the important public element of Beijing for the Qing narrative of legitimation can also explain why the Amherst mission was treated with less respect than the Macartney mission. As Amherst documented, the disregard with which his mission was treated was observed by other Qing subjects. Indeed, he had not been even allowed to enter through the main gate, but was brought in through a side gate – an act that indicated his embassy's inferiority. Bruce's refusal to acquiesce to a Qing request to enter a similar side gate was what led the Chinese to fire on British forces on the Peiho River. Instead of allowing Bruce public entry through the main gate, the Qing regime had been willing to reinitiate war with a foreign power that had already defeated them twice. Qing dependence on symbolic practices can help us to understand this otherwise seemingly self-destructive behavior.

Furthermore, whenever these practices were violated by outsiders, the regime made sure to disguise this from domestic audiences as much as possible, before finally banning any European embassies from traveling to Beijing. For instance, in 1795 Isaac Titsingh, an emissary from the Dutch East Indian Company, was sent to try to establish a permanent embassy in Beijing. Unlike Macartney, Titsingh was not offended by Chinese demands for ritual prostration (Duyvendak, 1938). However, unknown to Titsingh, the Qing intended to use him as a prop in a symbolic performance designed to make up for the diplomatic mess created by Macartney in the previous year. The Dutch ambassadors were subject to the harshest form of treatment prescribed for envoys, including spending long periods of time outside in the early morning, and being dragged and whipped in public settings (Van Braam Houckgeest, 1798: 186–188). According to the records kept by the Board of Rituals, Britain was technically inferior to the Netherlands (Fairbank, 1942). Thus the Qing were able to disseminate internal propaganda claiming that the Dutch were coming to apologize for Britain.

Conclusion

Following the destruction of the Summer Palace in 1860, the British (as well as other European powers) demanded that the Qing regime engage in Westphalian diplomatic practice. They claimed the diplomatic right of legal recognition with full ambassadorial rights. A now thoroughly weakened and impotent Qing administration tried one last time to dispute the audience question but the issue was finally resolved on February, 24 1873. Upon the ascendancy of the new emperor to his throne, the ambassadors of England, France, the United States, Russia, and Germany were received by him in the throne room. There the ambassadors placed their credentials directly in the hand of the emperor, and, in accordance with European standards, lightly bowed (Wang, 1971). The entire audience ceremony lasted less than five minutes. Europe had finally forced China to accept Westphalian diplomatic practice.

The consequences of this conflict over diplomatic practice were far-reaching. Although Qing China had already been under threat from European economic and military power, the disputes over diplomacy delegitimized the entire cosmology of Chinese imperial rule. Internal court politics centered on the issue of assimilating to Westphalian standards and resulted in the formation of a newly minted ministry of foreign affairs along European lines. As Seo-Hyun Park shows elsewhere in this volume, the collapse of Qing influence (both political and cultural) triggered significant dynamics in the domestic politics of Japan and Korea. In an effort to protect their political power the Qing had helped to ensure its complete annihilation by the political and cultural forces of Europe.

Notes

1. In addition to embassies, states also sometimes maintained consular missions abroad, which had a much more explicitly commercial role.
2. It was not until its success in its war against Russia in 1904–1905 that Japan's missions were upgraded to embassies in Western capitals.
3. The word *angeloi* is derived from the Greek for 'messenger'.
4. The ambassador died en route.
5. Amherst to Foreign Office, 8 August 1816, FO/17/3.
6. Amherst to Foreign Office, 8 August 1816, FO/17/3.
7. Amherst to George Canning, 10 February 1817, FO/17/3.
8. Amherst to George Canning, 7 March 1817, FO/17/3.
9. Amherst to British Prince Regent, 7 January 1817, FO/17/3.
10. China had been held up as the ideal form of a rational state in the eyes of philosophers such as Voltaire and Leibniz, who were impressed by the bureaucratic sophistication of the Chinese empire (Hillemann, 2009).
11. Amherst to George Canning, 22 March 1817, FO/17/3.
12. Amherst to Viceroy of Pe-che-lee, 8 August 1816, FO/17/3.
13. Elgin received a note from American and Russian ministers that the Chinese envoys would be executed if they conceded on this issue (Elgin, personal diaries, June, 29 1858).
14. Elgin, personal diaries, October 25, 1860.

15 Common knowledge exists "among a group of people if everyone knows [something, and] that everyone knows that everyone knows it, etc...." (Chwe, 2001: 9). It is the knowledge that others know that others know what others know. Common knowledge occurs when an act is public and the meaning of the act is readily interpretable.
16 Six times during his reign, the Qianlong emperor went on tours: in 1751, 1757, 1762, 1765, 1780, and 1784.
17 Unless the mission could be suitably disguised, as the Russian one was.

Bibliography

Anglo, Sidney. (1969) *Spectacle, Pageantry, and Early Tudor Policy*. Oxford: Oxford University Press.

Berridge, G.R. (2001) Grotius. In G.R. Berridge, Maurice Keens-Soper, and T.G. Otte, eds., *Diplomatic Theory from Machiavelli to Kissinger*. New York: Palgrave.

Buzan, Barry, and Richard Little. (2000) *International Systems in World History: Remaking the Study of International Relations*. New York: Oxford University Press.

Chang, Michael G. (2007) *A Court on Horseback: Imperial Touring & the Construction of Qing Rule, 1680–1785*. Cambridge, MA: Harvard University Press.

Cranmer-Byng, J.L., ed. (1963) *An Embassy to China: Being the Journal Kept by Lord Macartney during his Embassy to the Emperor Ch'ien-lung 1793–1794*. Hamden, CT: Archon Books.

Croxton, Derek. (1999) The Peace of Westphalia of 1648 and the Origins of Sovereignty. *International History Review* 21(3): 569–591.

De Wicquefort, Abraham. (1716) *The Embassador and his Functions*. Translated by John Digby. https://play.google.com/books/reader?id=VGlUAAAAYAAJ&printsec=frontcover&output=reader&authuser=0&hl=en&pg=GBS.PP13.

Der Derian, James. (1987) *On Diplomacy: A Genealogy of Western Estrangement*. New York: Basil Blackwell.

Duyvendak, J.L.L. (1938) The Last Dutch Embassy to the Chinese Court (1794–1795). *T'oung Pao*, Second Series 34(1/2): 1–137.

Edelman, Murray. (1964) *The Symbolic Uses of Politics*. Urbana: University of Illinois Press.

Elliot, Mark C. (2001) *The Manchu Way: The Eight Banners and Ethnic Identity in Late Imperial China*. Stanford: Stanford University Press.

Fairbank, J.K. (1942) Tributary Trade and China's Relations with the West. *Far Eastern Quarterly* 1(2): 129–149.

Foreign and Commonwealth Office Correspondence and Records from 1782, National Archives, Kew, *Letter from Amherst to Foreign Office*, 8 August 1816, FO/17/3/44–51.

Foreign and Commonwealth Office Correspondence and Records from 1782, National Archives, Kew, *Letter from Amherst to Viceroy of Pecheli*, 8 August 1816, FO/17/3/57.

Foreign and Commonwealth Office Correspondence and Records from 1782, National Archives, Kew, *Letter from Amherst to George Canning, President of the Board of Commissioners for India*, 10 February, 1817, FO/17/3/75–87.

Foreign and Commonwealth Office Correspondence and Records from 1782, National Archives, Kew, *Letter from Amherst to George Canning, President of the Board of Commissioners for India*, 7 March 1817, FO/17/3/89–98.

Foreign and Commonwealth Office Correspondence and Records from 1782, National Archives, Kew, *Letter from Amherst to George Canning, President of the Board of Commissioners for India*, 22 March 1817, FO/17/3/100.

Foreign and Commonwealth Office Correspondence and Records from 1782, National Archives, Kew, *Letter from Amherst to British Prince Regent*, 7 January 1817, FO/17/3/116.

Geertz, Clifford. (1973) *The Interpretation of Cultures*. New York: Basic Books.

Gernet, Jacques. (1987) Introduction. In S.R. Schram, ed., *Foundations and Limits of State Power in China*. London: School of Oriental and African Studies.

Graham, Gerald S. (1978) *The China Station: War and Diplomacy 1830–1860*. Oxford: Clarendon Press.

Greenwald, David E. (1973) Durkheim on Society, Thought and Ritual. *Sociological Analysis* 34(3): 157–168.

Hamilton, Keith, and Richard Langhorne. (2011) *The Practice of Diplomacy: Its Evolution, Theory, and Administration*. New York: Routledge.

Hevia, James L. (1989) A Multitude of Lords: Qing Court Ritual and the Macartney Embassy of 1793. *Late Imperial China* 10(2): 61–84.

Hillemann, Ulrike. (2009) *Asian Empire and British Knowledge: China and the Networks of British Imperial Expansion*. New York: Palgrave Macmillan.

Hsü, Immanuel C.Y. (1964) Russia's Special Position in China during the Early Ch'ing Period. *Slavic Review* 23(4): 688–700.

Kang, David. (2012) *East Asia before the West: Five Centuries of Trade & Tribute*. New York: Columbia University Press.

Kaufman, Stuart J. (2001) *Modern Hatreds: The Symbolic Politics of Ethnic War*. Ithaca: Cornell University Press.

Lake, David, and Robert Powell, eds. (1999) *Strategic Choice in International Relations*. Princeton: Princeton University Press.

Macartney, George. (1963) *An Embassy to China: Being the Journal Kept by Lord Macartney during his Embassy to the Emperor Ch'ien-lung 1793–1794*. Edited by J. L. Cranmer-Byng. Hamden, CT: Archon Books.

Mann, Michael. (2012a) *The Sources of Social Power: Volume 1, A History of Power from the Beginning to AD 1760*. New York: Cambridge University Press.

Mann, Michael. (2012b) *The Sources of Social Power: Volume 2, The Rise of Classes and Nation-States, 1760–1914*. New York: Cambridge University Press.

Marshall, P.J. (1993) Britain and China in the Late Eighteenth Century. In Robert A. Bickers, ed., *Ritual and Diplomacy: The Macartney Mission to China 1792–1794. Papers Presented at the 1992 Conference of the British Association for Chinese Studies*. London: British Association for Chinese Studies and Wellsweep Press.

McCaffree, M.J., and Pauline Innis. (1989) *Protocol: The Complete Handbook of Diplomatic, Official and Social Usage*. Washington, DC: Devon Publishing.

Mercer, Jonathan. (2005) Rationality and Psychology in International Politics. *International Organization* 59(1):77–106.

Mitzen, Jennifer. (2006) Ontological Security in World Politics: State Identity and the Security Dilemma. *European Journal of International Relations* 12(3): 341–370.

Naquin, Susan. (1982) Connections between Rebellions: Sect Family Networks in Qing China. *Modern China* 8(3): 337–360.

Nicolson, Harold. (1954) *The Evolution of the Diplomatic Method*. London: Constable & Co Ltd.

Oliphaunt, Laurence, Esq. (1970) *Narrative of the Earl of Elgin's Mission to China and Japan in the Years 1857,'58,'59*. New York: Praeger Publishers.

Osiander, Andreas. (2001) Sovereignty, International Relations, and the Westphalian Myth. *International Organization* 55(2): 251–287.

Pritchard, Earl H. (1943) The Kowtow in the Macartney Embassy to China in 1793. *Far Eastern Quarterly* 2(2): 163–203.

Rockhill, William Woodville. (1897) Diplomatic Missions to the Court of China: The Kotow Question II. *American Historical Review* 2(4): 627–643.

Schwartz, Benjamin I. (1987) The Primacy of the Political Order in East Asian Societies: Some Preliminary Generalizations. In S.R. Schram, ed., *Foundations and Limits of State Power in China*. London: School of Oriental and African Studies.

Sharp, Paul. (2009) *Diplomatic Theory of International Relations*. New York: Cambridge University Press.

Singer, Aubrey. (1992) *The Lion & the Dragon: The Story of the First British Embassy to the Court of the Emperor Qianlong in Peking, 1792–1794*. London: Barrie & Jenkins.

Spence, Jonathan D. (1990) *The Search for Modern China*. New York: W.W. Norton & Co.

Ssu-ming, Meng. (1960–1961) The E-lo-ssu kuan (Russian Hostel) in Peking. *Harvard Journal of Asiatic Studies* 23(1): 19–46.

Swidler, Ann. (1986) Culture in Action: Symbols and Strategies. *American Sociological Review* 51(2): 273–286.

Van Braam Houckgeest, Andre Everard. (1798) *An Authentic Account of the Embassy of the Dutch East-India Company, to the Court of the Emperor of China, in the Years 1794 and 1795*.

Wakeman, Frederic, Jr. (1997) *Strangers at the Gate: Social Disorder in South China, 1839–1861*. Berkeley: University of California Press.

Wakeman, Frederic, Jr. (1998) Boundaries of the Public Sphere in Ming and Qing China. *Daedalus* 127(3): 167–189.

Waley-Cohen, Joanna. (2006) *The Culture of War in China: Empire and the Military under the Qing Dynasty*. New York: Palgrave Macmillan.

Wang, Tseng-Tsai. (1971) The Audience Question: Foreign Representatives and the Emperor of China, 1858–1873. *Historical Journal* 14(3): 617–626.

Wendt, Alexander. (1999) *Social Theory of International Politics*. New York: Cambridge University Press.

Wood, John, and Jean Serres. (1970) *Diplomatic Ceremonial and Protocol: Principles, Procedures & Practices*. New York: Columbia University Press.

Zhang, Shundong. (1993) Historical Anachronism: The Qing Perception of Reaction to the Macartney Embassy. In Robert A. Bickers, ed., *Ritual and Diplomacy: The Macartney Mission to China 1792–1794. Papers Presented at the 1992 Conference of the British Association for Chinese Studies*. London: British Association for Chinese Studies and Wellsweep Press.

6 Ordering Europe

The legalized hegemony of the Concert of Europe

George Lawson

The world crisis

For the historian Chris Bayly (2004: 147), the late 18th and early 19th centuries were a period of 'cumulative turbulence' characterized by war, revolution, economic upheaval, and ideological fracture. Rival armies confronted each other from Moscow to Jogjakarta, and from Delhi to Washington, DC. And these wars were much bloodier than previous conflicts – battlefield deaths multiplied by a factor of ten between the 1750s and the early 1800s (Tilly, 1990: 165). Intensified warfare often went hand in hand with revolution. From the last quarter of the 18th century until the first quarter of the 19th century, anti-imperial uprisings were endemic to many parts of West, South, and East Asia (Armitage and Subrahmanyam, 2010). There were slave revolts in Haiti, Brazil, and Barbados, and constitutional revolutions across much of the Americas and Europe. These revolutions took place in a context of considerable economic dislocation triggered by intensified warfare, the extension of capitalist markets, particularly in cotton, and the deepening of agricultural commercialization through enclosures and plantations (Bayly, 2004: 125–132). This period was also one of wide-ranging ideological contestation, pitching advocates of constitutions and representative government on one side of the barricades, and those defending dynasticism and imperial rule on the other. It is within the fervent of this 'world crisis' that the Concert of Europe should be located. It was a settlement with its roots in Port-au-Prince and Cairo, as well as in Paris and Moscow.

If global turbulence provides a wide-angle lens on the Concert, European affairs offer more of a close-up. The meeting at Vienna followed two decades of war in Europe. Every European state had been militarized: each faced the need to demobilize often-substantial conscript armies. And every European state had incurred considerable war debts: each needed to rebuild their economies. At the same time, European polities were subject to significant domestic unrest courtesy of a heterodox array of challengers: peasants whose labor was increasingly subject to capitalist dynamics, a bourgeoisie pursuing a greater role in public life, and radical groups, from secret societies to republican movements, seeking to subvert the existing order (Rudé, 1964: 286–300).

No wonder that this period saw the advent of secret police forces. And no wonder that it witnessed violent bouts of state repression. As Bayly (2004: 126) puts it, in 1815, the primary form of political unit in Europe was the "dynastic police state."

The Concert of Europe emerged in the midst of this global and regional tumult. It is not surprising, therefore, that standard views of the Concert tend to see it as a reactionary affair, an attempt by dynastic police states to reassert stability in the midst of domestic and international disorder (e.g., Hobsbawm, 1962; Rudé, 1964). For some diplomatic historians and statesmen, the Concert was a largely successful attempt to reconstruct European order through the mechanism of the balance of power (e.g., Webster, 1919; Nicolson, 1946; Kissinger, 1957 and 1994; Kraeke, 1983). The strength of the Concert, it is argued, lay in the unusually prescient skills of its leading actors, most notably Metternich and Castlereagh (Jarrett, 2013). Such a view contrasts with those who associate the Concert not with balance of power politics, but with hegemony, whether this is represented by the 'dual hegemony' of Russia (as the guardian of monarchical order) and Britain (as the holder of the European balance) (Schroeder, 1994), or as a 'legalized hegemony' fostered by the emergence of a system of great power management (Simpson, 2004; see also: Bull, 1977; Osiander, 1994; Clark, 2011). Some accounts stress the moderate, even liberal, components of the Vienna settlement (e.g., Vick, 2014 and 2015); others point to the central, if occluded, role played by women in the Congresses (e.g., Sluga, 2014, 2015a, and 2015b). Scholarship in International Relations (IR) variously sees the Concert as an experiment in 'governance without government' (Holsti, 1992), as the first modern 'security regime' (Jervis, 1982 and 1985; Rendall, 2006), or as a proto 'security community' (Kupchan and Kupchan, 1991; Kupchan, 2010: 188–189). Others conceive of the Concert as an attempt to construct a "constitutional order" through "binding institutions" (Ikenberry, 2001: 24) or as an expression of "international public power" premised on a novel "consultative authority structure" (Mitzen, 2013: 5–11).

Following the rubric of this volume, this chapter approaches the Concert in a different way. As the Introduction to this book notes, the 19th century was bifurcated between a period of regionalism (1815–1856) and one of globalization (1871–1914), separated by a 'pivot' period (1856–1869) in which, to paraphrase Gramsci, the former was not yet dead and the latter had not yet been born. The Concert fits well with this narrative. The Concert represented a 'de-globalization' of world politics (Osterhammel, 2014: 473), a turning away from the era of 'world crisis' in favor of a reckoning with intra-European politics. Along with the 1823 Monroe Doctrine, the Concert served to compartmentalize world politics into regional spheres of influence. But this turn towards regionalism could not endure. During the course of the 19th century, particularly in the latter half of the century, transnational dynamics served to intensify interconnections and interdependencies between polities. This period witnessed a 'global transformation' in which industrialization, rational state-building, and 'ideologies of progress' generated the world's first global order (Buzan and Lawson, 2015). It is not surprising, therefore, that the Concert was something of a period piece. Its concerns with regional order made sense in a world of multiple, inward-looking regions. But they made little sense as the global transformation generated a single, if highly differentiated, world of competing empires. This chapter charts the emergence and maintenance of the Concert during the era of regional order-making before discussing how it unraveled as European powers became entangled in a new world crisis. It also charts the way in which one dimension of the Concert – the system of 'legalized hegemony' – became incorporated into international law and global governance.

The Concert of Europe

Carrying out an assessment of the Concert means taking a stand on three preliminary questions: First, when did the Concert operate? Second, what were its main characteristics? And third, how can its effectiveness be assessed?

First, when it comes to establishing the time horizons of the Concert, this chapter begins from the assumption that the roots of the Concert lay in the Congress system, which incorporated the 1814 Treaty of Paris as well as the Congresses at Vienna, Aix-la-Chapelle, Laibach, Troppau, and Verona. The start date of 1814 signifies that it was at Paris that the foundations for the later Congresses were laid, as well as key issues excluded from further discussion, particularly maritime rights and imperialism. The Congress system is seen as ending in 1822 because the Verona meeting of that year represented the last peacetime conference in which sovereigns and their main advisors met in person. After Verona, the system morphed into a wider 'Concert', which relied not on face-to-face interactions between sovereigns and their principal advisors but on forms of regularized bureaucratic exchange. The Concert ended in two mid-century events: the revolutions of 1848–1849, which represented the failure of the system to inoculate itself from revolution; and the Crimean War of 1853–1856, which represented the first interstate war between European great powers since 1815. Any attempt to broaden the scope of the Concert beyond these dates, for example to the onset of World War I (e.g., Kissinger, 1994; Schroeder, 2000; Vick, 2014), is a temporal stretching too far. Five wars were fought between European Great Powers in the third quarter of the 19th century. The following decades saw the rise of three new, revisionist Great Powers: a unified Germany, the United States, and Japan, the last of which fought – and defeated – Russia in 1904–1905. As the Introduction to this volume makes clear, the latter part of the 19th century saw the emergence of a 'new imperialism', underpinned by arms racing and 'scientific' racism, which produced a period of both heightened tension and, at times, considerable brutality. The emblematic conference of this period was not Vienna, but the 1884 conference in Berlin that both sanctioned and regulated the 'Scramble for Africa'.

Second, the main characteristic of the Concert was the establishing of networks of practices, treaties, and institutions headed by a governing council – the five Great Powers: Britain, Russia, Austria, Prussia, and, after 1818, a rehabilitated France.[1] This directorate was the head of a wider body of interlocking rights and responsibilities intended to foster mutual restraint between the Great Powers within Europe (Miller, 1994; Ikenberry, 2001; Kupchan, 2010; Bukovansky et al., 2012; Mitzen, 2013). A system of regular forums was established in order to settle disputes in Europe's trouble spots and generate collective security through 'group pressure' (Schroeder, 1994: 580–582, 801–803; Schroeder, 2000: 159–160; Simpson, 2004: 71; also see Mitzen, 2013). If the first half of the 19th century saw a continuation of Great Power competition, such as that between Britain and France in the Mediterranean, and between Austria and Russia in the Balkans, this competition did not lead to war. Rather, competition took place within a context of rules and practices that regulated interstate rivalries, transforming European international politics from "a game of poker to one of contract bridge" (Schroeder, 2000: 162). The Concert system can be defined as an assemblage of practices, norms, and rules that mitigated conflict and fostered co-operation between the Great Powers over a substantial period of time.

Third, any assessment of the Concert must begin with the task it was intended to perform: foster peace between the Great Powers *within* Europe. As noted above, this was to be achieved through face-to-face meetings between sovereigns and their principal advisors – what Brendan Simms (1997: 15) calls the "antechamber of power" – accompanied by mid-level diplomatic meetings and the establishing of committees on a variety of issue-areas. These mechanisms were so significant that they led some to argue that the Concert was the first modern form of international government (e.g., Mazower, 2012: xiv). Yet, those seeking to draw wider lessons from the Concert should be mindful of the context in which it was formed: the main actors that formed the Concert were dynastic empires, followed by a handful of constitutional monarchies, and a much larger group of statelets. And these actors operated in the uncertain climate prompted by the 'world crisis'. This was the paradox at the heart of the Concert. The retreat from the 'world crisis' served to stabilize Europe. But it did so only for as long as transnational vectors were containable within regional orders. Once the force of the global transformation was unleashed, the Concert came unstuck. The new world crisis of the second half of the 19th century needed a greater field of vision than the Concert's intra-European optic. If participants in the Concert failed to reach a full accommodation with these tumultuous times, this is hardly surprising – the scale of its transformative effects was virtually unprecedented in world history. However, their failure to do so tells us much about the limits of the Concert. The next section of the paper establishes the main components of the Concert. Subsequent sections assess its effectiveness and examine the ways in which the global transformation forged a transnational field that superseded the mechanisms established by the Concert, with one exception: the system of legalized hegemony.

Ordering Europe

So how did the Concert serve to 'order' Europe? In answering this question, it is worth starting with the system's first major Congress at Vienna, which was held over the course of a nine-month period in 1814–1815. Unsurprisingly, the intentions of the participants at Vienna varied. Some, notably Tsar Alexander, held maximalist visions of the Congress, seeing Vienna as the chance to foster European unity on a grand scale. The initial proposals put forward by Alexander included a single European army that could guard Europe's single 'political family'. For his part, Friedrich von Gentz, Secretary of the Congress and the main advisor to Prince Metternich, the Austrian Chancellor, wrote that the Congress would institute "a principle of general union, uniting all the states collectively with a federal bond" (in Mazower, 2012: 4). Britain had a more minimalist agenda, concerned primarily with containing France.[2] During the course of the Napoleonic Wars, some figures in Britain had promoted a more ambitious post-war agenda. In 1805, Prime Minister Pitt voiced support for a treaty in which the Great Powers 'bind themselves mutually' and promise to 'protect and support each other'. In 1813, the British Foreign Minister, Lord Castlereagh, proposed that the Great Powers forge a 'perpetual defensive alliance'. The following year, Britain signed the Treaty of Chaumont, which pledged that the Great Powers would 'concert together' for a period of twenty years. But Castlereagh did not envisage the Concert "as an Union for the Government of the World; or for the Superintendence of the Internal Affairs of Other States" (in Bew, 2011: 122). This reflected a general view amongst the British political class, both Whig and Tory, that the preservation of the balance of power and the 'law of nations' remained the central mechanisms for promoting both British interests and European stability (Bew, 2011; Jarrett, 2013).

If particular agendas varied, all parties agreed that Vienna must find a way to institute a period of extended peace. And although pre-Vienna discussions associated peace with defensive concerns about how to contain French expansionism, the escape of Napoleon and the ensuing '100 days' meant that the November 1815 meeting in Paris – and subsequent Congresses – assumed a more ambitious agenda: inoculating Europe against the revolutionary virus. The vast majority of participants at Vienna held the view that legitimacy was vested in the monarch, whether absolutist or constitutional, whose sovereignty was, in turn, appointed by Providence. Vienna was a settlement that rested on a 'syndicate of monarchs' who saw their authority as rooted in 'divine legitimacy' (Holbraad, 1970; Ghervas, 2014). The exemplar of this view was the Holy Alliance, instigated by Tsar Alexander and signed by Russia, Austria, and Prussia in September 1815. All three parties agreed to act as a supra-denominational Christian 'family', which would act on the basis of 'love, justice, and peace' in order to 'remedy the imperfections' of existing institutions. If neither Francis (of Austria) nor William (of Prussia) went along with Alexander's view that Napoleon was the living embodiment of the Antichrist, they did agree with him that their office had been assumed by divine right.

Castlereagh's verdict on the Holy Alliance illustrates well the differences between Britain and its Congress partners: "It is a piece of sublime mysticism and nonsense" (in Bew, 2011: 122). But this verdict did not arise from any kind of liberal credo; to the contrary, all of the main participants at Vienna were conservative, albeit of differing stripes (Holbraad, 1970; Holsti, 1992; Miller, 1994; Mazower, 2012). The basis for their agreement was widely held notions of 'organic' order sustained by an alliance of monarchs, nobles, aristocrats, high state officials, guilds, and clergy, and held together by birth, rank, and inherited privilege (Sperber, 2000: 292–297). For Congress attendees, the model social order was the patriarchal household (Sperber, 2000: 293; also see Owens, 2015). It is certainly the case that leading figures at Vienna were aware of Enlightenment texts and debates: von Gentz had studied under Kant, while Prince Czartoryski, one of the Tsar's principal advisors, saw constitutions as fundamental to collective security (Vick, 2015). In this sense, the Concert was embedded in a political culture within which discussion of rights, representation, and constitutionalism were commonplace (Vick, 2014). But none of the principal actors held truck with the notion that sovereignty was derived from the will of the people; rather, both territories and populations were seen as the property of the sovereign (Mazower, 2012: 40). Even when constitutions were used as forms of mediation and crisis management, as they were until the mid-1820s, these documents were restricted affairs. After the 1830 revolutions in France, Belgium, and elsewhere, the use of constitutions as forms of dispute settlement was dropped, being replaced by an alliance of 'throne and altar', a reassertion of monarchy, and high levels of both censorship and police suppression (Schroeder, 1994: 666).[3] If liberal ideas constituted an emergent field within which some of the discussions at Vienna took place, they were a background set of concerns rather than representative of an ideological consensus. As Metternich put it, 'There is only one serious matter in Europe, and that is revolution' (in Mazower, 2012: 6). The revolutionary threat was met by surveillance, censorship, suppression, and, at times, intervention.

If a reassertion of 'organic' conservative legitimacy lay at the heart of the Concert, so too did the notion that international order derived from the system's most powerful actors. For most participants in Vienna, it was self-evident who these actors were – the 'Quadruple Alliance' that had defeated Napoleon: Britain, Russia, Prussia, and Austria.[4] At the Treaty of Chaumont, in which the Quadruple Alliance put forward plans for a general Congress, proposals were made for a wide-ranging Congress, but with decision-making authority reserved for the four victorious powers. The Alliance agreed to consult regularly with Spain and France, and to show 'respect' for smaller powers. In reality, as Simpson (2004: 112) puts it: "The Great Powers made the law and the middle powers signed the Treaty … The smaller powers, meanwhile, were erased from consideration." At Vienna, France was invited to take part in most of the key decisions – as a result, the Quadruple Alliance became the 'Pentarchy'. The 'Committee of Five' met 41 times, the eight signatories of the Treaty of Paris (the Pentarchy, plus Spain, Portugal, and Sweden) nine times, and the full Congress not at all (Mitzen, 2013: 90). The Concert is best understood as "a multilateral directorial system in which the sovereign and foreign ministers of the Great Powers ... would reach agreement among themselves and then impose their will upon Europe – and call the result peace" (Armitage and Ghervas, 2014). Vienna represented a "freezing" of international order under the directorate of the five Great Powers (Osterhammel, 2014: 397).

Other aspects of the settlement were more novel. First was the breadth of actors involved in, and range of activities supported by, the Congresses. Over 200 plenipotentiaries and heads of state decamped to Vienna in the autumn of 1814; their retinues boosted the population of the city by a third (Jarrett, 2013: 95). Vienna and the other Congresses were major events, featuring jousting tournaments, balloon ascents, balls, and extensive cultural programs, including a performance of the 7th Symphony at Vienna conducted by Beethoven himself. As Brian Vick (2014) notes, these events were not incidental, but germane to the Congress system – there was no separation of politics from culture, but an awareness that culture *was* political. Multiple publics, from festival goers and lobbyists to pamphleteers and salonnières, took part in, and sometimes shaped, the Congresses. Vienna, in particular, was a celebration intended to wow its visitors through an extended festival of concerts, dancing, parades, opera, and theatre. These visitors included representatives of causes ranging from those advocating on behalf of the German Jews to those seeking to abolish the slave trade. Committees were established on the gathering of statistics, river navigation, and the activities of the Barbary corsairs. Particularly influential were the political salons, often run by women, which acted as "clearinghouses of information" and as sites of informal (and sometimes formal) exchange between diplomats and lobbyists (Vick, 2014: 132).[5] These salons, along with newspapers and pamphlets, formed part of a broader political ecology within which the formal, elite components of the Congresses were embedded.

Second was the set of peacetime rules and mechanisms that were devised to preserve European order. As noted above, these mechanisms began as face-to-face meetings between sovereigns and their main advisers – what Metternich called "Europe without distances" (in Vick, 2014: 9). As also noted above, following the last of the monarchical Congresses at Verona in 1822, face-to-face meetings between sovereigns and their principals were replaced by two decades of regularized ambassadorial exchanges. Whether resting on personal connections or more abstract mechanisms, the novel feature of the Congress system was the institutionalization of conference diplomacy as a basis for Great Power cooperation. Forums acted as a vehicle of both collective self-restraint and joint action (Mitzen, 2013: 28; also see Ikenberry, 2001). Rather than seeking to resolve conflicts bilaterally, the Concert forged a system of multilateral security sustained both through personal ties and the regularized interactions of professional diplomats (Schroeder, 2000: 159–160; Kupchan, 2010: 198–199).

Third was the *formal* recognition granted to the Great Powers (Bukovansky et al., 2012: 27; Osiander, 1994: 234). Rather than associating international order with a 'ranking of powers' based on precedence, title, and position, Vienna formed part of a wider shift towards the 'grading of powers' based on power capabilities (Bull, 1977; Osiander, 1994; Keene, 2013). The superior power capabilities held by the Great Powers meant that they possessed special rights (for example, over intervention) and responsibilities (such as a duty to maintain international order). The stratification between 'greater' and 'lesser' powers relied on a notion of 'dual authority' that tied together Great Powers horizontally, while constructing a vertical point of demarcation between them and other polities (Clark, 2011: 96–97). In this way, the Congress system represents the first example of an international political order governed by 'legalized hegemony': "the realization through legal forms of great power prerogatives" (Simpson, 2004: x). The most important of these prerogatives was intervention, which became a right afforded *to* the Great Powers *by* the Great Powers. This right played out in debates over whether to intervene in cases of unrest in Naples, Piedmont, Greece, Portugal, and Spain. After 1815, the great powers saw themselves, and were recognized by others as having, managerial responsibility for the maintenance of European order (Mitzen, 2013: 89).

The effectiveness of the Concert System

If these were the principal features of the Concert, to what extent did they succeed in meeting their objectives? The Concert was intended to tie together European polities in an interlocking system of rights and responsibilities at the apex of which stood the Great Powers. In terms of the primary aim of the Concert – avoiding war between the Great Powers – the system worked well. There was no general war between the European Great Powers between 1815 and 1914. In fact, there was no war of any kind between the Great Powers from 1815 to 1853. Considering the carnage of the world crisis that had preceded the Concert, this was no small achievement. Legalized hegemony, supported by a range of intermediary mechanisms, prevented Great Power competition from descending into outright war. But peace had a price. In this respect, three issues are worth highlighting.

First was the systematic repression of both reform and radical movements. Reform movements in Prussia and several other German states were violently suppressed in 1819, the same year as the Peterloo Massacre in Britain. Over the next three decades, European secret police forces placed a range of individuals and groups under surveillance and routinely arrested those considered to be subversive. Constitutions were suspended, radical groups banned, and the media censored. Rather than coalescing around a moderate "ideology of the middle" (Vick, 2014: 237),[6] the Concert was a settlement *between* nations that rested on the view that any such agreement required a settlement *within* nations. And this settlement was oriented around the model of the dynastic police state (Maier, 2012: 68; also see Bayly 2004). During the period of the Concert, the price to be paid for security between polities was the fostering of security states within polities.

Second, and linked to this point, is the way that Concert powers met the challenge of constitutionalism. During the early years of the Congress, constitutional revolutions took place in Spain (1820), Naples (1820), and Greece (1821). By the early 1820s, much of Spanish Latin America was free from Spanish rule; Brazil broke free of Portugal in 1822–1823. During the early 1830s, a second wave of uprisings took place in France, Belgium, Poland, Switzerland, and parts of Germany; in Britain, the unrest between mid-1830 and the 1832 Reform Act was so grave as to amount to a 'revolutionary situation' (Hobsbawm, 1962; also see Osterhammel, 2014: 541). A third wave of constitutionalist uprisings engulfed much of continental Europe in 1848, thereafter extending into a wider conflagration that stretched from the Americas to Ukraine, and from the Baltic to the Mediterranean (Sperber, 2000: 401). If the first wave of revolutions exposed fractures in the Congress, the second turned these fractures into breaks; the third prompted the entire framework to collapse.

From the outset, constitutionalist movements exposed tensions at the heart of the Concert. Britain reluctantly agreed to an intervention to suppress an uprising in Naples in 1821, but refused to go along with other counter-revolutionary interventions. As a result of tensions over the right to intervene, Britain and France sent only their local ambassadors to act as observers to the Congress at Troppau in 1820. Castlereagh was quick to repudiate the subsequent 'circular' issued by Russia, Austria, and Prussia, which contained a clause asserting that "every revolution becomes ... the object of a just and legitimate intervention by foreign powers" (in Jarrett, 2013: 263). British ambivalence hardened after Castlereagh's suicide in 1822 – his replacement as Foreign Secretary, George Canning, was deeply suspicious of the interventionist agenda promoted by Russia and Austria. There was to be, as Canning put it, "no doctrine of a European police" (in Mazower, 2012: 7). Under Canning, the British made a declaration of non-intervention towards the Latin American republics, an act that directly contravened the views of Britain's Concert partners. Canning rejected invitations to a congress to discuss Latin America, and refused to directly address tensions between the Ottomans and the Greeks. After the 1830 revolutions, Britain deepened its commitment to non-intervention and constitutional monarchy, while Austria, Russia, and Prussia reasserted their support for absolutism. Thereafter, no collective agreement could be reached on intervention against republican movements. Between 1830 and 1848, collaboration between the Great Powers was restricted to specific crisis points (Jarrett, 2013: 366). The 1848 revolutions forced the resignation of Metternich, the last living architect of the Concert. Five years later, Britain, France, and Russia went to war in the Crimea, and the Concert system was over.

Crimea was the result not just of increasingly diverse interests, but of increasingly diverse ideas of 'progress' (Buzan and Lawson, 2015: ch. 4). For Britain, mid-century Russia was a 'backward', 'semi-civilized' polity, a laggard in adjusting to rapidly changing times (Neumann and Sending, 2010: 106). As British power grew, the link between domestic regime type and international legitimacy hardened. It also became linked not to a social order characterized by the dynastic police state, but to 'modern' notions of 'good governance' and 'progress', particularly the capacity to administer and regulate social orders 'rationally' (Neumann and Sending, 2010: 156–157). Those 'outlaw states' that fell outside this group (Simpson, 2004: 6), whether because of 'backward' ideological disposition, cultural 'deviance', 'inappropriate' governance structure, racial 'inferiority', 'un-Christian' beliefs, or low levels of 'modernity' were no longer considered to be part of 'civilized' international society. And they could be treated accordingly.

The third price to be paid for European peace was neglect of the world outside Europe. The most immediate shortcoming prompted by the inward turn towards intra-European affairs was the exclusion of the Ottoman Empire – the 'Eastern Question' was an issue that destabilized European international order throughout the 19th century. More generally, the attempt to deracinate European politics from transnational vectors meant that there was a lack of fit between the regional concerns of the Concert and the wider 'global transformation' within which it was embedded.[7] During the second half of the 19th century, multiple regional international systems became engulfed in a 'full international system' in which all parts of the world became deeply connected economically, culturally, and in military-political terms (Osterhammel, 2014: 392–402). Although the world had been an 'economic international system' since the European voyages of discovery during the 15th and 16th centuries opened up sea-lanes around Africa, and across the Atlantic and Pacific Oceans (Buzan and Little, 2000: 96), only during the latter part of the 19th century did the world become a global system in which Great Powers could quickly and decisively project their power around the world. It was the unleashing of the global transformation that presaged the end of the Concert system.

The global transformation

The 'global transformation' contained three interrelated components. First, the extension of capitalism brought new opportunities for accumulating power, in part because of the close relationship between industrialization and dispossession. Indeed, industrialization in some states (such as Britain) was deeply interwoven with the forceful de-industrialization of others (such as India). Second, state-building projects accumulated and 'caged' administrative and bureaucratic competences within national territories (Mann, 1988). This process was not pristine. Rather, processes of state-building and imperialism were co-implicated. Finally, a number of political ideologies, rooted in Enlightenment notions of classification, improvement, and control, linked the promise of progress to a 'standard of civilization', which served as the legitimating currency for coercive practices against 'barbarians' (understood as peoples with an urban 'high culture') and 'savages' (understood as peoples without an urban 'high culture') (Gong, 1984; Keene, 2002; Anghie, 2004;

Suzuki, 2009; Millennium, 2014). During the 19th century, international order became composed of 'unequal sovereigns', which were differentiated not just by material capability, but also by ideology, religion, and race (Simpson, 2004: 64). The three dynamics that constituted the global transformation were mutually reinforcing. European imperialism was legitimized by 'ideologies of progress' and enabled through military superiority, mechanisms of state control, and infrastructural developments that were themselves facilitated by industrialization (Buzan and Lawson, 2015: 7).

Along with the 'world crisis' noted in the introduction to this chapter, the 'global transformation' provides the crucial context for the 19th century – and, thus, for understanding the Concert's limitations. A brief illustration makes clear why this is the case. During the period of the Concert, Britain was able to generate a considerable maritime advantage over its rivals: by 1840, the British navy possessed almost as many ships as the rest of Europe put together (Hobsbawm, 1962: 135). This period also saw Britain become the world's only major industrial economy. The crucial advance was the capture of inanimate sources of energy, particularly the advent of steam power, a process that enabled the biggest increase in the availability of power sources for several millennia (McNeill, 1991: 729; Christian, 2004: 421). Britain's lead in this field presented a major advantage – by 1850, 18 million Britons used as much fuel energy as 300 million inhabitants of Qing China (Goldstone, 2002: 364). Also crucial was the application of engineering to blockages in production, such as the development of machinery to pump water efficiently out of mineshafts (Parthasarathi, 2011: 151–152). Engineering and technology combined to generate substantial gains in productivity: whereas a British spinner at the end of the 18th century took 300 hours to produce 100 pounds of cotton, by 1830, the same task took only 135 hours (Christian, 2004: 346). As noted above, British industrialization went hand in hand with the de-industrialization of its rivals outside Europe. After 1800, the British government ensured that British products undercut Indian goods and charged prohibitive tariffs on Indian textiles. By 1820, British products were being exported in bulk to the subcontinent. By 1850, Lancashire was the center of a global textile industry, reversing centuries of subcontinental preeminence in this area (Parthasarathi, 2011: 151–153).

Britain's dual superiority in military and industrial power allowed the country to vastly increase its colonial possessions: between 1814–1849, the size of Britain's empire in India increased by over two-thirds (Hobsbawm, 1962: 136). During this period, Britain also accumulated a series of staging posts in Africa (e.g., Cape Town), the Middle East (e.g., Aden), and Asia (e.g., Singapore). These developments further enhanced Britain's military and industrial clout. During the 1830s, the British exported an average of 30,000 chests of opium from India to China each year, each of which carried 150 pounds of opium extract (Mann, 2012: 101). In 1840, Britain used the pretext of a minor incident involving the arrest of two British sailors to instigate the 'First Opium War', which it won easily. The Treaty of Nanjing that followed the war required China to cede Hong Kong to the British, pay an indemnity for starting the conflict, and open up five new treaty ports. The treaty also legalized the opium trade, forced China to accept British consuls, and guaranteed extraterritorial rights for British nationals. Such developments help to explain why Britain had no interest in intra-European conflicts – its interests were increasingly measured on a global scale.

These dynamics were not limited to Britain. In 1830, France invaded Algeria, instigating a conflict that lasted until 1847. During the same period, Russian claims in the Balkans and the Caucasus saw it either militarize or fight on several occasions. These incidents were the forerunners to the widespread conflicts that marked the 'pivot' period of 1856–1869. Within Europe, Prussia fought wars with Denmark, Austria, and France. France sought to extend its power in the Middle East and the Americas, most notably in Mexico. Spain annexed the Dominican Republic in 1861. Between 1810 and 1870, the US carried out 71 territorial annexations and military interventions (Go, 2011: 39). During the course of the century as a whole, the US became both a continental empire, seizing territory from Native Americans, the Spanish, and the Mexicans,[8] and an overseas empire, extending its authority over Cuba, Nicaragua, the Dominican Republic, Haiti, Hawaii, Puerto Rico, Guam, the Philippines, Samoa, and the Virgin Islands. A range of other settler states also became colonial powers in their own right, including Australia and New Zealand in the Pacific. Japan constructed an empire in East Asia, while Russian expansionism accelerated both southwards to Uzbekistan, Kazakhstan, and Turkmenistan, and eastwards to Sakhalin and Vladivostok. The globalization of imperialism was a bloody affair. The Belgians were responsible for the deaths of up to ten million Congolese (Rosenberg, 2012: 12). Germany carried out a systematic genocide against the Nama and Herero peoples in its South West African territories (Rosenberg, 2012: 12). Similar stories could be told about the conduct of the Americans in the Philippines and the Spanish in Cuba. In some parts of the world, such as Tasmania, Tahiti, and Southwest Africa, 'annihilation drives' resulted in the systematic extermination of the indigenous population (Bayly, 2004: 167). Overall, the casualty list of 19th century imperialism numbered tens of millions (Osterhammel, 2014: 124–127).

The escalation of inter- and intra-imperial conflicts went hand in hand with an escalation in civil conflicts. The mid-century Taiping Rebellion in China mobilized over one million combatants and spread to an area the size of France and Germany combined (Meier, 2012: 89). The rebellion destroyed both land and livelihoods: between 1850 and 1873, over 20 million people were killed and China's population as a whole dropped from 410 million to 350 million (Phillips, 2011: 185; Osterhammel, 2014: 120–121, 547–551). The American Civil War in the 1860s mobilized half of all white male Americans, of which a third lost their lives; the direct costs of the war are estimated at $6.6 billion (Belich, 2009: 331). Violent wars of national independence in Germany, Italy, Mexico, and elsewhere added to the death toll. Along with the Crimean War, these conflicts prompted the First Geneva Convention of

1864. The Geneva Convention and its successor Conventions at The Hague in 1899 and 1907 were attempts to impose limits on war, but only for those conflicts fought between 'civilized' polities (Mazower, 2012: 77). The codification of the laws of war distinguished between 'privileged belligerents' (inhabitants of the 'civilized' world) and 'unprivileged belligerents' (those who lived outside this zone). Privileged belligerents became subject to rules that determined the scope of legitimate violence, not least that it should be discriminate and proportional. Unprivileged combatants were considered to be outside such rules – violence in 'uncivilized' spaces took place without legal restrictions (Anghie, 2004: 241–242).

The bloody history of imperialism and the scale of the conflicts that took place *outside* Europe, particularly from the pivot period on, make clear the limits of focusing too tightly on the role of the Concert in fostering a 'long peace' *inside* Europe (e.g., Schroeder, 2000). Because such a focus is restricted to intra-European affairs, it occludes the experiences of those on the wrong end of the global transformation. Outside Europe, there was no 'long peace', but something more like a continuous war. Between 1803 and 1901, Britain alone was involved in 50 major colonial wars (Giddens, 1985: 223). The bifurcation between global crisis and European stability held major significance for the development of international order, reinforcing a sense of European cultural and racial superiority, which in turn facilitated its coercive expansions around the world (Anghie, 2004: 310–320; Darwin, 2007: 180–185, 222–229). Imperialism promoted the power of Britain and other European Great Powers with an intensity and scale that was unprecedented in world history. Because the stratification of international order between 'greater' and 'lesser' powers instituted in the Concert coincided with the global expansion of Western power, European hierarchy operated on a global scale, buttressed by a 'standard of civilization' that divided the world into civilized, barbarian, and savage peoples.

Legalized hegemony

Examination of the Concert, therefore, enables us to see the disjuncture that marks the 'bifurcated century'. In the first half of the century, the Concert stood as the emblematic institution of regional order – it is exemplary of the turn towards regionalism from 1815 to 1856. Yet the Concert's concern with intra-European affairs meant that it was deracinated from wider transnational vectors, not least the resurgence of British imperialism. The Concert unraveled as European powers once again competed globally, instigating a new world crisis that engulfed the entire planet. The result was the emergence of a single global order, albeit one that was highly stratified between polities and peoples. The different visions of empire that sustained this global order and the competition between imperialisms that marked its core dynamic reduced the Concert to relative impotence. If the origins of the Concert lay in a retreat from the first world crisis, its epitaph was written in the global transformation that took root in the early decades of the century, incubated during the mid-century pivot, and took off during the century's final decades.

In many ways, therefore, the Concert was a parochial settlement that belonged squarely to the first half of the bifurcated century. Its mechanisms for maintaining regional order were much more limited than those that sustained later forums of global governance. The Concert had no permanent secretariat, no enduring bureaucracy, no enforcement mechanism, and no general guarantee (Holbraad, 1970; Mazower, 2012: 94–95). It did not create standing legal organizations or constitute a new basis for international law (Simpson, 2004). It was an elite syndicate rather than a deeply embedded governance structure. But the Concert was not just a period piece. First, the Concert – or, at least, a particular vision of it – was appropriated and reproduced in diplomatic circles. The British diplomat Charles Webster wrote a widely circulated study of the Congress in his role as secretary to the military section of the British delegation at the 1919 Paris Peace Conference. Webster also later helped to frame British policy to the UN. Second, notwithstanding its focus on security issues, the Concert extended its reach to a number of issue-areas and actors in ways that were historically unprecedented: the slave trade, piracy, river navigation, and more.[9] In this sense, the Concert *was* nascent of later developments in international law and global governance. Third, and most importantly, the Concert was the incubator for the system of legalized hegemony. As noted in earlier sections, the Concert simultaneously recognized both equality (between the Great Powers) and inequality (between the Great Powers and other polities). From the Concert on, this notion of dual authority has been at the heart of international order, serving as the basis for the domination of international politics by a directorate of formally recognized Great Powers (Simpson, 2004: 67–68).

In this way more than any other, the Concert was embryonic of global governance, speaking to a bifurcation not just within European international order, but to the extension of the distinction between 'greater' and 'lesser' powers on a global scale.[10] Crucial here is the role played by the 'standard of civilization' in stratifying polities by culture, race, religion, and relative 'modernity' (Buzan and Lawson, 2015: ch. 4). As discussed in the previous section, the 'standard of civilization', institutionalized in legal distinctions between 'civilized', 'barbarian', and 'savage' peoples, helped to constitute a hierarchical international order during the second half of the 19th century. As also discussed above, the Hague Conferences of 1899 and 1907 established rules and restrictions about the conduct of war between 'civilized' polities. In such instances, positive law contained a dual purpose: regulating conduct amongst sovereign equals in the core, while policing 'difference' between unequal sovereigns globally. The interwar years maintained many of the practices of the 19th century, classifying territories on the basis of their 'primitive' (for which read racial) quotient (Mazower, 2012: 166–167). Of the 48 states that sent delegates to the first assembly meeting of the League of Nations, only four were from Asia (including the Raj) (Mazower, 2012: 254). Despite decolonization, many aspects of legalized hegemony lingered on, and some of these were significant. Particularly prominent was the formation of a permanent group of five Great Powers (the P5) within the UN Security Council and the granting of veto power to these alone. The P5 was a deliberate attempt to replicate the hierarchical management system of the Great Powers that had been instituted in the Concert: both Churchill and Roosevelt saw the Concert as the precedent for a system of global trusteeship under the jurisdiction of the Great Powers (Mazower, 2012: 196). Legalized hegemony also formed the backdrop to a range of debates that took place during the early years of the UN, not just the makeup of the Security Council, but also the formation of a Trusteeship Council to monitor readiness for self-determination, and the adjudication of responsibility between metropolitan powers and local authorities over human rights provisions (Reus-Smit, 2013).

In this way, the Concert pioneered a model of legalized hegemony that linked equality between the Great Powers to inequality between 'greater' and 'lesser' polities. This combination of hierarchy and equality was reproduced in many subsequent units of global governance, including the League of Nations and the UN. As a *specific* forum of international governance, the Concert lasted for less than half a century. As a *general* model of legalized hegemony, the system it pioneered became an enduring feature of world politics. What served to order European polities in a world of regions came to stratify global order in a world of empires.

Notes

1 The '100 days' that followed the escape of Napoleon from Elba led to the stationing of an occupation army in France. The removal of this army in 1818 permitted France to become a formally recognized Great Power.
2 This is not to say that Britain was not, on some matters, more ambitious than the other Great Powers. For example, it was Britain, largely due to the pressure exerted by a significant domestic abolitionist lobby, which pushed for an agreement on the slave trade. An abolitionist petition with over one million signatures was submitted to the British Parliament in June 1814; Parliament followed by passing an act declaring unanimous support for their cause. This put significant pressure on Castlereagh and other members of the British delegation to raise the issue in Vienna.
3 The activities of the secret police may have increased after 1830, but the activities themselves predate this period. At Vienna, for example, the Austrian secret police ran a network of spies and informants who opened and resealed mail, and collected the contents of bins and fireplaces. The findings from these activities were digested into a daily briefing for the Emperor (Jarrett, 2013: 96).
4 This is not to say that all members of the Quadruple Alliance were equal partners: Britain and Russia represented the top strata of the Alliance, Prussia and Austria its lower band.
5 The main roles of these 'salonnières' were as "brokers of patronage, political agents to foreign rulers, the hosts of underground political networks, and operators of informal news-related and networking activities" (Sluga, 2015b: 1–2; also see Sluga (2014 and 2015a).
6 For Vick, the "ideology of the middle" was an alliance of 'moderate liberals' and 'reformist conservatives', who convened a kind of grand bargain oriented around issues of citizenship and representation on the one hand, and historical rights and privileges on the other. But an "ideology of the middle" is a residual category, an act

of political bricolage rather than a coherent ideology. It was also a minority, elite persuasion, one that barely sustained the Congress system, let alone the Concert.
7 Some extra-European issues were discussed at the Congresses, from the future of French Guiana to the Latin American revolutions. But, for the most part, the British worked hard to keep these discussions off the agenda. This strategy, particularly the British refusal to countenance Concert intervention in Latin America, was intended to boost Britain's comparative advantage in maritime affairs and trade.
8 The purchase of Alaska from Russia in 1867 was also significant for securing hemispheric hegemony.
9 One useful illustration of the later extension of the Concert can be found in the realm of river navigation. Whereas the Concert was concerned with navigation of the Rhine, the settlement reached after the Crimean War included an agreement on the navigation of the Danube. The 1884 Berlin Conference went even further, including articles that established the right to navigate both the Congo and Niger.
10 This is not to say that European order simply scaled-up into global order. Rather, as diverse regional orders were forged into a single, if radically differentiated, global order, polities and regions were *incorporated* within a synthetic whole rather than *assimilated* within European legal orders (Benton, 2010; Phillips, 2016).

Bibliography

Anghie, Antony. (2004) *Imperialism, Sovereignty and the Making of International Law.* Cambridge: Cambridge University Press.
Armitage, David and Stella Ghervas. (2014) The Power of Peace: Why 1814 Might Matter More than 1914. *e-ir*, April 7, 2014. Accessed April, 28 2015. https://www.e-ir.info/2014/04/07/the-power-of-peace-why-1814-might-matter-more-than-1914/.
Armitage, David and Sanjay Subrahmanyam, eds. (2010) *The Age of Revolution in Global Context, 1760–1840.* London: Palgrave.
Bayly, C.A. (2004) *The Birth of the Modern World, 1780–1914.* Oxford: Blackwell.
Belich, James. (2009) *Replenishing the Earth: The Settler Revolution and the Rise of the Anglo-World, 1783–1939.* New York: Oxford University Press.
Benton, Laurie. (2010) *A Search for Sovereignty: Law and Geography in European Empires, 1400–1900.* Cambridge: Cambridge University Press.
Bew, John. (2011) 'From an Umpire to a Competitor': Castlereagh, Canning and the Issue of Non-Intervention in the Wake of the Napoleonic Wars. In Brendan Simms and David Trim, eds., *Humanitarian Intervention: A History.* Cambridge: Cambridge University Press.
Bukovansky, Mlada et al. (2012) *Special Responsibilities: Global Problems and American Power.* Cambridge: Cambridge University Press.
Bull, Hedley. (1977) *The Anarchical Society.* London: Palgrave.
Buzan, Barry and Richard Little. (2000) *International Systems in World History: Remaking the Study of International Relations.* Oxford: Oxford University Press.
Buzan, Barry and George Lawson. (2015) *The Global Transformation: History, Modernity and the Making of International Relations.* Cambridge: Cambridge University Press.
Christian, David. (2004) *Maps of Time.* Berkeley: University of California Press.
Clark, Ian. (2011) *Hegemony in International Society.* Oxford: Oxford University Press.
Darwin, John. (2007) *After Tamerlane: The Rise and Fall of Global Empires, 1400–2000.* London: Penguin.

Ghervas, Stella. (2014) The Congress of Vienna: A Peace for the Strong. *History Today* 64(9): 30–33.
Giddens, Anthony. (1985) *The Nation-State and Violence*. Cambridge: Polity.
Go, Julian. (2011) *Patterns of Empire*. Cambridge: Cambridge University Press.
Goldstone, Jack. (2002) Efflorescences and Economic Growth in World History. *Journal of World History* 13(2): 328–389.
Gong, Gerrit W. (1984) *The Standard of 'Civilisation' in International Society*. Oxford: Clarendon.
Hobsbawm, Eric. (1962) *The Age of Revolution, 1789–1848*. London: Abacus.
Holbraad, Carsten. (1970) *The Concert of Europe*. London: Longman.
Holsti, K.J. (1992) Governance without Government: Polyarchy in 19th Century European International Politics. In James N. Rosecrance and Ernst-Otto Czempiel, eds., *Governance without Government: Order and Change in World Politics*. Cambridge: Cambridge University Press.
Ikenberry, G. John. (2001) *After Victory*. Princeton: Princeton University Press.
Jarrett, Mark. (2013) *The Congress of Vienna and Its Legacy*. London: I.B. Tauris.
Jervis, Robert. (1982) Security Regimes. *International Organization* 36(2): 357–378.
Jervis, Robert. (1985) From Balance to Concert: A Study of International Security Cooperation. *World Politics* 38(1): 58–79.
Keene, Edward. (2002) *Beyond the Anarchical Society*. Cambridge: Cambridge University Press.
Keene, Edward. (2013) International Hierarchy and the Origins of the Modern Practice of Intervention. *Review of International Studies* 29(5): 1077–1090.
Kissinger, Henry. (1957) *A World Restored: Metternich, Castlereagh and the Problem of Peace, 1812–22*. New York: Houghton Mifflin.
Kissinger, Henry. (1994) *Diplomacy*. New York: Touchstone.
Kraeke, Enno. (1983) *Metternich's German Policy, Vol. 2: The Congress of Vienna, 1814–15*. Princeton: Princeton University Press.
Kupchan, Charles. (2010) *How Enemies Become Friends*. Princeton: Princeton University Press.
Kupchan, Charles and Clifford Kupchan. (1991) Concerts, Collective Security, and the Future of Europe. *International Security* 16(1): 114–161.
Maier, Charles S. (2012) Leviathan 2.0. In Emily S. Rosenberg, ed., *A World Connecting, 1870–1945*. Cambridge, MA: Belknap Press.
Mann, Michael. (1988) *States, War and Capitalism*. Oxford: Blackwell.
Mann, Michael. (2012) *The Sources of Social Power, Vol. 3: Global Empires and Revolution, 1890–1945*. Cambridge: Cambridge University Press.
Mazower, Mark. (2012) *Governing the World*. London: Allen Lane.
McNeill, William H. (1991) *The Rise of the West*. Chicago: University of Chicago Press.
Millennium (2014) Special Issue: The Standard of Civilization 42(3): 546–859.
Miller, Benjamin. (1994) Explaining the Emergence of Great Power Concerts. *Review of International Studies* 20(4): 327–348.
Mitzen, Jennifer. (2013) *Power in Concert*. Chicago: University of Chicago Press.
Neumann, Iver and Ole Jacob Sending. (2010) *Governing the Global Polity*. Ann Arbor: Michigan University Press.
Nicolson, Harold. (1946) *The Congress of Vienna*. New York: Viking.
Osiander, Andreas. (1994) *The States System of Europe, 1640–1990*. Oxford: Oxford University Press.

Osterhammel, Jürgen. (2014) *The Transformation of the World: A Global History of the Nineteenth Century*. Trans. Patrick Camiller. Princeton: Princeton University Press.

Owens, Patricia. (2015) *Economy of Force: Counterinsurgency and the Historical Rise of the Social*. Cambridge: Cambridge University Press.

Parthasarathi, Prasannan. (2011) *Why Europe Grew Rich and Asia Did Not*. Cambridge: Cambridge University Press.

Phillips, Andrew. (2011) *War, Religion and Empire*. Cambridge: Cambridge University Press.

Phillips, Andrew. (2016) The Global Transformation, Multiple Early Modernities and International Systems Change. *International Theory* 8(3): 481–491.

Rendall, Matthew. (2006) Defensive Realism and the Concert of Europe. *Review of International Studies* 32(3): 523–540.

Reus-Smit, Chris. (2013) *Individual Rights and the Making of the International System*. Cambridge: Cambridge University Press.

Rosenberg, Emily. (2012) Transnational Currents in a Shrinking World. In Emily S. Rosenberg, ed., *A World Connecting, 1870–1945*. Cambridge, MA: Belknap Press.

Rudé, George. (1964) *Revolutionary Europe, 1783–1815*. Glasgow: Fontana.

Schroeder, Paul. (1994) *The Transformation of European Politics, 1763–1848*. Oxford: Clarendon.

Schroeder, Paul. (2000) International Politics, Peace and War, 1815–1914. In T.C.W. Blanning, ed., *The Nineteenth Century*. Oxford: Oxford University Press.

Simms, Brendan. (1997) *The Impact of Napoleon*. Cambridge: Cambridge University Press.

Simpson, Gerry. (2004) *Great Powers and Outlaw States*. Cambridge: Cambridge University Press.

Sluga, Glenda. (2014) Madame de Staël and the Transformation of European Politics, 1812–1817. *International History Review* 37(1): 142–166.

Sluga, Glenda. (2015a) Sexual Congress. *History Today* 64(9): 33–39.

Sluga, Glenda. (2015b) Women, Men and the Making of Modern International Politics. Paper Presented at Columbia University, February.

Sperber, Jonathan. (2000) *Revolutionary Europe, 1780–1850*. Harlow: Pearson.

Suzuki, Shogo. (2009) *Civilization and Empire*. London: Routledge.

Tilly, Charles. (1990) *Coercion, Capital and European States, AD 990–1992*. Oxford: Blackwell.

Vick, Brian E. (2014) *The Congress of Vienna: Power and Politics after Vienna*. Cambridge, MA: Harvard University Press.

Vick, Brian E. (2015) Constitutions and Crises from the Congress of Vienna to the Concert of Europe. Paper Presented at Columbia University, February.

Webster, Charles. (1919) *The Congress of Vienna*. London: H. Milford.

7 Industrialization and competitive globalization after 1873

International thought and the problem of resources

Lucian M. Ashworth

In pretty much every social science the role of industrialization in the nineteenth century is viewed as a game changer. Two related 'industrial revolutions' are seen as changing human relations in very profound ways. International Relations (IR) is an exception to this rule. A quick glance in the main IR textbooks used today reveals how, with a few notable exceptions, even the broader topic of the nineteenth century is effectively ignored. In their survey of 48 IR texts and textbooks, Buzan and Lawson found only five with significant coverage of the nineteenth century (2013, 622). Turning from the textbooks to IR theory, it again becomes clear that, with a few notable exceptions, the study of world orders shows little awareness of the effects of industrialization.

There are, of course, exceptions. Perhaps the biggest can be found in international political economy (IPE) and in neo-Marxist IR, where the mode of production plays a bigger role (see Murphy 1994; Rosenberg 1994, 162; Cox 1981). While IPE is interested in industrial production, the interest tends to be focused on current relations, rather than the historical development of industrialization. In this sense, Murphy's work on the role of industrial change in global governance is an exception, rather than a rule. Yet, the importance of industrialization to global order has not just been the preserve of Marxism or IPE. It has also, on occasions, shown up within other approaches to IR, most notably, an intriguing piece by George Modelski in 1961. Modelski claimed that there were significant differences between the international orders found in agrarian and industrial societies. Using a more ecological model, rather than a Marxist one, Modelski's work represented a different route, where the wider social and physical environment was crucial to the development of systemic structures.

Having studied the emergence of western international thought in the nineteenth century I have become aware of how changes in industrial production had an effect on the nature of global order. I have also come to realize how resource and ecological questions play a larger role in our political life than post-1950 IR theory admits. There are, quite simply, resource and environmental frames and limits on our political life (Mitchell 2011; Morris 2015; Diamond 1997 and 2005). In this sense

Modelski, with his stress on the wider ecology, has something to say to IR. More to the point, I am interested in how the forces unleashed by industrialization *created* much of what we now know as international relations and the system of states, an interest which I share with Buzan and Lawson (2015). This has led me to hypothesize that the reason that we IR theorists have great difficulty in seeing how important industrialization is to IR is because the very subject we study is itself a product of industrialization (Ashworth 2014, chs. 4–5).

Interestingly, although I cover some of the same ground as Buzan and Lawson (2015), my argument concentrates on two different sources of evidence. The first of these is the role played by resources in the construction of the late nineteenth-century world order. The second is the use of 'eye-witness' accounts by international writers at the time. This concentration on both resources and contemporary analyses comes out of my primary interest in the history of international thought. Resources play a major role in late nineteenth- and early twentieth-century discussions of international order. Yet, concentrations on monetary amounts have tended to skew our appreciation of the importance of certain low-cost, yet vital, resources to the functioning of the global economy. This is nothing new. The availability of resources, and their rates of replenishment, is also key to Diamond's work. Similarly, the failure to properly engage with writers during the time has produced a rather stale and anachronistic account of world orders in IR theorizing. While it is true that contemporary authors need to be read critically, they do provide us with an invaluable insight into how these developments affected the thinking at the time.

This chapter will be divided into three sections, in which the role of resources and contemporary political thought will be central to the first and the second sections respectively. In the first section I examine how industrialization had lasting effects on the emergence of global order. Central here will be an exploration of how two waves of industrialization shaped and created the international system. I will argue that the monetary value of trade is only half the story. It is the dramatic shift in the trade in certain resources necessary for the new industrialized great powers that can help us understand the creation of large world powers locked into a balance of power that, in turn, overlays an increasingly two-tier world based on imperial control.

The second section looks at the eyewitness testimony of international theorists writing in the years after the second industrial revolution. In varying degrees these writers were well aware of the novelty of their global order, and of the politico-economic sources of the global system that they lived in. What is interesting is the extent to which there is a spike of interest in international affairs from 1880. I argue that this is due to the novelty of the international system that these writers faced, including the growing importance of international relations in the face of rapid interdependence and the mounting importance of resource needs.

The attempt to understand and to rebuild the global order in the first half of the twentieth century produced the concepts and ideas that still dominate current views of the international order in IR. In the third section I look at how central components of IR flow from industrialization. Part of the structural realist dismissal of industrialization stems from the view that economic interdependence did not greatly change the interactions of states in the state system – that a great power remained a great power. What this misses is that interdependence was one of twins born of industrialization. The modern nation-state, and especially the modern 'great' or 'world' power, was also a product of industrialization. In this sense, the early generations of IR scholars were studying a paradox: industrialization had produced two mutually antagonistic forces. Our conceptions of IR are not manifestations of a deeper transhistorical tragedy, but rather the results of the peculiarities of the new industrialized world that simultaneously produced strong states and global interdependence. This does not mean that all of what we study in IR is a product of industrialization: clearly much of the lexicon and issues such as the problem of war and the fear of hegemonic powers predate the late nineteenth century. What I do argue, though, is that key constituent parts can be traced from the playing out of the effects of industrialization.

From king coal to singing wires: how industrialization created our world

What role did imperialism and colonial control play in nineteenth-century political economy? Since the mass decolonization of the 1960s it has been fashionable to say that its role was limited. This argument has been ably summarized by James Foreman-Peck, who criticized the early Marxists on this point: "That this new colonisation was economically necessary for the European capitalism of the time, as Lenin and others maintained, is hard to square with the small volume of trade involved" (1995, 111). For those IR scholars, like myself, raised on a syllabus that included Hobson's *Imperialism*, this all made sense. A major part of Hobson's argument revolves around the claim, backed up by statistics, that the new colonial territories did little for the metropole by way of investment opportunities and trade when compared to the much larger levels of investment and trade flows between Britain and its main great power rivals of Germany, France, and the United States (Hobson 1902). This overlooks two points from Hobson's argument, however. First, he is specifically speaking about the colonies acquired in the last few decades of the nineteenth century (and the specific contemporary context was the Anglo-Boer wars). Hobson was happier with the economic use and viability of earlier colonies. Also, the one exception that Hobson singles out is also instructive. He mentions Malaya as the only one of the recent colonies to have any economic viability, and that was not to do with volumes of trade or investment, but rather to its climate that allowed for the establishment of plantations producing the now necessary strategic commodity of rubber. In short, Hobson was not saying that all colonies were economic drains, nor was he judging colonial acquisition by monetary worth alone. Hobson, like his contemporaries, was well aware that the dramatic changes in political economy during the nineteenth century had fundamentally altered the structure of the international system. Key to these changes were certain commodities linked to the processes of industrialization.

What do I mean by industrialization? I am referring to what has often been divided into the 'first' and 'second' industrial revolutions. The first, taking place before the mid-nineteenth century, usually refers to the advent of coal power, of malleable wrought iron smelting, and the development of the steam engine that was adapted for use on the new railways. The widespread growth of the cotton industry is also associated with this time period, and reference is often also made to an earlier and parallel agricultural revolution that produced food surpluses capable of supporting larger urban populations. The second industrial revolution, covering the late nineteenth century and the Edwardian period, is associated with the rise of steel, the exponential growth of railways, the development of electricity, the proliferation of the electronic telegraph, the revolution in chemical production, and finally the rise of petroleum and the internal combustion engine. Each of these developments brought about different resource needs, but perhaps the biggest of these was coal.

Timothy Mitchell has described our modern industrialized society as a 'hydrocarbon civilization'. The first key industrial commodity was coal, a form of easily transportable concentrated energy (Mitchell calls it 'buried sunshine') that created a whole new way of living (Mitchell 2009; Mitchell 2011, ch. 1). The abundance of cheap coal (and, increasingly in the early twentieth century, petroleum) led to an unprecedented social revolution. Coal made steam power cheap, and changed into coke, revolutionized the smelting of iron. Steam-driven iron trains and ships were able to transport coal cheaply and efficiently. Coal's highly concentrated levels of energy cut society's reliance on extensive tracts of land for energy production – whether in the form of woodlands or food for laborers and animals – and allowed the concentration of populations in industrial cities far from the sources of the raw materials that their industries used. In the 1801 UK census 20% of the population lived in towns (a high figure for Europe as a whole), by 1851 that figure was 50%, and by 1881 two-thirds of people were urban. Railways and steam-driven shipping delivered the raw materials and food required by these new industrial conurbations, and finally shipped out the finished industrial products of the new industries. For Mitchell the advent of coal as a necessary source of energy, as well as the use of iron railways, fundamentally altered the power relations in society (Mitchell 2011, ch. 1), an issue I return to below. The pivotal role of coal is the one missing element in Buzan and Lawson's otherwise excellent account of the origins of industrialization (Buzan and Lawson 2015, 626–627).

The advent of coal and wrought iron put a premium on the control and trade of coal and iron ore. Access to both of these became necessary to sustain an industrial economy. In Britain cotton was also an early industry reliant on the import of raw materials, and the system of guaranteeing supplies through political control, plantation economies, and free trade provided the template for the acquisition of other raw materials later in the nineteenth century. With the advent of the electric telegraph in the early nineteenth century and the building of the submarine cables that turned the telegraph into a single global system of cheap mass communication, copper became a vital commodity. This role for copper was only increased by the development of electricity later in the century, and even today it remains a vital material (see Blake 1992, 143–219). During much of the nineteenth century the center for copper wire production was Birmingham in the UK, but copper ores had to be imported. While the United States remained a major producer, the top sources in the British Empire were Canada, Australia, and Northern Rhodesia. The southern region of the Belgian Congo also became a major producer of copper ores in the nineteenth century, while Peru and Chile continued to produce copper for export. With innovations in chemical and metallurgical processes, a growing list of raw materials, some rare and not available through European or North American sources, became necessary for the industrial economies of the great powers. These included nitrates for fertilizers (and explosives), antimony, tin, zinc, and chromium for alloy production, and increasingly petroleum as first shipping and then land and air transportation started using it.

Yet, it was not just minerals that became vital resources. Increasingly industrial societies became dependent on the trade in foodstuffs and resources grown for export such as wool, cotton, and rubber. The opening up of the North American prairies for wheat production and export provided a cheap source of a common staple. Canning and refrigeration introduced Europeans to cheap South American meat, as well as New Zealand and Argentinian dairy products. By the late nineteenth century Britain was particularly dependent on imported food to feed its population (Parson 1999, 11), and by 1914 imports accounted for 60% of calories consumed in Britain (Dewey 2003, 271). All of this added up to a global dependence by industrial great powers on the international economy for the supply of products that were now key to the survival of their societies.

The dependence of industrial societies on certain resources does not necessarily turn those societies into imperialists. If a commodity can be acquired cheaply via trade, then the need to acquire it by force and direct control is costly and unnecessary. This point was certainly appreciated by many early international experts, and indeed Isaiah Bowman's advocacy of free trade was premised on the notion that, to an industrial economy, the only alternative to a global free market, where all raw materials could be purchased, was imperial competition where states strove to guarantee their stocks of resources by conquest (Bowman 1942). Indeed, the prevalence of a British sterling-dominated system of trade (and, from the 1880s, an international gold standard) in the late nineteenth century did in fact facilitate such trade. Thus, Europe became reliant on cheap American and Canadian grain that could be bought without resort to conquest. Similarly, the United States remained a major source of copper, while Sweden provided iron ore. Some nominally independent countries also supplied vital resources without becoming colonial territories, although the presence of capital and companies from the great powers did lead to a semi-colonial status. This, for example, happened to that other great source of copper, Chile. H.N. Brailsford would later refer to such societies as the equivalent of 'human cattle farms': nominally independent, but actually economically controlled (see the next section).

Yet, in these cases the societies were already fully linked up with the global political economy. What of other societies with 'necessary' resources in which the nature of their economy, or the unwillingness of their governments, made them poor trading partners? Foreman-Peck sums this problem up in chillingly bloodless fashion: "European trade with many tropical areas created a variety of problems, which from the viewpoint of the European powers could often best or most simply be dealt with by the extension of formal political control" (1995, 118). Thus taking over a region and altering its economic structure so that it provided large quantities of a resource for the growing global economy became a common occurrence (Cameron and Neal 2003, 195). This system had already been pioneered with cotton, where the development of cotton plantations in India, and then in the Caribbean and the American south, created a system of raw material trade that fed the major industrial cotton centers such as Lancashire. As with cotton, this could take one of two forms. A territory could be forced to export resources it already had, or only produced for local consumption, such as happened in the colonization of Burma.[1] It could also involve the taking over of a territory that had the right climate and soil for the production in plantations of a vital resource. Thus, Malaya provided ideal conditions for the production of rubber from a tree species originally native to Brazil.

This is not to say that all colonies were taken over for purely economic reasons. Indeed, by the late nineteenth century, colonial acquisitions also became an end in itself as a means of gaining prestige for a great power – specifically, to ensure its status as a world power, rather than just a regional one. Thus Germany's growing hunger for places in the sun, spurred on by the agitation of the *Kolonialverein*, was as much about German honor as economic exploitation. That said, though, the very fact that colonies were seen as important had its roots in their frequent importance as sources of resources, as well as markets and investment opportunities. Importantly though, as writers in international affairs often knew already, the benefit of a colony was not solely for the colonizing power, but (in a free trade sterling-based global order) for all industrial societies. Germans could get access to Malayan rubber, Chilean copper, or Newfoundland wood-pulp via trade. The important issue was that this was a system divided into two spheres. Wealthy industrialized societies obtained cheap resources via global trade, while poorer colonial and semi-colonial societies provided these resources either freely, but with very little say in the trade (as was the case with Chilean copper), or through colonial control of their economy in exploitative systems such as plantation economies. What was being created was a hierarchical system of societies, underpinned by racist ideas of civilization.[2] Imperialism marked the culmination of a process in which non-western societies also played an important, if subordinate, role in the shaping of global society (see especially Wolf 1982, ch. 11).

Looking back from 1926 to the highpoint of colonial expansion in the late nineteenth century, Parker Moon astutely summarized these forces that had encouraged the building of the large colonial and semi-colonial empires:

> Europe was converted to imperialism not by logic alone, nor by economic 'necessity' alone, but by a combination of argument and interest, arising from an almost revolutionary alteration of economic political conditions. The old order, the good old mid-Victorian order, had passed away, and if not a new heaven, at least a new earth was seen by the keen eye of business and politics.
>
> (Moon 1926, 25)

This development of a two-tier, economically interdependent world dominated by western or westernized industrial societies was also exacerbated by spinoffs from the processes of industrialization. Developments in communications technologies – especially steamships, railways the electronic telegraph, and the internal combustion engine – enabled states to increase their control within their territories, while also making their own projection of power over the globe easier (Buzan and Lawson 2015, 627 develop this argument in their discussion of the emergence of the rational state). The vast territories of the colonial empires were both conquered and controlled by a network of coaling stations, shipping lanes, and submarine telegraph cables. Similarly, land transportation and conquest, which had been only as fast as a soldier could walk or a messenger could ride in the Napoleonic wars, were now facilitated by networks of railways, telegraph lines, and (eventually in the early twentieth century) automobiles and airplanes. John Mearsheimer has made much of the 'stopping power of water', and the comparative ease of land conquest. While that may have been true of the twentieth century, the reverse was true in the eighteenth, where naval technologies allowed for easier sea transportation. Indeed, it was the initial ease of sea transportation that made the colonial empires possible in the first place. The 'stopping power of land', in the absence of rail and telegraph, was a very real problem for armies before then. It was the sharp reversal between the speeds of sea and land power that had led Mackinder to write his 1904 'Geographical Pivot of History' paper that heralded the end of what he saw as the 'Columbian Age' of sea-based exploration and empire (1904, 421–437).

I have already discussed how coal was crucial to the development of the modern industrialized economy. In fact, its importance as the primary source of industrialized energy remained unchallenged until the development of another hydrocarbon: oil. Coal played little direct role in the imperial conquests of the major world powers because Britain, France, Germany, and the United States already had access to large reserves. Coal, though, did play a vital role in the development of the western societies that relied on it, as Timothy Mitchell has argued. Basically, coal fostered mass democracy. The digging, transportation, and distribution of great 'quantities of energy' 'along very narrow channels' gave coal miners, iron workers, and railwaymen the power to threaten elites through trade union agitation and strikes. According to Mitchell, the modern mass democracy that emerged in the late nineteenth and early twentieth centuries was a creation of the power that unions had over the fragile energy flows of the new industrial economy (2009, 403–406; 2011, ch. 1). Coal-induced mass democracy both helped establish a new modern state based upon the sovereignty of the whole people, and also produced a challenge to this new emerging state in the form of an international socialist and trade union movement. Without the effects of this mass democracy the ideas of national interest and of total war, so central to the relations of states in the twentieth century, would have been of a very different order.

At the same time as coal was changing the political complexion of industrial societies, the new communications technologies, particularly the telegraph, were revolutionizing information flows. Particularly relevant here is how the telegraph flattened out market prices, creating the world's first global market, while at the same time allowing for heightened levels of state centralization and control.[3] Radio would also offer a vital tool in the manufacturing of political support in the decades following the end of the First World War. The era of mass communication brought the far corners of the world closer, but also helped divide people through centralized state communications, and control. Communications could be used as much to create identities as to break them down. "No system in world history," write Buzan and Lawson, "so united the planet, while simultaneously pulling it apart" (2013, 626).

On top of this, it was not just industrialization per se that created a puzzle for late nineteenth-century scholars, but also how it played out in creating world powers. By the 1870s Britain's global hegemony had given way to a 'concert' dominated by the new world powers. At one level this was a return to the old pre-industrial idea of the balance of power, and indeed reliance on a balance between the new world powers carried with it many of the hallmarks of an earlier agrarian world a century before. Eighteenth-century concerns with balancing alliances and the threat of growing powers remained, but the ecology that they now existed within had changed. It now involved: 1. a global hierarchical political economy in which revisionist powers were also seeking greater control over the colonial and semi-colonial world; 2. nationally mobilized states armed with modern militaries capable of unleashing system-destabilizing wars as a matter of course; and 3. changes to what Buzan and Lawson call "the mode of power" (2015, 307) – that is the social sources of power – that made the substance of the balance of power from the late nineteenth century so fundamentally different from that of the eighteenth century. This is explored in more detail in the next section.

In all, what emerges from the developments of the political economy of the nineteenth century is a sharp break with the agrarian past. Key here is the role of a growing number of resources necessary for industrial processes, as well as an increasingly global trade in food to feed industrial urban centers. Behind all this is the development of a hydrocarbon civilization, in which societies become dependent first on coal and then on oil for the energy required to run their economies. These developments create a two-tier, fully global political economy, but they also help centralize the state, usher in populist politics in both its socialist and nationalist forms, and create military structures and technologies that overcame the problem of 'the stopping power of land'. These developments lead to a world dominated by two opposing forces: growing interdependence, on the one hand, and state formation and centralization, on the other. Thus, the legacy of industrialization is an equivocal one, producing forces that are in permanent tension with each other. Not surprisingly these developments did not go unnoticed by political writers and journalists of the time. Indeed, it is the very tension between these legacies that made the international so interesting (and worrying) to the generations between the 1880s and 1940s. Increasingly the idea of the importance of the global political economy and of international affairs emerges as a genre of political writing. It is to this development of international thought that we now turn.

Clutching for certainties in a world in flux: international thought comes of age

There is an odd peak in interest in international affairs and the dynamics of global political economy from the 1880s (Knutsen 2008; Schmidt 1998; Ashworth 2014). While the First World War certainly did much to popularize international relations, the debates (and many of the international experts) in the interwar period had already matured in the four decades before the war (Sylvest 2005). Earlier still, in the mid-nineteenth century, several key political economists, philosophers, and public figures had realized that fallout from the first industrial revolution of coal, iron, and railways had marked a change in the relations between states (Ashworth 2014, ch. 4). Yet, it was in the last fifth of the nineteenth century – in the wake of the second industrial revolution – that a new genre of writing began to emerge: works that were either focused on international matters, or were exclusively international in nature. In the earlier generation of writers in mid-century, international affairs was still an adjunct or an afterthought to the main concerns of the author. Thus, List's interpretation of an emerging system of states and of imperial competition over non-western territories was part of his central concern about the development of coherent and industrial national societies through specific public policy choices (List 1966 and 1983). By the last two decades of the nineteenth century, a growing number of writers began to see the study of the foreign policy of the great powers within a global system as a worthy object of study.

Much of the work at the end of the century focused on what defined a 'world power': a new form of great power that had adjusted to take into consideration the global realities of industrial needs. For Friedrich Ratzel, the new centralized states were analogous to organisms competing with other states over the spatial environment. For Germany to acquire world power status it would need three things: possessions in all parts of the world for economic and strategic reasons, a blue-water navy to service this empire, and a 'space perception' amongst the German population that allowed Germans to see why this expansion was necessary (1897, 11–12 and 357; 1898, 1–2; 1899, 2; Ashworth 2014, 99–100). In the United States the same problems were being explored by the political scientist Paul Reinsch. For Reinsch the stable balance of power was now being challenged by an impersonal struggle for power between states. The source for these forces was changes to economic and industrial relations that used emotive nationalism to promote an imperialism driven by commercial (rather than territorial) interests. Colonialism for Reinsch offered a safety valve for conflicting financial and commercial interests, and he hoped that it could be used to prevent direct great power conflict (1900, 11–80; Ashworth 2014, 108–109).

Although both Ratzel and Reinsch were attempting to extract general rules for international behavior, they were doing this against the backdrop of what they realized were epochal changes. Both incorporated ideas of an expanding and powerful state competing in an increasingly interdependent world. Interdependence, though, was a double-edged sword. While it could form the basis of peaceful cooperation, as Reinsch would argue in his later work (Reinsch 1911), it was more likely just to exacerbate rivalry and competition. Central to Ratzel and Reinsch – as both competition and safety-valve – was the acquisition of colonies. Indeed, Reinsch's other major research interest was colonial government (Reinsch 1902 and 1905). Even ostensibly anti-imperial works, such as J. A. Hobson's *On Imperialism*, recognized the importance of the colonial relationship, and its interaction with the problem of war. Hobson's book was an attack on the 'new imperialism' of the late nineteenth century, which (Hobson argued) only served sectional interests at home (especially among the rentier class), and not the colonial power as a whole (Hobson 1902). Despite this, though, Hobson did recognize the economic value of the previous wave of imperialism, and even in criticizing the current crop of imperial adventures, he was aware that the roots of it lay in the nature of capitalism in the industrial powers. Norman Angell's different take on the international economy started from the other direction from Hobson. Less concerned with imperialism, which he largely accepted as part of a broader globalization of the world economy, he worried that the military competition between the great powers (based on outdated ideas of conquest from a pre-industrial age) threatened to undermine the fragile global links that made the global industrial economy function (Angell 1911).

Throughout all these studies, the primary problems of international affairs emerged as both the problem of war and the management of empire, both of which were made increasingly problematic by the interdependence of the global economy. The two spheres of the international system – the great power security balance and the global imperial-based political economy – were recognized as the sources of its two major problems: war and colonial administration. Thus, by the end of the nineteenth century it was widely accepted that a central part of the reality of global politics was a two-tiered world in which an industrialized and predominantly western world ruled and extracted resources from a dependent non-western world. In essence, international society was recognized as a hierarchical, not an anarchically egalitarian, system.

Two very different writers who captured the nature of this new two-tiered global order were the American admiral Alfred Thayer Mahan, and the British journalist and political activist Henry Noel Brailsford. Mahan was an advocate of a higher level of armaments, an opponent of widening the scope for peaceful arbitration, and a pro-imperial racist. Brailsford, by contrast was a socialist classics scholar who opposed great power diplomacy, and advocated stronger representative international organizations. Despite the wide divergence in their political opinions, both came to not incompatible conclusions about the nature of the global order before the First World War, and both understood the two-tier nature of the global political economy. The major difference in approach was that Mahan supported the imperial status quo, while Brailsford opposed it.

As an admiral Mahan's first concern was naval geo-strategy, and the book he is most famous for was a history of the role of sea-power (Mahan 1890). The underlying assumption in Mahan's writings, which justified his view of the importance of history for the understanding of contemporary problems, was that a constant human nature meant that the determinants of strategy and military thinking were also unchanging. The tactics employed might vary because of changes in technology, but strategic thinking rooted in human nature obeyed the same laws throughout history (1890, 88–89). For Mahan the sea remained a 'great highway', and industrious nations had always used it as a means to build an imperial order. Industry led to trade, which produced shipping, and finally produced a colonial empire – and a colonial empire based on trade needed a strong navy to defend it (1890, 25–28; 1918, 87). Thus, Mahan recognized that colonial expansion was a direct result of any modern industrial society.

It was upon the basis of this view of the strategy of the great powers that Mahan built his model of the international system. Competition between states and societies was a natural part of human life for Mahan, but in the world he saw around him this competition took two very different forms. The first involved the relations between what Mahan called the European great powers (including the United States). The European great powers formed a global balance of power in which war and armaments played an important role in maintaining the health of this international society. For Mahan each of the great powers could be seen as analogous to a living organism, with its own sense of morality (1912, 142). Wars were fought between the great powers over matters of honor and vital interest, so war and the balance of power should be seen, he argued, as moral conflicts over matters of justice. The balance of power was, therefore, a means of settling claims of justice between states (Mahan 1907, xvii and 38–39; 1912, 12). For Mahan this military balance acted as a sort of European constitution in which the smaller states were protected by the balance between the great powers, and the competition between the great powers became analogous to the competition between companies vying for market share, but in the act of following their self-interest they benefit the well-being of all. It was, therefore, a system for maintaining the health of the European body politic (Mahan 1912, 10, 13–14, 86–87, 107–109, and 145). The balance of power, though, served another important function for Mahan: through competition in armaments and over colonies the European great powers were able to refine their skills and technology so that they could defend themselves against their common enemy: the non-western world.

The second form of competition that Mahan saw was the conflict between the European and non-European worlds. This, for Mahan, was also a moral conflict because the non-European world was 'barbaric', and the preservation of a European and Christian civilization was for him the highest goal of international affairs. Civilized societies have a natural tendency to expand, he argued, and the easiest form of expansion remained that into the territories of 'incompetent' and 'inferior' races. This imperial use of force was morally justified, since it brought superior European organization to parts of the world were the inhabitants were unable to develop superior forms of organization on their own (Mahan 1898, 165–166; 1912, 113–117). Yet, while the Europeans possessed superior organization, technology, and morality (all of which had been honed and perfected through the balance of power between European great powers), the non-western world had its own strengths through which it could threaten European civilization. As Mahan saw it, European civilization's power came from its armaments ('velocity') and its superior self-assertion ('spirit'), the non-Europeans relied on their greater population ('mass'). Armaments were, therefore, needed to preserve European civilization in order to counteract the superior numbers of the non-white races (1912, 9).

Although Mahan's ideas are primarily the rantings of a bigot displaying what John M. Hobson has categorized as a 'racist siege mentality', (Hobson 2012, 129) it is how those rantings are organized and justified that shows Mahan's underlying understanding of the structure of the pre-1914 global political economy. The system is a two-tier one, in which global security is maintained by a predominantly European balance of power. This balance of power exists alongside an economic system in which industrialized powers reduce the non-industrialized to a dependent colonial status intended to provide the industrialized with raw materials, markets, and financial opportunities. Mahan's notion of the importance of a colonial empire to a world power is also echoed in the work of Friedrich Ratzel.

Mahan's perception of global order reappears in the writing of H.N. Brailsford. The crucial difference, however, is that while Mahan supported and advocated the system he explained, Brailsford opposed it. Similar to Mahan, Brailsford saw the global political economy as split between a politico-military balance of power between states, and a politico-economic order run upon the principles of a capitalist mode of production. These were not hermetically sealed systems, however, and the nature of the balance of power, according to Brailsford, was directly affected by the nature of wealth accumulation in the wider political economy. Thus, in the agrarian eighteenth century, wealth was based on land, and therefore the balance of power manifested itself as a conflict over the control of territory. In the industrial era, however, wealth came from the acquisition of capital, and as a result the balance of power was now a struggle over investment opportunities and market share (Brailsford 1917, 29–32). Thus, for Brailsford power within a balance of power system was not an end in itself, but rather a means towards the end of the acquisition of wealth. As the form of wealth changed so would the political competition between states in the balance of power.

Yet, for Brailsford it was both the colonial territories of the global south and the smaller nominally independent small powers that were the victims of the competition between capitalist great powers. Although in formal political terms the smaller and weaker state within the global system remained independent, in informal and economic terms it was now turned into 'a human cattle farm', where wealth was extracted for the benefit of capitalist elites in the great powers (1917, 72). Thus, the form of the global political economy was not wholly reducible, as it was in Mahan, to a racialized north–south division, although that was also part of the explanation. Rather, the international system was changing from one obsessed with the sovereign control of territory, to a less formal set of imperial ties where even formally independent states were caught up in a system of domination. Brailsford had aptly described the semi-colonial status of nominally independent states, such as the copper and tin exporters Chile and Peru. The crucial point about the international system as Brailsford saw it was that the balance of power between the great powers was a means by which those great powers competed over capital, and armaments were used as a means of putting pressure on rivals to concede market share or financial control over specific territories or states. This, Brailsford argued, was a system of 'armed peace', where ideally the great powers achieved their ends through military threats, while avoiding a single great military conflagration that would threaten to destroy the system as a whole. What Brailsford had laid out, although he did not have a name for it, was what half a century later analysts would call neo-colonialism. For Brailsford the only way out of this exploitative system that disadvantaged both the colonized and the working classes of the great powers, was to replace capitalism with democracy and socialism (Brailsford 1917).

Both Mahan and Brailsford portray a world order based on two very different relationships: a balance of power among great powers that manages the security of the system,[4] and a global political economy that makes one part of the world subservient to the economic needs of another. Although Mahan supported this system and Brailsford opposed it, both could agree that this was generally a stable system. Yet, it was the very fact that the July crisis of 1914 was a surprise to Mahan and Brailsford – as it was for much of the rest of the world too – that points us in the direction of a key piece of evidence that the First World War was less the culmination of an imperialist international system, as it was a shock and disruption to that system. This idea of the outbreak of war as a threat to the system comes out most clearly in the works of Norman Angell. Angell was an opponent of Mahan's. The two had earlier clashed over the utility of war (see Mahan, 1912, 122–123), and while he shared much with Brailsford, the latter regarded Angell's approach as at best only half an argument because Angell had not directly addressed the problems of capitalism and imperialism. Yet, one part of Angell's argument is germane to Mahan and Brailsford's view of the durability of the pre-1914 global order. Angell, too, saw the interdependent world economy as a stable and successful system, but that system was threatened by an 'optical illusion' among the broader public and policy communities in the great powers: the fallacy that wealth could be captured by war between the great powers. This, for Angell, was an idea inherited from an agrarian past when wealth could be conquered (1911, 27–28, 46–47, 54; 1913, 24–25; 1914, 89, 95–98). Now, in a global and industrial world, where wealth was in intangible things like finance, war had the opposite effect: it threatened to ruin the very processes that created wealth in an industrial society. An agrarian mentality, armed with the power of the new industrialized 'world powers', endangered the system of imperial control and interdependence.

Thus, Mahan and Brailsford's view of the stability of the global system was premised on both the stability of the imperial economic system (which seemed valid), and on the self-restraint of the great powers (which, in hindsight, broke down by 1914). Angell provides the missing piece here. It was the failure of the great powers to maintain a secure armed peace that stands out, so rather than the war being the result of the imperialism of the great powers, it is probably fairer to say that it was their failure to maintain the restrained armed peace explored by Mahan and Brailsford that undermined their imperial projects. This is even lent much credence by the nature of the July crisis in 1914 itself. While colonial irritants in Morocco, Egypt, Persia, and China had caused crises to erupt between the powers, these had all been resolved one way or another by 1914. What had not was the hardening of the European alliance systems, and the increasingly volatile politics of the Balkans and Serb irredentism against Austria-Hungary. The weakness of the system proved to be not its imperial nature, but rather its Europe-focused balance of power.

The shock of war did not remove the resource problem for industrial societies, and it is the problem of resources that dominates discussions of international affairs between 1919 and 1945. It became commonplace to see the war as the final destruction of a pre-war liberal laissez-faire order (Reynolds 2014, 124ff). For John Maynard Keynes in 1920, the world from 1870 to 1914 had been a thoroughly interdependent liberal order. Premised on low wages for labor and self-restraint by capitalists (Keynes called this a 'double-bluff or deception'), the system had appeared to be stable to those living through it, but the war had destroyed the self-restraint that had maintained it (1920, ch. 2). By 1926 Keynes felt confident enough to declare the death of laissez-faire liberalism (Keynes 1926). The same argument appears in Norman

Angell's assessment of the post-war realities. Even before the war, Angell had argued that the free-trade interdependent global economy was particularly vulnerable to the pressures of war (1914, 61–68). By 1921 he was arguing that the pre-war liberal order was dead, and that the consequence of this was that interdependence (and with it prosperity) was being reversed and rolled back towards a less efficient and nationalistic order (1921, 61–70, 300–301). Through all of this, however, it was recognized that the problem of resources remained, even if the order that had distributed them was in its death throes. Indeed, the rollback of interdependence would exacerbate the problem, as great powers attempted to control resources within their own economic spheres of influence. Much of the work of the peacemakers in Paris during 1919 revolved around drawing boundaries that would guarantee economic viability by assigning adequate resources (especially coal) to the newly emerging independent states (see the discussion in Macmillan 2001).

Mistaking flux for permanence: industrialization in the history of IR

Perhaps it was because of the success of the immediate post-1945 reconstruction that the problems of resources and industrialization played such a minor role in the study of IR in the decades after 1950. With the problem of resources and industrial needs solved for now, IR could safely accept it as just latent background, and turn instead to abstract discussions of power for the sake of power. Indeed, it was not really until the oil shock of 1973 that the problem of resources in an industrial economy climbed up the list of priorities in the field. Even then, much of the development in this area came from the newly minted IPE community. Perhaps, though, it is worth pausing to reflect that in the decades between the 1880s and 1940s, issues of industrialization and resource access were important to the major writers on international affairs. Indeed, elsewhere I have argued that, prior to 1945 much of what we know as early IR was really what we would now call IPE (Ashworth 2011). It has become commonplace in IR textbooks to present the history of IR as being 'idealist' before 1945, but 'realist' thereafter. A perusal of the record suggests that a more accurate description was that it was materialist before 1945, but distinctly idealist in a philosophical sense after 1950. The classical realist and English School IRs that emerged in the 1950s and 1960s seemed to distance their analysis from the broader political economy approaches of the past, but in so doing they unconsciously constructed views of the international system that were still based on the norms of international affairs that had been crafted by industrialization.

Perhaps the most basic of these was the idea of the reality of the international being a system of states. While this state-centrism, and idea of a society of states, was stronger amongst English School 'international society' scholars than it was amongst US classical realists, the very idea that it was possible to base an interpretation of IR on the idea of national interest assumed a society of states dominated by the mass politics that had come out of the hydrocarbon age. Equally, the idea of a global system of centralized states engaged in a balance of power assumed the existence of new world powers. Along with the rise of the modern state, industrialization through growing interdependence had created a global system in which the contacts between states were also exponentially increased. New welfare and development states became responsible for more areas of policy at a time when many of those same areas had become internationalized and globalized.[5] This was the state system that IR theorists sought to understand from the 1950s.

Even the security role of the state was premised on an industrialized military that was very different from that which had been available in the seventeenth century. John Mearsheimer has made much of the 'stopping power of water' and the corresponding ease with which land power can be applied. Yet, this notion of land power is a recent product of industrialization. Before the advent of the railway and telegraph the advantage in terms of travel and the projection of power lay with sea power. The 'stopping power of land' – the way that the environment of the land applied friction to the projection of land power – was a reality that restricted the damage that land power could inflict on bodies politic. Throughout the almost continuous wars of the seventeenth and eighteenth centuries in *Ancien Regime* Europe, for example, very few polities were wiped off the map. The partitions of Poland stand out as the major exception that proves the rule (Anderson 1998, 66ff).

Perhaps, as well, even the very conception of offensive realism, as described by Mearsheimer, is a feature of industrial society. Returning to Bowman's argument discussed above, industrial societies, by the very nature of their economies and of their chronic vulnerability due to interdependence and resource needs, are looking to expand. Whether that expansion is manifest as overt political imperialism, or as covert commercial and financial links, the onus remains on growth. By contrast, agrarian societies, based as they are on wealth extracted from land and agricultural surpluses, have no such imperative. This does not necessarily mean that they need not expand: after all both Rome and ancient China were empire builders. It does, though, mean that they encountered limits to their expansion based on the ability to extract agricultural surpluses from conquered land. The case of *Ancien Regime* Europe shows how militarized and war-prone societies that engaged in brutal acts of violence need not necessarily follow the logic of offensive realism when their societies are primarily agrarian. Industrial societies, however, are locked into a logic of growth.

This is not to say that the international relations of the industrial world were completely developed without any reference to the world before it. Many of its logics are shared with an early agrarian world, and indeed the late nineteenth-century concern with the balance of power is an example of this continuity. It is rather that key aspects of the substance of post-1870s international affairs are the result of its industrial ecology. The works of early IR scholars between the 1880s and 1940s reveal this important link between industrial ecology and 'world-power' politics.

Above all, though, our global order is still largely a two-tier one, separating a 'developed north' from an 'underdeveloped south'. Underdeveloped is a misnomer, however, since the societies we describe in this way were actually developed to serve a particular (albeit subservient) role within a global industrial order. Despite the rise of NICs in the latter part of the twentieth century, and BRICS in the first part of the twenty-first, our global order remains one divided along lines created during industrialization. IR, with its gaze still mainly on a state-centric order regulated by an abstract disembodied conception of power, needs to be aware of the unusualness of this order, and the extent to which the modernity it studies rests on certain basic material and ecological forces that are more elemental than an abstract will to power.

Notes

1 The role of business interests in the British annexation of Burma is explored in Webster (2000, 1003–1025).
2 For a discussion of the hierarchical nature of international society and 'standards of civilization', see both Hobson 2014 and Keene 2014.
3 The revolution in communication launched by the telegraph is explored in Standage 1998.
4 The origins of this diplomatic system are explored in Mitzen 2013.
5 This approach to the state and global politics was popularized by David Mitrany. For a good summary of Mitrany's thought on this, see Ashworth 2013, 59–68.

Bibliography

Anderson, M.S. (1998) *War and Society in Europe of the Old Regime 1618–1789*. Stroud: Sutton.
Angell, Norman. (1911) *The Great Illusion. A Study of the Relation of Military Power in Nations to their Economic and Social Advantage*. Toronto: McClelland and Goodchild.
Angell, Norman. (1913) *War and the Essential Realities*. London: Watts.
Angell, Norman. (1914) *Foundations of International Polity*. London: William Heinemann.
Angell, Norman. (1921) [1972] *The Fruits of Victory*. New York: Garland.
Ashworth, Lucian M. (2011) Missing Voices: Critical IPE, Disciplinary History and H. N. Brailsford's Analysis of the Capitalist International Anarchy. In Stuart Shields, Ian Bruff, and Huw Macartney, eds., *Critical International Political Economy. Dialogue, Debate and Dissensus*. Basingstoke: Palgrave.
Ashworth, Lucian M. (2013) "'A New Politics for a Global Age': David Mitrany's A Working Peace System." In Henrik Bliddal, Casper Sylvest, and Peter Wilson, eds., *Classics of International Relations*. London: Routledge.
Ashworth, Lucian M. (2014) *A History of International Thought. From the Origins of the Modern State to Academic International Relations*. London: Routledge.
Bowman, Isaiah. (1942) "Geography vs. Geopolitics." *Geographical Review* 32: 646–658.
Blake, B.C. (1992) *Copper Wire and Electrical Conductors – The Shaping of a Technology*. Chur: Harwood.
Buzan, Barry and George Lawson. (2013) "The Global Transformation: The Nineteenth Century and the Making of Modern International Relations." *International Studies Quarterly* 57: 620–634.

Buzan, Barry and George Lawson. (2015) The Global Transformation: History, Modernity and the Making of International Relations. Cambridge: Cambridge University Press.
Brailsford, H.N. (1917) *The War of Steel and Gold. A Study of the Armed Peace*. 9th edition. London: Bell.
Cameron, Rondo and Larry Neal. (2003) *A Concise Economic History of the World*. 4th edition. Oxford: Oxford University Press.
Cox, Robert W. (1981) "Social Forces, States and World Orders: Beyond International Relations." *Theory Millennium – Journal of International Studies* 10(2): 126–155.
Dewey, Peter. (2003) Agriculture, Agrarian Society and the Countryside. In Chris Wrigley, ed., *A Companion to Early Twentieth Century Britain*. Oxford: Blackwell.
Diamond, Jared. (1997) *Guns, Germs and Steel*. New York: Norton.
Diamond, Jared. (2005) *Collapse. How Societies Choose to Fail or Succeed*. New York: Viking.
Foreman-Peck, James. (1995) *A History of the World Economy. International Economic Relations since 1850*. 2nd edition. New York: Harvester.
Hobson, John A. (1902) *Imperialism. A Study*. London: Nisbet.
Hobson, John M. (2012) *The Eurocentric Conception of World Politics. Western International Theory, 1760–2010*. Cambridge: Cambridge University Press.
Hobson, John M. (2014) "The Twin Self-delusions of IR: Why 'Hierarchy' and Not 'Anarchy' is the Core Concept of IR." *Millennium* 42(3): 557–575.
Keene, Edward. (2014) "The Standard of 'Civilisation', the Expansion Thesis and the 19th-century International Social Space." *Millennium* 42(3): 651–673.
Keynes, John Maynard. (1920) *The Economic Consequences of the Peace*. London: Macmillan.
Keynes, John Maynard. (1926) *The End of Laissez Faire*. London: Hogarth Press.
Knutsen, Torbjørn. (2008) "A Lost Generation? IR Scholarship Before World War I." *International Politics* 45: 650–674.
List, Friedrich. (1966) *The National System of Political Economy*. New York: Augustus Kelly.
List, Friedrich. (1983) *The Natural System of Political Economy, 1837*. London: Frank Cass.
Mackinder, Halford J. (1904) "The Geographical Pivot of History." *The Geographical Journal* 23: 421–437.
Macmillan, Margaret. (2001) *Peacemakers. The Paris Conference of 1919 and Its Attempt to End War*. London: John Murray.
Mahan, Alfred Thayer. (1890) *The Influence of Sea Power upon History 1660–1783*. Boston: Little, Brown & Co.
Mahan, Alfred Thayer. (1898) *The Interest of America in Sea Power. Present and Future*. Boston: Little, Brown & Co.
Mahan, Alfred Thayer. (1907) *Some Neglected Aspects of War*. Boston: Little, Brown & Co.
Mahan, Alfred Thayer. (1912) *Armaments and Arbitration or the Place of Force in the International Relations of States*. New York: Harper.
Mahan, Alfred Thayer. (1918) *The Interests of America in International Conditions*. Boston: Little, Brown & Co.
Mearsheimer, John J. (2014) *The Tragedy of Great Power Politics*. Updated edition. New York: Norton.
Mitchell, Timothy. (2009) "Carbon Democracy." *Economy and Society* 38(3): 399–432.

Mitchell, Timothy. (2011) *Carbon Democracy. Political Power in the Age of Oil.* London: Verso.

Modelski, George. (1961) "Agraria and Industria: Two Models of the International System." *World Politics* 14(1): 118–143.

Moon, Parker Thomas. (1926) *Imperialism and World Politics.* New York: Macmillan, 1947.

Morris, Ian. (2015) *Foragers, Farmers, and Fossil Fuels. How Human Values Evolve.* Princeton: Princeton University Press.

Murphy, Craig N. (1994) *International Organization and Industrial Change. Global Governance since 1850.* Cambridge: Polity Press.

Parson, Timothy H. (1999) *The British Imperial Century 1815–1914. A World History Perspective.* Lanham, MD: Bowman and Littlefield.

Ratzel, Friedrich. (1897) *Politische Geographie.* Munich and Berlin: Oldenburg.

Ratzel, Friedrich. (1899) *Anthropogeographie.* Stuttgart: J. Engelhorn.

Ratzel, Friedrich. (1898) "Flottenfrage und Weltlage." *Münchner Neueste Nachrichtung* 51: 1–2.

Reinsch, Paul S. (1900) *World Politics at the End of the Nineteenth Century. As Influenced by the Oriental Situation.* New York and London: Macmillan.

Reinsch, Paul S. (1902) *Colonial Government. An Introduction to the Study of Colonial Institutions.* New York: Macmillan.

Reinsch, Paul S. (1905) *Colonial Administration.* New York: Macmillan.

Reinsch, Paul S. (1911) *Public International Unions. A Study of International Administrative Law.* Boston: Ginn.

Reynolds, David. (2014) *The Long Shadow. The Legacies of the Great War in the Twentieth Century.* New York: Norton.

Rosenberg, Justin. (1994) *The Empire of Civil Society. A Critique of the Realist Theory of International Relations.* London: Verso.

Schmidt, Brian. (1998) *The Political Discourse of Anarchy. A Disciplinary History of International Relations.* Albany: SUNY Press.

Sylvest, Casper. (2005) "Continuity and Change in British Liberal Internationalism, c.1900–1930." *Review of International Studies* 31: 263–283.

Standage, Tom. (1998) *The Victorian Internet.* New York: Bloomsbury.

Webster, Anthony. (2000) "Business and Empire: A Reassessment of the British Conquest of Burma in 1885." *The Historical Journal* 43(4): 1003–1025.

Wendt, Alexander. (1999) *Social Theory of International Politics.* Cambridge: Cambridge University Press.

Wolf, Eric R. (1982) *Europe and the People without History.* Berkeley: University of California Press.

8 Between European Concert and global status

The evolution of the institution of great powers, 1860s to 1910s

Thomas Müller

Introduction

The institution of great powers, understood as the collective hegemony and special managerial role of the group of great powers, is usually depicted as a product of the early 19th century. Scholars point to the Concert of Europe as the origin and first embodiment of the practice of joint order management by the group of great powers in the name of international society as a whole (see Schroeder, 1994; Simpson, 2004; and Mitzen, 2013).[1] In fact, International Relations (IR) tends to equate the history of the institution of great powers with the history of the Concert of Europe for most parts of the 19th century. However, most IR narratives privilege the first half of the century by associating the actual practice of the Concert mainly with that era and narrating the second half in terms of the "demise" of the Concert and the rise of great power conflict (see Clark, 2011; Bisley, 2012; and critically Marcowitz, 2006: 91–95). These narratives are, in other words, based upon a bifurcated-century interpretation, with the period from the Crimean War (1853–1856) to the Franco-German War (1870–1871) as the transition from the first to the second phase.

This chapter analyzes how the institution of great powers evolved in the second half of the century. While basically agreeing with the "two worlds" interpretation, it argues that the demise-narrative downplays the dynamic character of the Concert. The demise-narrative reduces the evolution of the Concert to the gradual degeneration of practices that characterized it in the (late) 1810s and 1820s, rather than approaching it as a set of understandings and practices which changed over time as the Concert adapted to new situations. Although great power relations were considerably more shaped by conflicts and (imperial) competition in the second half of the 19th century, both halves witnessed both great power cooperation and great power conflict. Moreover, a decisive difference between the institution of great powers in the first and second half of the century is that the former was based on a stable set of five great powers while the latter was shaped by an enlarging group of great powers which gradually admitted Italy, the USA, and Japan into its ranks. By focusing on the degeneration of the Concert and treating the rise of the USA and Japan mainly as part of a great power conflict narrative – which emphasizes imperial competition, (naval) arms races, and growing inequalities among the great powers (see Buzan and Lawson, 2013) – IR tends to neglect the co-evolution and interrelation between the growing number of great powers and changes in the practice of the institution of great powers.

To provide a better account of the evolution of the institution of great powers in the second half of the 19th century, this chapter analyzes two important dimensions: The *first dimension* relates to the *shifting set of practices through which the institution of great powers was performed*. The set of practices became broader insomuch as the Concert, which continued to be the main element of the institution of great powers, was complemented by what might be called an extended concert for certain colonial affairs. Nevertheless, with the sole exception of the collective intervention of the eight (great) powers in China during 1900–1901, collective action by the group of great powers continued to be centered on Europe. Notwithstanding some important globalizing trends, the institution of great powers thus remained foremost a European – and thus regional – institution despite the ongoing shift from a European to a global international society.

The *second dimension* relates to the *interaction between the "grading of powers" and the "managerial function of the great powers"* (Wight, 1977: 136). As the chapter will show, great power status and membership in the Concert were essentially conceived of as one and the same within Concert discourses of the 1860s. This thick interlinkage was loosened, however, by the globalization of the classification of powers and the recognition of the USA and Japan as new great powers, since both became great powers without becoming Concert members. At the same time, growing inequality among the powers gave rise to the distinction between (eight) great powers and (one to five) "world powers." Importantly, however, this conceptual development within the classification of powers did *not* translate into the supersession of "great powers" by "world powers" as the relevant status category for the allocation of special rights and duties. Rather, as the negotiations at the Second Hague Conference in 1907 showed, "great powers" remained the decisive status category to which managerial rights and functions were ascribed. In this sense, these little-studied interactions between classification and managerial functions contribute to a better understanding of the elasticity of the institution of great powers to changing patterns of stratification.

The chapter proceeds in five steps. The first section outlines the theoretical framework which, based upon the English School and sociological theories of stratification, conceptualizes the institution of great powers as the epitome of status-differentiated allocations of special rights and duties in international society. The second section uses archival material on the eventually unsuccessful French proposal to nominate Spain as the sixth great power to illustrate the interlinkage between great power status and Concert membership. The third and fourth sections discuss the shifting patterns of practices, with the third section focusing on the Concert activities in Europe and the fourth section on the extended concert and the partial globalization of concert practices. The fifth section then turns to the shifting patterns of stratification, the emergence of "world power" status and the persistent relevance of great power status for special managerial functions in international society. The conclusion finally reflects on the implications for the study of the 19th century as a bifurcated century.

Theoretical framework: patterns of stratification and the institution of great powers

In the English School, the institution of great powers denotes the allocation and performance of special managerial functions to and by the group of great powers (see Bull, 2002: chap. 9; Clark, 2011). While these special managerial functions build upon the material preponderance of the most powerful states, they are a quintessentially social role, as they are constituted through the recognition of special rights and duties. As Hedley Bull put it: "To say that a state is a great power is to say not merely that it is a member of the club of powers that are in the front rank in terms of military strength, but also that it regards itself, and is regarded by other members of the society of states, as having special rights and duties" (Bull, 1980: 437). The institution of great powers thus represents a form of collective hegemony exercised by a subgroup of members, namely the group of great powers, for and in the name of international society as a whole (see also Simpson, 2004). The English School stresses that this special role is a potential role, both because the great powers do not always behave like "great responsibles" and because the legitimacy of the special rights and duties is "constantly subject to challenge" (Bull, 1980: 438).

The present chapter proposes a refined conceptualization of the institution of great powers. It retains Bull's emphasis on special rights and duties and the management of international order in the name of international society as key characteristics of the institution of great powers. At the same time, it *reconceptualizes the institution of great powers as a status-differentiated allocation of special rights and duties to a particular status category, namely "great powers"*. This reconceptualization follows Martin Wight's suggestion that the *relation between the "grading of powers" and the "managerial function[s] of the great powers"* (Wight, 1977: 136) *is an open (empirical) question* rather than presupposing, as Bull did, that great power status is inseparable from, and indeed constituted by, the accordance and practice of special rights and duties.

This reconceptualization is based upon two main reasons: Firstly, while special rights and duties are important status markers, great power status forms part of broader patterns of stratification in international society that are not reducible to the institution of great powers (see also Volgy et al., 2011 and Paul et al., 2014). The classification of powers, additionally, historically predates the emergence of the institution of great powers and can therefore not be reduced to it (see Keene, 2013). Wight's more open conceptualization instead allows investigating and reconstructing how the classification of powers became and remained the prevalent classification scheme for the allocation of special managerial functions. The allocation of special managerial functions has not always been reserved for great powers (see also Bukovansky et al., 2012).

Secondly, as Gerry Simpson emphasized, Bull's conceptualization overlooks the element of recognition involved in the equality among the great powers. "It strikes me that formal equality between the hegemons operates in a similar way to sovereign equality among states generally; it overlays a regime of equality upon a highly differentiated material reality" (Simpson, 2004: 71). In other words, the members of the group of great powers are equal not because they necessarily have to possess roughly equal material capabilities (as Bull posits) but because they recognize each other as equals despite their (potentially) differing material capabilities. Who is part of the group of great powers – and who is not – then depends on "struggle[s] over classification" (Bourdieu, 1985: 734) and practices of recognition which give rise to the "grading of powers", that is, the stratificatory ordering of the members of international society in terms of classes of powers.

The present chapter therefore conceives of the institution of great powers as the product of (ongoing) struggles over classifications and practices of recognition which mark certain aspects of the multidimensional patterns of stratification shaping international society as important for its political organization and consequently allocate special managerial rights and duties to the "great powers," understood as the members of the upper stratum within these patterns of stratification. The distinction between great, middle, and small powers – that is, the classification of powers – is thereby but one classification scheme among others which orders these patterns of stratification (see also Keene, 2014). For instance, the distinction between developed, underdeveloped, and least developed countries is an alternative classification scheme. Different classification schemes are likely to be more advantageous for some states than for other states. The allocation of special rights and duties therefore entails struggles over classifications insofar as the members of international society have to select some stratificatory aspects over others and have additionally to decide on the classification scheme through which the selected stratificatory aspects are ordered and invested with institutional meaning.

The identity of great power status and Concert membership in the 1860s

In May 1860, France proposed to elevate Spain to the rank of the sixth great power. While the French proposal was ultimately unsuccessful, it triggered a three-month debate via diplomatic correspondence about a possible enlargement of the Concert. The debate – which has so far not been analyzed by IR or History – illuminates two crucial aspects of the prevalent understandings about great powers and the Concert. Firstly, its shows that the diplomatic discourse was shaped by a multilayered and ambivalent set of understandings about "great powers" which combined (realist) notions of great powers as the most powerful states qua their material capabilities, with more normative notions of great powers as bearers of the right (and duty) to manage the general affairs of Europe. Interestingly, "great powers" was labeled as a position, rank, and role but not yet as a "status" (as is common today). Secondly, the basic premise of the debate was that great power status and Concert membership were one and the same. Great powers – in contrast to non-great powers – were conceived of as possessing the right to participate in the regulation of the general affairs of Europe. Admission to the Concert conferred that right and thus symbolized recognition as a great power.

On May 30, the French Foreign Minister Thouvenel sent a letter to the four other great powers in which he proposed that Spain should be granted the "right to be consulted in general affairs" and consequently to "resume its place in the deliberations of the great courts".[2] Thouvenel's argumentation tied together the special right to participate in deliberations on general affairs, the Concert of Europe, and great power status. For Thouvenel, the "European concert is formed by the powers which, by the extension of their interests, find themselves necessarily involved in all great affairs, and whose capabilities enable them to exercise an influence in all communal deliberations." The special role of the great powers, Thouvenel noted, derived its legitimacy from the "good which it produces for the ensemble of other states." Accordingly, Thouvenel described the Concert and its members not only in terms of interests and capabilities but also in terms of privileges and responsibilities. Membership in the Concert entailed both "advantages" and "sacrifices": "[I]f it constitutes a privilege, it entails a vast responsibility, because the custody which it requisites applies to all the essential interests of the European community."

At the same time, Thouvenel proposed to more strongly link Concert membership to changes in the patterns of stratification and capabilities. He argued that the number of Concert members ought to "decrease and increase depending on the vicissitudes which shape the relative forces and which determine the international position of governments" (ibid.). Thouvenel listed several characteristics that qualified Spain to be a great power: in addition to Spain's regained strength, he mentioned Spain's participation as one of six great powers at the Congress of Vienna, the importance of its colonial empire and a more comprehensive representation of the general interests if Spain would participate in the Concert of Europe.

Thouvenel's proposition was met with reluctant approval by the other four great powers. They agreed in principle that there were very strong reasons for elevating Spain to the rank of a great power by admitting it to the Concert of Europe provided that Spain itself would apply for that position. Yet, Prussia questioned that Spain had been recognized as a great power at the Congress of Vienna, arguing that great power status had been inaugurated at the Congress of Aix-la-Chapelle in 1818.[3] More importantly, all four powers voiced their concerns that the French proposal was meant to establish precedence for an eventual inclusion of other states and especially for the French protégé Sardinia/Italy. While Austria had communicated its approval in early June 1860 (conditional on the non-acceptance of Sardinia), especially Prussia and Great Britain adopted a more reserved stance. Prussia lobbied for the inclusion of Sweden and questioned Spain's wish to become a Concert member. As the French minister in Berlin reported home, Prussia had doubts that Spain was ready to shoulder the sacrifices associated with the "role of a great European power" which, according to the Prussian Foreign Minister von Schleinitz, entailed both "advantages" and "imposed certain obligations and even certain sacrifices".[4] Great Britain, in turn, refused its approval on the ground that the admission of Spain would lead to further admissions and a concert of nine powers which would strongly undermine the efficiency of Concert deliberations and decision-making. In face of these reservations and public Spanish statements that it did not want to apply for Concert membership, the French government ended the debate in late August 1860.

While most diplomats seem to have accepted the basic premise that admission to the Concert equated with recognition as a great power (and vice versa), this premise was however not unquestioned. Notably, the Russian Foreign Minister Gorchakov explained to Otto von Bismarck, then the Prussian minister in St. Petersburg, that while Russia would not veto the nomination of Spain, the idea of nominating a great power was in principle faulty. According to Bismarck, Gorchakov posited that "a power is not created through nomination, but rather it reveals itself".[5] Informally, high Spanish officials conveyed a similar interpretation to a Prussian diplomat in Madrid, maintaining that one did not ask for great power status but took it and that the growing strength of Spain would soon enable it to make its voice heard in the councils of Europe.[6]

All in all, while unsuccessful, the debate can be seen as an important transition point from a stable towards a growing set of great powers. For the first (and arguably only) time, the great powers engaged in a substantial debate about Concert enlargement. The arguments, though, were still more about past power constellations rather than ongoing or future power shifts. All candidates discussed as potential new Concert members were European and, with the exception of the rising Sardinia, the other three candidates, Spain, Sweden, and Portugal, were the three powers that together with the five great powers had formed the Committee of Eight at the Congress of Vienna in 1814/1815.

The first actual enlargement of the Concert then happened in May 1867 with the admission of Italy. Sardinia had already exceptionally participated in the negotiations on the Treaty of Paris 1856 as a member of the alliance and also in subsequent meetings on the Eastern Question in its capacity as a party to the Treaty of Paris. It was however only in May 1867, on the occasion of the conference on the affairs of Luxembourg, that the five great powers granted Italy the status of a regular member endowed with the right to participate in all Concert deliberations on the general affairs of Europe. Thereafter, Italy was regarded as the sixth great power (see Dülffer, 2003: 56). In this sense, the admission of Italy affirmed and enacted the basic premise of the debate about Spain: great power status was still inextricably tied to (regular/permanent) membership in the Concert to such an extent that great power status and Concert membership were essentially conceived of as being identical.

The evolution of the Concert of Europe

IR (and also History) often employs a twofold demise- and degeneration-narrative for the evolution of the Concert and the institution of great powers in the second half of the 19th century. On the one hand, the middle of the century is often considered as a crucial period in which the Concert "ceased to function" (Clark, 1989: 131; see also Mitzen, 2013). For Paul Schroeder, the Crimean War "simultaneously revived European bellicism and imperialism" (Schroeder, 2009: 35) thus breaking with two fundamental principles of the Vienna settlement: the Crimean War reintroduced war as a solution to problems – as the subsequent Italian and German wars of unification underscored – and recoupled European and non-European affairs which the Vienna Settlement had purposively decoupled. In this perspective, the middle of the century marked the shift from a concert based on a normative consensus on cooperative order management to an increasingly destabilized competitive balance of power as the base of order management (e.g., Clark, 1989). Some authors even paint the difference between the two halves as the existence and then non-existence of a functioning institution of peace/order management (e.g., Osterhammel, 2009: 675).

On the other hand, the Concert and the idea of special and exclusive rights and managerial functions of the great powers were increasingly delegitimized by growing demands for sovereign equality and by the rise of the practice of inclusive, multilateral conferences and international organizations based on sovereign equality as an alternative mode of regulation and management of international relations (see Reus-Smit, 1999: 140–145; Simpson, 2004: 115–164; Finnemore and Jurkovich, 2014). The demands for more equality were especially voiced by (new) states from the periphery, notably Latin American states. The Second Hague Conference in 1907 is often identified as the culmination of the clash between the institution of great powers and the new mode of governance (Simpson, 2004: 137).

While these demise- and degeneration-narratives capture important aspects of the evolution of great power relations and of the decreasing legitimacy of the institution of great powers in the second half of the 19th century, they nevertheless downplay and underestimate the further evolution of the practices through which the Concert and the institution of great powers were performed. Importantly, despite the growing conflicts among the great powers, they frequently returned to the use of concert practices to resolve crises and also at several times engaged in joint actions.[7] The great powers also continued to consult each other on important European questions. In fact, according to the historian Martin Schulz, 22 of the 42 conferences under the auspices of the Concert occurred after the Treaty of Paris of 1856 until the London conference in 1912–1913 (see Schulz, 2009: 684; see also Schulz, 2012). Instead of distinguishing the first and second half of the century in terms of a simple existence/non-existence narrative, it would thus be more appropriate to analyze the evolution of the Concert in terms of continuities and changes in its practices, its operability, and its salience (see also Bridge and Bullen, 2005: 5).

The Concert crisis in the middle of the century is a case in point. The Concert failed to operate and/or was bypassed in several crucial affairs, yet it did not cease to exist. In the period from 1853 to 1871, the great powers fought several wars against each other, notably the Crimean War of 1853–1856, the Franco-Austrian War of 1859, the Austrian-Prussian War of 1866, and the Franco-Prussian/German War of 1870–1871. In addition, two crucial European questions – the Italian and German unifications – were resolved through wars and unilateral actions instead of through concert consultations and decisions. Nevertheless, consultations among the great powers continued and *in parallel* to its failures the Concert also jointly managed several affairs. In 1860–1861, the Concert mandated a collective intervention, mostly carried out by France, in Syria to protect Christian minorities. In 1867, the great powers convened to resolve a minor affair about the duchy of Luxembourg. And during the Franco-Prussian war, a conference met in London in early 1871 to discuss the Russian attempts to remilitarize the Black Sea and negotiated a new agreement which allowed the Russian remilitarization while upholding Ottoman control of the Dardanelles.

In important respects, the London conference of 1871 ended the Concert's crisis period and inaugurated the second phase of concert politics which would last until the First World War. In particular, the London conference reaffirmed, to quote the French plenipotentiary, the "salutary rule of the European family of nations," namely "that no essential change should be introduced into the relations of nations towards one another without the examination and consent of all the Great Powers" (House of Commons, 1871: 38). The great powers thus renewed their commitment to concert practices as the primary means for managing and resolving important European affairs.

The second Concert phase was, like the first, characterized by the absence of war between the Concert members and by the ongoing use of concert practices. To name but the more important Concert activities: the Concert resolved the Eastern crisis of 1877–1878 over a Russian war against the Ottoman Empire through a collectively sanctioned agreement at the Congress of Berlin 1878. It met in a series of two conferences pertaining to the delimitation of the Greek-Ottoman boundaries in Berlin and Constantinople in 1880–1881. In 1886, it enacted a sea blockade against Greece to avert a Greek war against the Ottoman Empire. In 1896–1898, the Concert managed the crisis over the Greek-Ottoman War, again employing a sea blockade against Greece (in 1897) and then collectively occupied Crete. The collective occupation was carried out by Great Britain, France, Russia, and Italy and lasted until 1908. For important questions, though, the other two Concert powers were also consulted. In 1912–1913, finally, the Balkan wars led to a conference in London which decided upon the political order in the Balkans (and inter alia recognized Albania as a new state independent from the Ottoman Empire).

The second phase was characterized both by continuities and changes in the Concert practice. The continuities related primarily to the basic Concert principles and procedures. General European affairs, defined as fundamental questions of European (territorial) order and balance, were considered the collective purview of the great powers, to be dealt with through collective consultations, negotiations, and decisions. Non-great powers were only arbitrarily invited by the great powers to these deliberations and decision-making processes. The changes, in turn, were mainly in the following aspects. Firstly, the subject matters changed, both because the Eastern Question was now almost the only intra-European subject matter and because the extended concert now also dealt with colonial questions, that is, extra-European affairs. Secondly, conferences of ambassadors became the primary conference format through which the Concert managed its common affairs. The Congress of Berlin of 1878 represented the last Concert conference on the level of statesmen. What is more, the Concert started to establish what might be called a system of sub-commissions, in that it designated special commissions for the management of certain affairs. Examples are the financial commissions created to supervise the public finances of Egypt (established in 1880) and Macedonia (established in 1906) as well as the management of the occupation of Crete through a council of admirals and later a conference of ambassadors in Rome. Thirdly, the culture of intervention changed. Interventions no longer served to support monarchs against revolutions – as the Concert of the 1820s had done – but were carried out in the name of the protection of minorities (e.g., Syria 1860–1861), the pacification of conflicts (e.g., the occupation of Crete), and the reorganization of relations between the newly created Balkan states and the Ottoman Empire. Furthermore, the financial commissions constituted a new form of Concert interference in the internal affairs of states which had not been practiced in the first half of the century.

As the demise- and degeneration-narratives rightly emphasize, the practice of the Concert was fourthly increasingly shaped and complicated by power political considerations. The great powers showed less restraint regarding their individual interests in the promotion of the allegedly common good of Europe to which the Concert subscribed in this self-legitimation. For instance, at the Congress of Berlin in 1878, Great Britain and Austria-Hungary secured zones of occupation and thus de facto territorial gains for themselves (see Schulz, 2012: 269). More importantly, the great powers increasingly relied on armaments and alliances to pursue their interests and security. By the middle of the 1900s, these alliances had coalesced into two competing alliance formations, one comprising Austria-Hungary, Germany, and Italy and the other France, Great Britain, and France (see Clark, 2013: 121–167). This antagonistic group formation within the Concert seriously undermined Concert unity and thus the search for common solutions for European problems.

The emergence of more global managerial practices, though not yet of a global concert

To map the evolution of the institution of great powers, it is helpful to distinguish – depending on the circle of participants – between the Concert, an extended concert, and a potential global concert of all eight great powers. What emerged in the 1880s – besides and in addition to the Concert of the six European great powers managing general European affairs – was an extended concert format comprising the great powers plus some select secondary powers for certain colonial affairs. The conferences in Madrid in 1880, in Berlin in 1884–1885, and in Algeciras in 1906, as well as the Suez Convention of 1888, are examples of this extended concert. This suggests an implicit form of division of labor in which European and non-European affairs were dealt with through different concert formats. What did not yet emerge in the late 19th century, with the exception of the collective intervention in China in 1900–1901 and the London conference of 1908/1909 was, however, a regularly practiced global concert comprising all eight great powers. While becoming broader than the Concert of Europe, the institution of great powers did therefore not yet assume the form of a global concert.

This distinction also allows qualifying Gerry Simpson's argument that starting with the 1870s "status gives way to interest as the key principle" for participation in the managerial functions (see Simpson, 2004: 128). On the one hand, great power status and the idea of special rights and duties continued to be cornerstones of the Concert practice within Europe. Regarding general European affairs, great powers status was thus not replaced by interested states as a criterion for the allocation of managerial functions. On the other hand, the conferences on colonial questions did indeed witness a broader allocation of managerial rights which went beyond the great powers to also encompass select interested powers. Nevertheless, with the exception of the Madrid conference in 1880 (where Russia was not present), the circle of participants always comprised all the European great powers and most of the time also the USA (with the exception of the conferences relating to the Suez Canal in the mid-1880s). Japan was not yet invited to these conferences. To give an example: at the invitation of Germany and France, the Berlin conference of 1884–1885 dealt with colonial questions in Africa and especially the situation in the Congo and the abolition of the slave trade. The final document was signed by the six great powers and additionally Belgium, Denmark, Spain, the USA, the Netherlands, Portugal, Sweden, and the Ottoman Empire. These states were invited because of their interests as maritime powers (e.g., the USA, the Netherlands, Denmark, and Sweden) and their colonial possessions in Africa (e.g., Spain and Portugal) (see Albrecht-Carrié, 1968: 311–315). It was thus more an extended concert rather than a replacement of great power status as the important status for the allocation of managerial functions, since the great powers were always present and still dominated the negotiations.

In addition to this broadening of the managerial functions to include select colonial affairs, the practice of spheres of influence was adapted to the new imperial setting. While spheres of influence constituted important elements of the practice of the institution of great powers within the Concert and balance of power system, the practice of spheres of influence now also increasingly shaped deliberations on colonial empires in Africa and Asia (see Keal, 1983: 16–17). As the political scientist Paul Reinsch noted in 1900, "the term spheres of influence or sphere of interest, has been given an extended meaning by recent developments" (Reinsch, 1900: 60). Whereas spheres of influence had so far connoted neighboring territories under the control and influence of a power, they now also referred to territories claimed for future control and exploitation. The bilateral unequal treaties which several European powers concluded with China exemplify this extended use. These spheres of exclusive commercial rights were opposed by the USA, which favored free trade and equal commercial rights for all nations (whereas in the political dimension, the USA still insisted on the Monroe Doctrine and even construed a right of intervention within the Latin American sphere with the Roosevelt Corollary of 1904).

In 1900, a coalition of eight powers – the very eight powers associated with (potential) great power status at the time, that is, the six European powers plus the USA and Japan – intervened as a coalition in China in reaction to attacks on foreigners and a siege of the diplomatic mission in Peking by Chinese imperial forces (see Silbey, 2012; Otte, 2013). The coalition troops remained in the country for more than a year until the end of the negotiations with the Chinese government in September 1901. During that time, the coalition troops conducted various brutal reprisal missions against alleged Boxer rebels. While Great Britain had considered limiting the negotiations to the eight nations (to increase the relative influence of Great Britain and Germany), the negotiations were eventually conducted between the eleven nations with diplomats in Peking on one side, and China on the other.[8]

This intervention in China in 1900/1901 constituted the only instance of concerted collective action by all of the great powers in the imperial context. Regular concerted collective action by the great powers thus remained essentially a feature of the management of European affairs through the Concert while the imperial game to a large degree was characterized by the competition and struggles of the different colonial powers (notwithstanding some attempts at finding common rules, e.g., at the Berlin Conference of 1884–1885). These rivalries also shaped the intervention in China. The different national contingents often deviated from the joint plans and tried to secure key locations for themselves. For instance, the Russians seized a section of the British-built Chinese Northern Railway, causing "a full-blown international crisis" which the joint Commander in Chief von Waldersee eventually resolved after several months of frictions in late January 1901 (Otte, 2013: 1289, see 1286–1289 in general).

Another factor contributing to the differentiation of managerial practices in international society was the rise of inclusive, multilateral international conferences and organizations. Contrary to conventional wisdom, this development did not always result in equal rights for all participants. In some conferences and organizations (e.g., the Universal Postal Union) not only states but also colonies were admitted and sometimes accorded the same rights as other members, thus overlaying the stratification into states and colonies with a regime of situational equality. In combination with the use of majority rule, this practice favored colonial powers. Some conferences and organizations consequently capped the number of colonial votes. In 1906, for instance, the International Radiotelegraphic Conference stipulated a maximum number of six colonial votes so that the most favored countries – in this case Germany, France, Great Britain, the USA, and Russia – possessed their own plus five colonial votes (see Myers, 1914).

Shifting status practices and the continuing relevance of great power status

These developments were underpinned by the transformation from a European to a global system of international politics, in which colonialism and the imperial ambitions of some powers became a decisive factor in great power interaction (see Dülffer, 2003; Buzan and Lawson, 2013). While this transformation was considerably shaped by the growing power differentials between European powers and other parts of the world, it also witnessed the rise of two non-European great powers, the USA and Japan (it is thus misleading to portray this transformation simply as the extension of European power). Importantly, during this transformation the power differentials within the status group of great powers greatly increased (for the following figures see Kennedy, 1989: 198–202). In 1890 the iron/steel production of the different powers – considered an indicator of war potential – ranged from 10.3 million tons (USA) and 6.3 million (Germany) to 0.02 million (Japan) and 0.01 million (Italy). In 1910, the gap had widened to 26.5 million (USA) vs. 0.16 million (Japan). Likewise, by 1913 the total industrial potential of the USA and Germany had surpassed that of Great Britain which, in turn, was more than three times the potential of the three "minor" great powers (Austria-Hungary, Italy, and Japan). Industrialization had tightened the links between economic potential, political power, and military potential, and thus intensified the differences and conflicts among the great powers (see Kennedy, 1989: 198; Buzan and Lawson, 2015: 4).

This shifting frame of reference affected the status of the great powers, which became to a considerable degree decoupled from membership in the Concert of Europe and additionally embedded within a reformulated classification of powers distinguishing between great powers and world powers. Membership in the Concert of Europe no longer represented the main status marker, as had been the case in the Spain debate of 1860 and in the recognition of the Italian great power status. While colonies and large navies evolved into significant status markers associated with first-rate powers, the institution of diplomacy turned into an important practice through which great powers recognized the great power status of rising powers. The Vienna Règlement of

1815 and its modification in Aix-la-Chapelle in 1818 had introduced a diplomatic rank system ranging from ambassadors, ministers/envoys, and minister residents to chargés d'affaires. While the Règlement gave each state the right to choose the ranks of its diplomats, an informal practice developed in the 1870s in which all of the great powers mutually represented themselves in their respective capitals with ambassadors while employing lesser ranks for other powers (see Hamilton and Langhorne, 1995: 109–115 and Nickles, 2008: 288–294). This informal practice closely linked the mutual sending and receiving of ambassadors to the recognition of high political status and, as it was habitually understood, to great power status. In this sense, the elevations of the embassies of several European great powers in Washington in 1892/1893 and in Tokyo in 1905/1906 were widely regarded as the recognition of the new status of the USA and Japan. This informal practice was, however, to some degree ambiguous, especially because some great powers appointed more than seven ambassadors and because Spain and the Ottoman Empire were likewise represented with ambassadors at the courts of most great powers, without usually being considered to be great powers.

At the same time, the differences in power and assumed future prospects of the eight commonly recognized great powers were reflected in late 19th century political discourses in the distinction between great powers and world powers. While the term "world power(s)" was already used by some authors in the 1850s, it only became a prominent concept in the 1890s and 1900s (see Faber, 1982: 930–933 and Dülffer, 2003: 63–64). Scholars and political observers differed in their analysis about the exact number of world powers, with lists ranging from one to five world powers. Among the actual or potential world powers were counted the British Empire, Russia, the USA, Germany, and France. World power status was usually associated with worldwide interests and colonial possessions in several parts of the globe, with Italy, Austria-Hungary, and Japan being identified as more regionally confined great powers. Discourses about world powers often combined insights into the power differentials between the great powers with reflections about the supposedly conflict-prone future between these world powers. The fast pace of high imperialism since the 1880s, combined with the idea that the world was being divided up among a small number of powers, led to forecasts that the expansionist ambitions of the world powers were likely to clash more vehemently in the near future. This theme was complemented by a second which portrayed these imperial rivalries in social Darwinist logics, as a relentless life-or-death struggle in which only the strongest could survive. These logics were especially visible in Germany's striving for world power status but likewise influenced the foreign policy discourses of other great powers (see Bönker, 2012 for German and US naval policies). And as the example of the International Radiotelegraphic Conference shows, in some international organizations special privileges were de facto allocated to the group of world powers rather than all of the great powers.

Nevertheless, these shifts in the classification of powers did *not* result in a general shift from great to world power status as the main status category for the allocation of status-differentiated rights in international society. In fact, while a variety of classification schemes were proposed at the Second Hague Conference in 1907 for the allocation of judges on the Permanent Court of Arbitration as well as the International Prize Court, the great powers ultimately proposed for both courts' classification schemes to designate the eight great powers as the only members of the highest class and as the only states awarded permanent representation. And none of the multiple competing classification schemes aimed at limiting permanent representation to "world powers," but rather usually advanced conceptions of the highest class that were broader than the category of great powers (for the proceedings of the conference, see Scott, 1921; also Davis, 1975: 251–276). This facet of the Second Hague Conference is usually neglected, especially as the Second Hague Conference symbolizes the rejection of special rights and duties on the part of the smaller powers. The smaller powers, especially those from Latin America, strongly opposed any form of differential allocation of rights for the Permanent Court of Arbitration. The Second Hague Conference is therefore usually interpreted as a highpoint for the rejection of special rights for the great powers by the small powers (see Simpson, 2004: 132–164).

Yet, in addition to the persistent salience of the category of "great powers," the Second Hague Conference also marked the first acceptance of a global allocation of special rights to the eight great powers. In the parallel negotiations on the International Prize Court, the small powers accepted the principle of differential allocation. Even the Brazilian delegate Rui Barbosa, arguably the most fervent proponent of sovereign equality at the Conference, declared that because the Prize Court affected only the interests of maritime powers "it is in proportion to the value of such a fleet that their rights should be measured in this matter" (Scott, 1921: 827). The deliberations therefore centered on finding the most "equitable classification," Barbosa stated (Scott, 1921: 827). For instance, the British proposal to use the total tonnage of the fleets as criteria was rejected. Great Britain, Germany, and the USA then introduced a joint draft proposal which awarded permanent seats on the Court to the eight nations which happened to be the recognized great powers of the time and which allocated the mandates of other seats proportionally to the maritime interests of the other states. While this scheme was criticized for its inconsistencies in the classification of individual small powers, the Prize Court convention was accepted by the plenary meeting on September, 21 1907 with 37 affirmative votes, 1 negative vote (by Brazil), and 6 abstentions (see Scott, 1921: 164–169).

One year later, the great powers attempted to further substantiate the maritime law of war at the London Conference of 1908–1909. The conference resembled the extended concert format, with all eight great powers – now also including Japan – plus Spain and the Netherlands as participants. For the international law scholar T.J. Lawrence, the International Prize Court and the

London Conference signified the emergence of a "World Concert" (Lawrence, 1910: 278). Yet, the International Prize Court was never ratified, and the eight great powers did not practice a global form of the concert in the years until the First World War. Neither the allocation of special rights and duties nor the concert practice were thus fully globalized at the end of the long 19th century. The global version of the institution of great powers only emerged with the establishment of the League of Nations in the form of the League's Council.

Conclusion

On the whole, this chapter substantiates the "two worlds" interpretation of the 19th century. Despite important continuities regarding concert practices, both the classification of powers and the practice of the institution of great powers differed considerably in the two halves of the century. Importantly, the chapter showed that concert practices continued to be used by the great powers during and after the Concert's crisis in the middle of the century. The difference between the first and second half of the century is therefore neither the existence/non-existence of the Concert nor the transition from great power cooperation to great power conflict, although the element of great power conflict was certainly more pronounced in the second half. Rather, what changed was the relevance of the Concert within the institution of great powers, the practices of the institution of great powers, and the classification of powers.

While the first half was characterized by a stable number of great powers, the second half witnessed a growing number of great powers. This broadening of the group of great powers broke the identity of great power status and Concert membership prevalent until the 1860s, as the two new great powers became recognized members of the group of great powers without becoming Concert members. Second, starting with the 1880s the institution of great powers, until then essentially identical with the Concert, became more diverse. While the Concert continued to govern European affairs, an extended concert met on several occasions to manage certain colonial affairs. However, the attempt to create a global concert of the eight great powers largely failed at the Second Hague Conference in 1907 so that the intervention in China remained the sole joint action by the enlarged group of eight. The classification of powers, in other words, globalized faster than the institution of great powers. Third, the growing inequalities among the great powers gave rise to "world powers" as a new status category. However, the practice of special managerial functions continued to be mainly linked to "great powers" as the relevant status category, as especially the Second Hague Conference demonstrated. This persistent salience of the category of "great powers" despite the changing classification of powers stands in some contrast to the evolution of the institution of great powers during the Cold War, in which a change in the classification of powers (the emergence of the category of "superpowers") strongly reshaped the practice of the institution.

In addition, the evolution of the institution of great powers also testifies to the importance of the pivotal transition period in the middle of the century. The 1850s and 1860s saw several decisive developments which shaped the further evolution: (a) the crisis of the Concert marked by several wars between great powers; (b) the beginning of the transition from a stable to a growing number of great powers (Spain debate and admission of Italy); and (c) the emergence of a new mode of governance based on inclusive, multilateral conferences and the first public international unions (e.g., the International Telegraph Union in 1865). At the same time, the chapter suggests that a second pivotal transition period began in the 1880s. The diversification of the institution of great powers beyond the Concert, the further development of the classification of powers through the differentiation between world powers and great powers, and the diplomatic recognition of the first non-European great powers all happened after 1880 and lasted until 1906/1907. From the perspective of the evolution of the institution of great powers, the second half of the bifurcated century was thus itself marked by a further bifurcation.

Notes

1 In the following, the capitalized "Concert" is used as shorthand for the "Concert of Europe" as a specific institution, while "concert" with a lowercase "c" refers to the broader practice of concerting that was extended beyond the original Concert in the second half of the 19th century.
2 S.E.M. Thouvenel to Prince de la Cour d'Auvergne, Paris, 30 May 1860, Geheimes Staatsarchiv Preußischer Kulturbesitz, Berlin, III. Hauptabteilung: Ministerium der auswärtigen Angelegenheiten, I, Nr. 7175 „Spanien. Vorschlag Frankreichs, Spanien in den Rang einer Großmacht aufzunehmen" (hereafter: GSPK Nr. 7125), translation TM.
3 See Von Schleinitz to von Bernstorff, Berlin, 3 July 1860, GSPK 7175.
4 La Tour d'Auvergne to S.E.M. Thouvenel, Berlin, 7 June 1860, Archives diplomatiques du ministère des Affaires étrangères, La Courneuve, Correspondance politique, Prusse, 336, Mai à Juillet 1860, translation TM.
5 Otto von Bismarck to Baron de Schleinitz, St. Petersburg, 27 June 1860, GSPK Nr. 7125, translation TM.
6 Graf Galen to Baron de Schleinitz, (Madrid), 5 September 1860, GSPK Nr. 7125.
7 Relevant studies include Hoffmann (1954: 23–116); Albrecht-Carrié (1968); Verosta (1988); Sédouy (2009: 324–466); and Schulz (2012). For conflict resolution among the great powers more broadly, see also Dülffer et al. (1997).
8 In addition to the eight great powers, these were Spain, the Netherlands, and Belgium: see Lehner and Lehner (2002: 498).

Bibliography

Albrecht-Carrié, René. (1968) *The Concert of Europe.* New York: Harper & Row.
Archives diplomatiques du ministère des Affaires étrangères, La Courneuve, Correspondance politique, Prusse, 336, Mai à Juillet 1860.
Bisley, Nick. (2012) *Great Powers in the Changing International Order.* Boulder: Lynne Rienner.

Bönker, Dirk. (2012) *Militarism in a Global Age: Naval Ambitions in Germany and the United States before World War I.* Ithaca: Cornell University Press.
Bourdieu, Pierre. (1985) The Social Space and the Genesis of Groups. *Theory and Society* 14(6): 723–744.
Bridge, F.R. and Roger Bullen. (2005) *The Great Powers and the European States System 1814–1914.* 2nd edition. Harlow: Pearson Education Limited.
Bukovansky, Mlada, Ian Clark, Robyn Eckersley, Richard M. Price, Christian Reus-Smit, and Nicholas J. Wheeler. (2012) *Special Responsibilities: Global Problems and American Power.* Cambridge: Cambridge University Press.
Bull, Hedley. (1980) The Great Irresponsibles? The United States, the Soviet Union, and World Order. *International Journal* 35(3): 437–447.
Bull, Hedley. (2002) *The Anarchical Society: A Study of Order in World Politics.* 3rd edition. Basingtoke and New York: Palgrave.
Buzan, Barry and George Lawson. (2013) The Global Transformation: The Nineteenth Century and the Making of Modern International Relations. *International Studies Quarterly* 57(3): 620–634.
Buzan, Barry and George Lawson. (2015) *The Global Transformation: History, Modernity and the Making of International Relations.* Cambridge: Cambridge University Press.
Clark, Christopher. (2013) *The Sleepwalkers: How Europe Went to War in 1914.* London: Penguin Books.
Clark, Ian. (1989) *The Hierarchy of States: Reform and Resistance in the International Order.* Cambridge: Cambridge University Press.
Clark, Ian. (2011) *Hegemony in International Society.* Oxford: Oxford University Press.
Davis, Calvin DeArmond. (1975) *The United States and the Second Hague Peace Conference: American Diplomacy and International Organization 1899–1914.* Durham, NC: Duke University Press.
Dülffer, Jost. (2003) Vom europäischen Mächtesystem zum Weltstaatensystem um die Jahrhundertwende. In Jost Dülffer, *Im Zeichen der Gewalt. Frieden und Krieg im 19. und 20. Jahrhundert*, edited by Martin Kröger, Ulrich S. Soénius, and Stefan Wunsch. Köln: Böhlau Verlag.
Dülffer, Jost, Martin Kröger, and Rolf-Harald Wippich. (1997) *Vermiedene Kriege. Deeskalation von Konflikten der Großmächte zwischen Krimkrieg und Erstem Weltkrieg, 1865–1914.* München: Oldenbourg Verlag.
Faber, Karl-Georg. (1982) Macht, Gewalt. In Otto Brunner, Werner Conze, and Reinhart Koselleck, eds., *Geschichtliche Grundbegriffe. Historisches Lexikon zur politisch-sozialen Sprache in Deutschland: Band 3.* Stuttgart: Ernst Klett Verlag.
Finnemore, Martha and Michelle Jurkovich. (2014) Getting a Seat at the Table: The Origins of Universal Participation and Modern Multilateral Conferences. *Global Governance* 20(4): 361–373.
Geheimes Staatsarchiv Preußischer Kulturbesitz, Berlin, III. Hauptabteilung: Ministerium der auswärtigen Angelegenheiten, I, Nr. 7175 "Spanien. Vorschlag Frankreichs, Spanien in den Rang einer Großmacht aufzunehmen" (= GSPK Nr. 7125).
Hamilton, Keith and Richard Langhorne. (1995) *The Practice of Diplomacy: Its Evolution, Theory and Administration.* London: Routledge.
Hoffmann, Stanley. (1954) *Organisations internationales et pouvoirs politiques des états.* Paris: Armand Colin.
House of Commons. (1871) *Protocols of Conferences Held in London Respecting the Treaty of March 30, 1856. Presented to Both Houses of Parliament by Command of Her Majesty.* London: Harrison and Sons.

Keal, Paul. (1983) *Unspoken Rules and Superpower Dominance*. London: Macmillan.
Keene, Edward. (2013) The Naming of Powers. *Cooperation and Conflict* 48(2): 268–282.
Keene, Edward. (2014) The Standard of 'Civilization', the Expansion Thesis and the 19th-century International Social Space. *Millennium* 42(3): 651–673.
Kennedy, Paul M. (1989) *The Rise and Fall of the Great Powers: Economic Change and Military Conflict from 1500 to 2000*. London: Vintage Books.
Lawrence, T.J. (1910) *The Principles of International Law*. Fourth edition, revised and rewritten. Boston: D.C. Heath & Co.
Lehner, Georg and Monika Lehner. (2002) *Österreich-Ungarn und der "Boxeraufstand" in China*. Mitteilungen des Österreichischen Staatsarchivs, Sonderband 6. Wien: Österreichisches Staatsarchiv.
Marcowitz, Reiner. (2006) Von der Diplomatiegeschichte zur Geschichte der internationalen Beziehungen. Methoden, Themen, Perspektiven einer historischen Teildisziplin. *Francia* 32(3): 75–100.
Mitzen, Jennifer. (2013) *Power in Concert: The Nineteenth-Century Origins of Global Governance*. Chicago: Chicago University Press.
Myers, Denys P. (1914) Representation in Public International Organs. *American Journal of International Law* 8(1): 81–108.
Nickles, David Paul. (2008) US Diplomatic Etiquette during the Nineteenth Century. In Markus Mössling and Torsten Riotte, eds., *The Diplomats' World: A Cultural History of Diplomacy, 1815–1914*. Oxford: Oxford University Press.
Osterhammel, Jürgen. (2009) *Die Verwandlung der Welt. Eine Geschichte des 19. Jahrhunderts*. München: C.H. Beck.
Otte, T.G. (2013) From "Can-Can Diabolique" to "Sitzkrieg": The International China Expedition. *Journal of Military History* 77(4): 1277–1302.
Paul, T.V., Deborah Welch Larson, and William C. Wohlforth, eds. (2014) *Status in World Politics*. Cambridge: Cambridge University Press.
Reinsch, Paul S. (1900) *World Politics at the End of the Nineteenth Century. As Influenced by the Oriental Situation*. London: The Macmillan Company.
Reus-Smit, Christian. (1999) *The Moral Purpose of the State: Culture, Social Identity, and Institutional Rationality in International Relations*. Princeton: Princeton University Press.
Schroeder, Paul W. (1994) *The Transformation of European Politics, 1763–1848*. Oxford: Oxford University Press.
Schroeder, Paul W. (2009) The Transformation of European Politics: Some Reflections. In Wolfram Pyta, ed., *Das europäische Mächtekonzert: Friedens- und Sicherheitspolitik vom Wiener Kongreß 1815 bis zum Krimkrieg 1853*. Köln: Böhlau Verlag.
Schulz, Matthias. (2009) *Normen und Praxis. Das Europäische Konzert der Großmächte als Sicherheitsrat, 1815–1860*. München: Oldenbourg Verlag.
Schulz, Matthias. (2012) "Defenders of the Right"? Diplomatic Practice and International Law in the 19th Century: An Historian's Perspective. In Luigi Nuzzo and Milos Vec, eds., *Constructing International Law: The Birth of a Discipline*. Frankfurt am Main: Vittorio Klostermann.
Scott, James Brown, ed. (1921) *The Proceedings of the Hague Peace Conferences. Translation of the Official Texts. Volume II: Meetings of the First Commission*. New York: Oxford University Press.
Sédouy, Jacques-Alain de. (2009) *Le concert européen: aux origines de l'Europe, 1814–1914*. Paris: Fayard.

Silbey, David J. (2012) *The Boxer Rebellion and the Great Game in China.* New York: Hill and Wang.

Simpson, Gerry. (2004) *Great Powers and Outlaw States: Unequal Sovereigns in the International Legal Order.* Cambridge: Cambridge University Press.

Verosta, Stephan. (1988) *Kollektivaktionen der Mächte des europäischen Konzerts.* Wien: Verlag der Österreichischen Akademie der Wissenschaften.

Volgy, Thomas J., Renato Corbetta, Keith A. Grant, and Ryan G. Baird, eds. (2011) *Major Powers and the Quest for Status in International Politics.* Basingstoke: Palgrave Macmillan.

Wight, Martin. (1977) *Systems of States.* Leicester: Leicester University Press.

9 Reordering East Asian international relations after 1860

Seo-Hyun Park

Introduction

What makes the nineteenth century such an important critical juncture in East Asian international relations? One obvious reason is the arrival of Western powers and the process of organizing Asia into the Westphalian system of modern territorial states during this period. But existing studies of this period have tended to claim transformative change in East Asian countries, in the aftermath of and in response to the "shock" of Westphalia, without careful consideration of the nature of these changes. In this chapter, I examine the transition process from the traditional Sinocentric order to the Westphalian state system as experienced by Japan and Korea, two countries forced to navigate and negotiate between China and the West. Even though the regional system of interstate relations had been challenged in multiple ways – in the realms of diplomacy and commerce, for example – through interaction with Western powers since the beginning of the nineteenth century, Chinese presence and influence remained strong in the region, including in Japan and Korea. The different foreign policy responses shown by Japan and Korea reflected attempts to adjust to changes in both the traditional regional order and the Europe-based but expanding "international society" during this critical period in East Asia (Bull and Watson, 1984).

This chapter builds on, and adds nuance to, earlier scholarship on this period, which puts an emphasis on how Westphalian sovereignty was a powerful new legitimating idea that transformed Asian state behavior thereafter (Gong, 1984a). At the same time, it departs from a Eurocentric view of global normative diffusion and instead highlights intra-regional variation in the types of political crises generated by the crystallization of a new global hierarchy in the latter half of the nineteenth century (Keene, 2014; Zarakol, 2011; Suzuki, 2009). That is, the preexisting regional hierarchy and the emergence of a new global hierarchy led to a complex politics surrounding these competing standards of statehood and sovereign status. We see evidence of such contestation and change in the evolving concept of sovereignty in the late nineteenth century. These processes of political crisis, reflecting paradigmatic shifts in the sociopolitical context, both domestic and international, constitute this "critical juncture" (Mahoney, 2001; Mahoney and Rueschemeyer, 2003) in the history of international relations in the East Asian region.

I make two central claims. First, I argue that a fundamental transformation during this period was the creation of a regionally shared language of sovereign autonomy to discuss the accelerating hybridity of regional diplomatic practices. Contemporary security concepts, such as sovereignty, autonomy, and state power, were reimagined through translation, transliteration, or recombination following regional encounters with Western powers in the nineteenth century (Howland, 2002; Liu, 1999a). Past security discourses and regional diplomacy in East Asia had been conducted in a transnational but elite-centered language common to a select bureaucratic corps educated in Confucianism. The newly fashioned concept of autonomy allowed the political participation and mobilization of new elites and interest groups that was the basis for the creation of a national citizenry.[1] Seen from this regional perspective, the challenge was not so much a choice between the normative moral obligations within the Sinocentric world and the pressures (or, strategic deployment) of Western, mostly material, power and institutions. Rather, the regional context in the late nineteenth century, until the end of the Sino-Japanese War (1894–1895), was one of legal and institutional pluralism, which determined the nature and timing of subsequent domestic political battles and outcomes.

Second, I show that domestic political crises began with the delegitimation of existing policies and political ideologies as Japanese and Korean leaders sought to redefine their status in the newly internationalizing hybrid regional order. By adding important empirical details and variations to the more structural perspectives on various global transformations during the nineteenth century (for example, Buzan and Lawson, 2015), this study recognizes the critical elements of agentic participation, in addition to the environmental shaping, of local political change. The different paths of Japan and Korea were not predetermined by their structural positions or cultural differences. Too often, Japan is touted as a "success" case, the first Asian country to "enter" international society dominated by Western countries, unencumbered by strong "nativist" reactions to Westernization. Rather, ideas and interests were constantly in flux during multiple stages of transition, resulting in legitimacy crises for ruling regimes in both countries. The varying degrees of policy rigidity shown by Japanese and Korean leaders were contingent on the outcome of such domestic legitimacy politics. These initially fluid outcomes, however, had long-lasting consequences. As the Qing Empire disintegrated into different political-military factions, Japan began its quest to "catch up" with European Great Powers, while Korea lost its sovereignty to the expanding Japanese empire.

Expansion of international hierarchy in late nineteenth-century East Asia[2]

How did the arrival of Westphalian sovereignty in East Asia in the nineteenth century affect traditional diplomatic practices based on Sinocentric hierarchy in East Asia during the Ming (1368–1644) and Qing (1644–1912) empires? It is important to note that formal rules and rituals acknowledging a hierarchy of power and status notwithstanding, relations with China were interdependent and negotiable, with variable modes of autonomous status for non-dominant states within the Sinocentric order (Ku, 1988: 6; Schmid, 2007; Hevia, 1995; Womack, 2006; Kang, 2010; see also Burbank and Cooper, 2010). A hierarchical order did not negate or obviate political autonomy for independent, if not equal, units. There were different *types* of autonomy that were negotiated between China and its weaker neighbors.

The ruling regime's autonomy was established bilaterally through informal rules and roles in interstate relations. For example, Joseon Korea's (1392–1910) deferential policy of *sadae*, or revering Great Powers, effectively secured autonomy in domestic rule as well as military protection from China. The Tokugawa regime (1600–1868) in Japan took a different route to maximize its autonomy from the Chinese mainland: by monopolizing and closely regulating, through a series of edicts severely limiting foreign contact and travel (what is now known as Japan's *sakoku*, or national seclusion, policy), its indirect trade with China. In short, both *sadae* (ritualistic participation) and *sakoku* (regulated trade) were means to secure autonomy and distance from China.

They were also informal in the sense that stated goals often differed from actual practice and exceptions were more than tolerated. Despite heavy emphasis on elaborate rhetorical formalities and seeming intimacy with each other at the abstract level to add to their political legitimacy, Chinese and Korean rulers sought to limit mutual contact as much as possible in reality – to avoid entanglement and to protect autonomy respectively (Ku, 1988). The essence of Joseon Korea's *sadae gyorin* policies, Hara argues, was "to bar all intercourse ... except for formalized ceremonial exchanges of envoys and limited trade conducted under close official supervision" with China and Japan based on a "desire to keep these two neighbors at a safe distance" (Hara, 1998: 392). Similarly, its policy of prohibiting Christianity and overseas travel notwithstanding, Tokugawa Japan was not closed off from the outside world, as the word *sakoku* (literally, closed country) implies. Japan continued to indirectly trade with China and Korea, even without formal recognition or diplomatic relations (Toby, 1984; Toby, 1977).

While this long and contested history of negotiating autonomy with the region's dominant power had existed in the past, what changed by the late nineteenth century was the context in which autonomy would be interpreted and practiced. At stake for regime legitimacy was no longer dynastic succession but state sovereignty (and strength). In addition, the kind of multilayered political autonomy that was bilaterally negotiated in traditional East Asian diplomacy was no longer tenable in the face of modern "global standards," dominated by Western legal principles and institutions.[3] In other words, this period saw the narrowing – indeed, erasure – of political space for multivocal definitions of autonomy as well as practices of legal and institutional pluralism.

A comparison of Japan and Korea during this period shows that their processes of transition into Westphalian statehood occurred in multiple stages. There was no single "shock" that suddenly and uniformly reshuffled the Asian state system or interstate relations within it.[4] The first stage of political crisis was the delegitimation of *sakoku* and *sadae* as policies and ideologies in Tokugawa Japan and Joseon Korea respectively. By the late nineteenth century, *sakoku* and *sadae* were stigmatized due to major foreign policy failures. They were criticized as being anachronistic – not what modern, sovereign states are supposed to do. The context and rules of the game had changed, leading to a crisis of legitimacy for ruling regimes in Japan and Korea. The anti-regime opposition movement in each country contested existing sources of regime legitimacy with an alternative state-strengthening, autonomy-enhancing project – with varying degrees of success. It was the outcome of this domestic legitimacy contestation – rather than direct structural pressures or the degree of cultural resistance (or ideological inflexibility) – which led to different paths for Tokugawa Japan and Joseon Korea.

Hybrid regional order

The late nineteenth century is a critical political-historical turning point for East Asian international relations because Westphalianization was a shared regional experience. While the transition from feudal societies to modern nation-states was a varied experience for each individual country, their encounters with European powers during this period necessitated changes in regional diplomatic relations and domestic legitimacy politics in China, Japan, and Korea. Practices and statuses that had been bilaterally negotiated between each country fell victim to the new "script" of Westphalian sovereignty (Oksenberg, 2001). Recognition of the new context of statehood and international relations was reflected in the new diplomatic language in East Asia. Sovereign autonomy became the new keyword by the 1880s. It was the shared language to discuss diplomacy and security. The new language of sovereign autonomy helped reshape the legal and institutional context for conducting foreign relations in the region. As China, Japan, and Korea deepened their interactions with the Western powers, gaining recognition as capable modern states and enhancing status vis-à-vis other Great Powers became a shared concern.

At the same time, it is important to recognize that the new rules and principles of Westphalian sovereignty did not simply replace, but were rather juxtaposed against, traditional diplomatic practices. That is, discourses of Westphalian autonomy and international law emerged in the context of legal pluralism in the last phase of the Sinocentric order (Cassel, 2012). As a consequence, a central problem facing East Asian state officials was not merely responding to Western demands for trade and extraterritoriality, but dealing with intra-regional complexities arising from this dual political-institutional context. Western standards of statehood transposed another layer of international hierarchy rather than erasing or replacing the existing hierarchical order in the region.

What is notable about the nineteenth century, and what makes it such a "critical" juncture for studying regional order, is this mixed legacy of Westphalianization. Reaching advanced-nation status through a "rich nation, strong army" (*fukoku kyōhei* in Japanese, *pukuk kangbyŏng* in Korean) became an all-important agenda, but within the context of a reimagined and reified hierarchical order. In other words, to be a truly sovereign state was to be judged favorably against civilizational standards, as promoted by dominant powers in the international system.[5] The new regional hierarchy, however, differed from the traditional Confucian norms-based hierarchical order in that international relations were no longer negotiated bilaterally on a case-by-case basis. The new language of sovereignty and the Westphalian state system presented an alternative multilateral context in which rules of interaction and mutual obligations were made public and shared. The mutual understandings that undergirded the mutually obligatory/distancing relations of *sadae-jaso* or *sakoku* were no longer acceptable, or feasible, practices.

It is in this context that the concept of autonomy continued to be contested. Multiple, and possibly contradictory, lessons were learned by Japanese and Korean reformers. Autonomy was interpreted simultaneously as asserting equal status with neighboring countries, on the one hand, and overcoming the discriminatory application of international law by European members of "international society" against non-members, on the other.[6] Such interpretations reflected both the new context and existing ideas about status-seeking in a world of Great Power politics. On the surface, sovereign autonomy was defined as having international legal sovereignty and Western-style domestic institutions befitting a modern nation-state. But within these basic parameters, autonomy also continued to be contested, drawing on past status-seeking frames. Thus, we see neither complete rupture nor path dependence during the nineteenth-century critical juncture in East Asia.

Domestic legitimacy crises in nineteenth-century Japan and Korea[7]

The immediate trigger for each regime's legitimacy crisis in nineteenth-century Japan and Korea was the challenge to the ability of the ruling regime to defend the existing status-securing strategy, weakening their political legitimacy. Perry's demands to the Tokugawa rulers for trade and diplomatic relations in 1853 and Chinese abandonment of the principle of domestic autonomy for its tributaries in the quelling of the 1882 Imo Rebellion in Seoul threatened to undermine Japanese autonomy. Central to the subsequent unleashing of legitimacy contestation was the constraint posed on the regime's attempts to contain the crisis and maintain political power.

Domestic legitimacy politics in Japan and Korea in the late nineteenth century took place in the context of institutional crises that resulted from the processes of *extremization* and *entrapment*. Legitimacy crises were triggered in both countries by attempts to change the existing status-seeking frame under conditions of extreme political competition. Debates between alternative security frames became polarized when leaders experienced "competitive outbidding" from domestic political opponents.[8] In both Japan and Korea, accommodation attempts by the ruling regime allowed previously excluded actors onto the political scene – regional lords from the outer domains in the case of Tokugawa Japan and lower-ranking reform-minded literati in Joseon Korea. Ensuing political competition resulted in a polarization of ideas on legitimacy. Tokugawa rulers had to battle against and incorporate elements of *jōi* (expel the barbarians) thought in order to demonstrate their commitment to protecting imperial authority (*sonnō*).[9] Similarly, the Min clan-dominated Korean government was forced to defend the advanced status of the Sinocentric civilization against progressive ideas on Western civilization and enlightenment (*munmyeong gaehwa*).[10]

In this context of political polarization, regime leaders faced the narrowing of their range of policy options and found themselves pushed to a more extreme position than the initial status quo. In what may be called the entrapment effect of legitimation, rulers were forced to defend their strongest and most salient source of legitimacy, especially during crises. Entrapment was particularly likely for the Tokugawa and Joseon governments in late nineteenth-century Japan and Korea since regime legitimacy was so closely tied to the legitimating ideologies of *sakoku* and *sadae*. Japanese and Korean rulers could not easily or inconsequentially diverge from their mandate even in the face of changing strategic conditions. Pushed by conservative factions within the government, *bakufu* leaders continued to adhere to the ideal of independence through insulation from the global order, even though the formula of formal diplomatic closure and informal trade relations was no longer tenable. On the other hand, King Gojong (Kojong) and his officials during the late Joseon period agreed that the foremost strategic priority for Korea was to avoid isolation. In a continuation of past *sadae* policies, Korean rulers saw the United States as a replacement "elder brother" and a means to protect Korea's autonomy from other Western powers as well as emerging signs of Chinese imperialism.

The ruling regimes in Japan and Korea met with varying levels of success in their attempts to protect their political legitimacy against the opposition. The Tokugawa regime in Japan was forced into power-sharing compromises early on and eventually lost its power through defeat in a civil war. The Min faction within the Joseon court was able to maintain its power through sustained alliance with the Qing and cracked down on its opposition, which included both orthodox Confucian conservatives and progressive reformers. Whereas anti-regime forces in Japan were able to coalesce into an "overthrow the *bakufu*" (*tōbaku*) movement against a weak central government, the early failure of the 1884 coup by Korean progressives skewed the domestic balance of power in favor of the ruling regime and its traditionalist forces.

From sakoku to civilization in Japan (1853–1877)

For the Tokugawa regime, *sakoku* was more than a policy; it symbolized the national ideology of "Japan as Middle-Kingdom," which "allowed *bakufu* leaders to extricate Japan from subservience to a China-dominated diplomatic world order of universal empire and culture" (Wakabayashi, 1986: 8). In order to continue to protect its autonomy, the *bakufu* leaders sought to avoid war with the Western powers by offering minimal concessions in the form of a small number of designated open ports, as they had done with Dutch and Chinese merchants for centuries. The Tokugawa regime's conciliatory stance toward foreigners, however, was not widely endorsed among the *daimyo* (regional lords).

Perry's arrival in 1853 had the effect of creating open political divisions on how to proceed with American demands for trade. In the hopes of garnering consensus, the *bakufu*'s chief councilor, Abe Masahiro, made an unprecedented foreign policy consultation to all the *daimyō*, requesting that they submit in writing their opinion on how best to deal with the Americans (Gordon, 2003: 49; Beasley, 1995). While the *fudai* (inner domain) lords dominating the *bakufu*'s Senior Council favored a more pragmatic foreign policy of compromise while strengthening the country, the Tokugawa regime faced opposition from the frustrated, and traditionally the most anti-Tokugawa, *tōzama han* (outer domains) such as Satsuma, Chōshū, Hizen, and Tosa (Craig, 1961: 17–18; Totman, 1980a: xv–xvii). These previously excluded actors began to coalesce into a coordinated *jōi* (expel the barbarians) movement, based on earlier Confucian scholarship such as *Shinron* (New Thesis, 1825)[11] and National Learning (*kokugaku*), which focused on the imperial institution as the center of the national tradition (Tsuzuki, 2000: 49–51; Huber, 1975, 79–81). *Jōi* activism grew stronger even in the face of repression from the regime.[12]

Increasing pressure from the British and the French in the 1860s, however, revealed the futility of both *sakoku* and *jōi*. The *bakufu* and the *daimyo* were well aware of their weakness vis-à-vis Western gunships but continued to talk of driving out foreigners because of pressure from *jōi* activists, who championed their cause in the name of the Japanese emperor. In 1863, a significantly weakened *bakufu*, for the sake of protecting *sakoku* and their own legitimacy, was pushed to set a starting date for enacting *jōi* but could not actually enforce it in the face of the continuing threat from the British. Satsuma and Chōshū, the headquarters for the *jōi* movement, tried to repel the foreigners on their own and were met with retaliatory attacks in 1863 and 1864. As a result, Chōshū was forced to pay indemnities to the British, Americans, Dutch, and French and to agree to provisions for foreign ships at Shimonoseki (Jansen, 1985: 10–11; Tsuzuki, 2000: 47–49).

In order to maintain their power and legitimacy, the *bakufu* also attempted to placate the *jōi* loyalists by introducing reforms that would allow the imperial court's participation in national politics, a shift from its earlier ceremonial role. Tokugawa officials, realizing that *sakoku* could never be restored, sought to regain their control and authority through *kōbu gattai* (literally, unity between court and *bakufu*), "a concept that proposed to achieve national unity through a coalition of high-ranking members of the imperial nobility and samurai class" (Totman, 1980b: 12). An unintended consequence of this institutional innovation, however, was the decentralization of power and "major shift of decision-making authority to a council of lords centered in Kyoto" away from Edo (present-day Tokyo), where the *bakufu* was located (Gordon, 2003: 55–56).

While the Tokugawa government was further weakened through various factional struggles and intricate court politics, the opposition led by the newly forged Satsuma-Chōshū alliance consolidated its power by rallying around the newly extended slogan, "revere the emperor, expel the barbarians" (*sonnō jōi*).[13] The *bakufu*'s abandonment of *sakoku* was portrayed as a repudiation of the *sonnō* principle and a betrayal of the emperor. Having secured the backing of Kyoto, the anti-regime forces gained a new layer of legitimacy and radicalized into a movement to overthrow the *bakufu* (*tōbaku*) (Craig, 1961: 235–236).

The beginning of the end for the Tokugawa regime came in 1866, when Satsuma and several other domains refused to aid the *bakufu* forces in a second punitive expedition against Chōshū in the summer of 1866. Yoshinobu stepped down as shogun in November 1867, but in December the joint forces of Satsuma and Chōshū took control of the imperial palace in Kyoto, abolished the *bakufu*, and announced an imperial "restoration" in January 1868. The civil war lasted another 18 months, but the anti-*bakufu* forces had succeeded in militarily overthrowing the Tokugawa regime by capitalizing on the latter's failure to protect Japan's self-reliant autonomy, which had been an important source of Tokugawa political legitimacy for over 250 years.

Upon taking power, however, the Meiji oligarchs embarked on a new course, jettisoning a traditionalist, particularistic notion of autonomy in favor of attaining Great Power status as an active member of "international society." Whereas in the past, Japan had surreptitiously attempted to build a parallel universe alongside China, the new Meiji leadership now sought to "catch up" and integrate with the advanced European civilization. The Meiji government dissociated itself from the *jōi* movement and forcibly carried out new reforms, persuading its citizenry that Japan must emulate and adopt Western institutions and culture in order to rival their power (Tōyama, 1985: 36). The Meiji State Council declared that the new Japanese government would conduct itself according to "international law" (*bankoku kōhō*).[14]

Japan's reverse course policy was not merely a continued accommodation of the West, which had been the de facto policy during the late Tokugawa period. In sharp contrast to Qing China's status quo aspirations, the worldview of Japanese elites changed dramatically from the late 1860s until the 1870s, owing in large part to the influx of Western Learning (*yōgaku*), led by reformers who had been part of state missions dispatched abroad to learn European institutions (Kang, 2004: 27). In addition, the past failures of *sakoku* and *jōi* paved the way for active *kaikoku* (opening the country) by the new Meiji regime. Between 1853 and 1868, *sakoku* underwent a dramatic conceptual transformation, from idealization to stigmatization: "As of 1853 *sakoku* was an expression of ethnic virtue ... By 1867 *sakoku* was well on the way to becoming an expression of archaic parochialism, and *kaikoku* was rapidly acquiring credibility as an expression of ethnic virtue and sound strategy" (Totman, 1980b: 7). Yet, attachment to insular autonomy did not easily disappear; *jōi* loyalists remained active until they were finally crushed in the 1877 Satsuma rebellion led by Saigo Takamori. In addition, many intellectuals and party activists were still firmly opposed to the unequal treaties signed with the Western powers and demonstrated against their revisions in 1887 and 1889 (Vlastos, 1989: 387–388; Gluck, 1985: 114).

Amidst this newly intensified political competition, the new political leadership in Japan attempted to consolidate their power through external standards of power and authority. The Meiji leaders believed that the strength and autonomy of the Japanese state could not be maintained through insular self-reliance, but by enhancing its competitiveness and standing within the greater international system. The legitimacy of the regime was increasingly tied to the new slogan of *bunmei kaika* (civilization and enlightenment) and the building of a "modern" state. State-strengthening was to be accomplished by achieving civilizational status through Westernization. Westernization was discussed and promoted primarily as industrialization and acquiring technology and scientific knowledge but also as cultural change. The most famous public discussions on cultural change were held by the so-called Meirokusha (Meiji Six Society) intellectuals, created in 1873 and composed of leading philosophers, educators, legal scholars, and political economists such as Katō Hiroyuki, Fukuzawa Yikichi, and Nakamura Keiu, all of whom had started their careers in the Tokugawa schools for Western learning (Howland, 2002: 12–13).

Notably, Western political concepts such as privilege, right, and sovereignty were carefully studied and reconstructed during this time to connote the power of the state (*kokken*). For instance, sovereignty was interpreted as the power and authority of the state, "a term representing a country's esteem and prosperity, its unlimited powers, its unrestricted *kokken*" (Howland, 2002: 139). Even the imperial institution was linked to *kokken* in that Shinto was made a state religion (Najita, 1985: 83–85). The symbolism of the emperor changed from its emphasis on the "national essence" (*kokutai*) to the external civilizational status of the Japanese state.

At the same time, the Meiji leaders also went to great lengths to accommodate the rules and norms of the international system, pressing for the adoption of Westernized legal codes in order to demonstrate the civilized progress of Japan and to accelerate the revision of unequal treaties (Pyle, 1989: 688–690). Attacks against foreigners were banned, and violations were severely dealt with in order to prevent diplomatic incidents and the undermining of the government's stature in the international arena. The Meiji government also improved its system of law enforcement and embarked on an extensive propaganda campaign to inform the public that anti-foreign attacks were against "the laws of the world." Such strategies were calculated to consolidate the government's authority and prestige – both domestically and internationally (Iriye, 1989: 734–735).

Joseon Korea's dual status problem (1882–1895)

More embedded in the Sinocentric diplomatic order, Korea's initial interactions with the Western powers were guided by Chinese directives. Wanting to avoid another military confrontation, and with the advent of Japanese influence, China pushed Korea to accommodate, rather than aggravate, the Western powers. Despite reservations about taking advice from a weakened China to sign treaties with the West, King Gojong (r. 1873–1907), and his Min clan-dominated government, abandoned his father's isolationist policy in favor of modest reforms. But the Min regime faced harsh opposition from conservative Confucian scholar-bureaucrats, who viewed Western religion and influence as disrupting the traditional sociopolitical order. Gojong and his reform-minded officials had to rely on Chinese authority and influence to deflect domestic opposition from the xenophobic conservative factions (Kim, 1976: 238–239). By tying their legitimacy even closer to the protection of the Sinocentric civilizational order and showing deference to Qing China, the Min government was able to slowly introduce self-strengthening reforms, such as the establishment of the Tongnigimu Amun, a Western-style Office for the Management of State Affairs (Kang, 1994: 177–189).

The Korean regime's reformist path, as well as its traditional relationship with China, came to an abrupt end with the soldiers' mutiny of July 1882 (Imo Rebellion), when China militarily interfered in Korean domestic affairs for the first time in their history of *sadae* relations (Kim, 1980: 326–327). At the request of the Min government, China's de facto foreign minister Li Hongzhang sent 3000 troops to Korea to help quell the Imo Rebellion, but went on to abduct the Daewon-gun (Taewŏn'gun), the Korean King's father, who opposed opening up the country to Western powers, and assumed absolute authority over the country to enforce Korea's foreign relations. Li had a Chinese garrison stationed in Seoul under the command of Yuan Shikai and hired various foreign advisors to control Korea's financial and foreign affairs (Shin, 2000: 34–36).

China's military intervention and continued stationing of troops on Korean soil effectively ended the policy of "benign" leadership by China.[15] The Qing court ordered the Min government to abolish all Japanese-style reforms and insisted on being consulted before making any foreign policy decision. For example, in 1887, the Qing court insisted that Korea obtain permission from the Chinese Ministry of Protocol before dispatching any permanent diplomatic missions to Europe and America (Zhou, 2007: 40–41). In October 1882, the Joseon-Qing commercial treaty was signed to promote Chinese commercial activities and to strengthen its influence in Joseon (Choe, 1993: 128–129). Such unprecedented changes in Chinese policy indicated an attempt to turn Korea into a Western-style protectorate (Larsen, 2008; Fujimura, 1977: 426–427). Therefore, in late nineteenth-century Joseon Korea, dealing with China – rather than Japan or the West – was the most important foreign policy "crisis."

The unprecedented intervention by the Chinese court had serious consequences for the reform movement in Korea. After 1882, progressive reformers split from the gradualists within the government in their frustration with the pace of and Qing influence over modernizing reforms (Deuchler, 1977: 204–211; Hwang, 1978: 72–73; Chung, 2004a: 51–52; Chung, 2004b: 163–168). Against the ruling Min clan, who continued to rely on Chinese support in order to maintain their own power and authority, emerged an opposing coalition of the so-called "Enlightenment leaders" who formed their own Enlightenment (Independence) Party. The Enlightenment Party stated as its policy objectives "independence" from the Qing and continued implementation of reforms modeled after Europe and Japan. Dependent on China, the Min faction, which had formerly opposed the xenophobic policies of the Daewon-gun, now found itself as the conservative, pro-Chinese party (Hwang, 1978: 76–77).

It is at this juncture that *sadae* became reformulated as antithetical to sovereign autonomy. In order to promote their own reform agenda against the powerful Min clan, the progressives labeled the gradualist reformers the Sadae Party and criticized their Great-Power-worshipping and anti-reform stance, despite the fact that they had once been on the same side – advocating reform – against the traditionalist Confucian scholar-bureaucrats.[16] In doing so, what used to be a sign of propriety in the traditional East Asian order – or, at the very least, a long-term security strategy to protect autonomy and to fend off unwanted interference from a much stronger neighbor – was transformed into an affront to Korean independence. The principle of *sadae* and the logic of civilization in promoting state security and legitimacy were now stigmatized as compromising Korean sovereignty.

Aided by a tacit alliance with the Qing military commanders stationed in Korea, the Min clan attempted to neutralize the power of the monarchy and the progressives. The Min clan leaders schemed to block the Enlightenment Party, whose members were mostly mid to low rank government officials, by cutting off funds for their modernization projects (Kang, 2003: 461). According to Martina Deuchler, a major factor in the launching of the 1884 Gapsin (Kapshin) coup d'état by progressives was the Min clan's strong hold on government power; progressive reformers were outside the decision-making level of government politics and could not reach the apex of power by traditional means (Deuchler, 1977: 211; Kang, 1994: 252). Against Chinese interference, and without military backing from the Japanese, on which the coup organizers had relied, the attempt at regime change failed after just three days.

Neither the regime nor reformers were able to consolidate their power after 1884. Most reformist officials had been purged or exiled. The legitimacy of the regime's ruling ideology and Korea's international status were in question. Yet, the Korean government remained dependent on Chinese (and other outside) support for their hold on power, and until the end of the Sino-Japanese War, maintained a dual presence in both the traditional East Asian world and the European state system as a paradoxically "autonomous-yet-dependent" *sokbang* (vassal).[17]

Korean intellectuals debated the best strategy to negotiate between traditional *sadae* relations and the rules of Westphalian sovereignty. For instance, Kim Yun-sik advocated a continuation of *sadae* policy, arguing that a weak country like Korea could survive only by forming multiple alliances with other Great Powers, China being one of them. Yu Gil-jun (Yu Kil-chun), on the other hand, viewed Chinese encroachment as threatening and argued that it was necessary to balance against Chinese influence by aligning with Russia or the United States (Chung, 2004: 202–211). Although a series of reforms were undertaken in the period between 1882 and 1895, Korean leaders continued to face the problem of maintaining a precarious balance between "equality" in relations with Europe and "semi-autonomy" vis-à-vis the Qing (Hamashita, 2002).

Contrasting outcomes of Japanese and Korean status-seeking strategies

One of the most visible signs of change in Japanese foreign policy after the Meiji Restoration was in language use. Wanting to participate equally with the Great Powers, the Japanese government used French and English in its international diplomacy, recognizing the power and importance of language (Dudden, 1999: 166–167). The Japanese also eschewed traditional diplomacy in favor of the European "law of nations" when dealing with their Chinese and Korean neighbors. Meiji officials recognized that international law would empower Japan over China and were determined to avoid a repeat of the signing of the Sino-Japanese Protocol in 1871–1872, during which the Qing court had hampered negotiations based on traditional Chinese etiquette, expressing scorn for the "Dwarf Nation" of Japan (Stern, 1979: 107–109).

In addition, Japan began to compete with China for influence over Korea and leadership in the region – another sign of Japan's concern with external status. The Treaty of Ganghwa (Kanghwa) signed in 1876 symbolized Japan's status as a "Western" nation-state and brought prestige to the Meiji rulers (Iriye, 1989: 746). Despite resistance from conservative officials, King Gojong resumed formal diplomatic relations with Japan by signing the treaty.[18] This was Japan's attempt to make Korea "independent" and "to dismantle the vestiges of the East Asian international order and its diplomatic institutions, the Tribute System" (Suzuki, 2009: 10). It also acted as Japan's formal challenge to China, igniting their rivalry over Korea until it was forcefully resolved in 1894–1895 (Oh, 1980: 37). Following its victory over China in the war of 1894–1895, Japanese leaders distanced themselves from the traditional Sinocentric order to achieve greater "civilization" – above and beyond China and Korea – among the Western powers. The desire for Great Power status continued through the experience of the Triple Intervention in 1895 (Kim, 1980; Suganami, 1984), when Britain, France, and Russia forced Japan to give up some of its gains in China. An important moment of recognition as a Great Power came in 1902 with Japan's signing of an alliance with Britain (Iriye, 1989: 773).

In Korea, after the failure of the 1884 coup, the anti-*sadae* movement of the progressive Enlightenment Party emphasized the humiliation of Chinese suzerainty over Joseon and prioritized gaining complete independence from Qing China (Kim, 1989: 167–168; Chung, 2004b: 113–114). But it was the outcome of the Sino-Japanese War that catapulted the Korean nationalist movement's project to "de-center" the Middle Kingdom and erase Chinese cultural influence from all aspects of Korean society. China's loss symbolized "the defeat of 'old knowledge' (*guhak*) by 'new knowledge' (*sinhak*)," according to editorials from all three nationalist newspapers, the *Dongnip sinmun* (Independent, 1896–1898), the *Hwangseong sinmun* (Capital Gazette, 1898–1910), and the *Jeguk sinmun* (Imperial Post, 1898–1910) (Schmid, 2002). China was constantly cited as an example of country that did not engage in the "civilizing" process, witnessed in the corrupt nature of Chinese law and its inhumane penal institutions as well as the dirty streets and hospitals and even the lazy and idle national character of the Chinese. Reports of Chinatowns both abroad and at home reinforced such images of a nation of "savage" customs (Schmid, 2000: 85–87).

Departing from the traditional Sinocentric order also meant the reformulation of an alternative nationalist identity for an independent Korea. Korean modernizers felt it necessary to break with the transnationalism of traditional East Asian elite culture in favor of a "pure" national culture (Schmid, 2002: 29). In order to "clear the way for new institutions and values upon which to ground a modern Korean nation," nationalist intellectuals such as Jang Ji-yeon, Pak Un-sik, and Sin Chae-ho actively engaged in the *sadae* debate, the "*cause célèbre* at the time" (Robinson, 1991: 207–209; see also Shin, 2006). As part of this project, Confucian scholar-bureaucrats were blamed for their obsequiousness before the now-foreign Chinese culture and their inability to modernize Korean society. Enlightenment modernizers started to argue that Confucianism and its traditions were Chinese – and therefore, foreign. Even though "Confucian precepts had been a part of the Korean intellectual tradition for over a millennium and had become thoroughly Koreanized, nationalists blamed the plight of the failing Yi political system on its excessive veneration of a foreign cultural system" (Robinson, 1991: 207).

Enlightenment leaders such as Yi Sang-jae, Yun Chi-ho, Syngman Rhee (Yi Seung-man), and Philip Jaisohn (Seo Jae-pil) created the Independence Club as a means to protect national sovereignty "by promoting national unity, economic and military strength, and modern culture, not relying on foreign powers" (Nahm, 1988: 191). The club members advocated the destruction of Yeong-eun Gate (present-day Independence Gate in Seoul), a "symbol of Korea's subservience to and dependence on China" (Nahm, 1988: 195). They also persuaded King Gojong to adopt the imperial title (on equal status with the Qing court) and to stop granting concessions to foreigners. Despite such efforts, Korea's independent status remained nominal, as strategic rivalry over the Korean peninsula and Japan's increasing ambitions for regional leadership in Asia led to the latter's claiming of protectorate rule over Korea in 1905 and finally annexation in 1910.

Conclusion

At first glance, Japan and Korea showed clearly contrasting responses to the European state system. Japan initially rejected and then strived to become part of the West. Korea, on the other hand, sought to maintain the status quo, as an autonomous-yet-dependent kingdom within the China-centered world, which significantly constrained its future options and prospects for transitioning into the Westphalian system of modern states. At the same time, leaders in both countries recognized and debated the critical role of China in regional as well as their own security. Japanese and Korean interpretations of the consequences of a weakened China were, in turn, shaped by their previous positions, reflecting their different degrees of identification with China and different sources of regime legitimacy within the traditional Sinocentric order.

The delegitimation of the *ancien regime*, however, did not lead to a clear adoption of a "Westphalian script." In other words, Westphalianization was a contested process and contained elements of foreign policy thought from traditional patterns of hierarchical relations. What did emerge was a new set of political vocabularies and concepts to express old and new notions of autonomous status for states. Even in Europe, by the nineteenth century, "notions of sovereign equality were more widespread but still had to contend with the perceived reality of hierarchy, initially in the form of Great Power Concert, and theoretical counter-arguments" (Stirk, 2012: 643). We now know in hindsight that the peace of Westphalia was not an epochal turning point for sovereign equality. Similarly, in East Asian international relations in the nineteenth century, we see a mix of multiple frames of thought and policy ideas at work amidst evolving political contexts. That is, the content of sovereignty remained contingent in different temporal and spatial contexts (Suganami, 2007).

Moreover, the legacy of the regional transformations described above has had far-reaching consequences beyond this period. Late nineteenth-century experiences have created a distinct "problem-space" (Scott, 2004: 4), in which modern international relations in East Asia have been dominated by the question of state-strengthening via status enhancement. Autonomy has remained a particularly important security concept, discussed in conjunction with sovereignty, state power, and national "advancement." It is this late nineteenth-century context of a reconstituted regional hierarchy which provides the politically "identifiable stakes" and continues to motivate contemporary security dilemmas. Hierarchical ranking and status, especially their country's standing in the world, remain all-important to the Japanese and Koreans. For instance, Japanese elites situate their country not only horizontally (in unipolar or multipolar international systems) but also in the stratified international order (for example, asymmetric alliance relations) (Ikenberry and Inoguchi, 2003: 10–11; Hunsberger, 1997). Since the Meiji period, Japanese leaders strove to "catch up with and surpass" (*oitsuku* or *oikosu*) the West and become a "first-class nation" (*ittō koku*) (Samuels, 2003: 12). In other words, the nineteenth-century political experience of compromised sovereignty – both perceived and real – continues to inform Japanese and Korean security debates.

Notes

1 On the bureaucratic "incorporation" of various members of society by aristocratic elites via grafting of symbols and myths through wars, mobilization, and administrative and fiscal incorporation, see Smith, 1996: 106–130.
2 This section draws from chapter 3 of Seo-Hyun Park, *Sovereignty and Status in East Asian International Relations* (Cambridge: Cambridge University Press, 2017).
3 On the politically contested process of replacing multilayered authority in the kingdom of Siam (present-day Thailand) with Westphalian principles of indivisible sovereignty during the nineteenth century, see Winichakul, 1997.
4 Even Perry's arrival in Japan was not a shock, as commonly believed, but anticipated for years. Dutch merchants had warned the *bakufu* leaders of future "visits" from England or the United States. On the myth of Perry's "sudden" opening of Japan, see Kohno, 2001; Tsuzuki, 2000, 38. On the building up of Japan's sense of crisis since the early nineteenth century, see Mitani 2006, 23–39.
5 On the application of a European "standard of civilization" to other regions of the world in the nineteenth century, see Gong, 1984b. On the continued relevance of "externally established benchmarks for socio-political self-organization" within the current globalization debate, see Bowden and Seabrooke, 2006: 5–7; Zarakol, 2011.
6 According to Shogo Suzuki (2009), East Asian elites were very much aware of the dualities inherent in the European "society of states."
7 Much of the next two sections also draw from chapter 3 of Park, *Sovereignty and Status in East Asian International Relations*.
8 In their study of political mobilization in ethnic conflicts, Lake and Rothchild (1996: 44) argue that "political outbidding" occurs when moderates, faced with an electoral challenge from extremists, are driven to "ethnicism." One reason, as presented by Kaufmann (2001), may be that extremists within ethnic groups denounce and sanction middle-grounders, forcing them to choose ethnically based identities.
9 In Jeffrey Legro's (2005) portrayal of the Meiji Restoration, the lack of new, reformist ideas delayed consolidation of shock-induced collapse and change. The problem with this analysis is that powerful alternative ideas did exist in Japan, but the ideology that toppled the regime, "revere the emperor, expel the barbarians" (*sonnō jōi*) was not the ideology that consolidated the new Meiji regime, "rich country, strong army" (*fukoku kyōhei*). It was not the case that alternative ideas for consolidation were unavailable, but that it was not until after the Meiji Restoration that Westernization could be fused onto a legitimate ruling ideology.
10 The Min clan refers to the family members of King Gojong's queen, who came from the Min family. Late Joseon Korean politics had been dominated by a series of such consort clans.
11 Written by the nationalist writer from the Mito school, Aizawa Seishisai, *Shinron* became "a virtual bible to activists in the 'revere the Emperor, expel the barbarian' movement." See Tsuzuki, 2000: 33; Jansen, 1985: 5–6.
12 When the issue of receiving the court's approval for Japan's treaty with the United States became mixed up with the issue of shogunal succession in Kyoto in 1858, the *bakufu*'s Senior Councilor Ii Naosuke signed Townsend Harris's commercial treaty on his own and purged his opponents from the outer domains of western Japan. On the Ansei Purge of 1858–1859, see Tsuzuki, 2000: 39; Gordon, 2003: 52; Craig, 1961: 167–168.
13 The Sat-Chō alliance was the result of a secret mediation by the Tosa domain's Sakamoto Ryōma between Satsuma and Chōshū in the mid-1860s.
14 *Bankoku kōhō* was also the title of the translation text *Elements of International Law* by Henry Wheaton, which was first translated into Chinese in 1864 as *Wanguo gongfa* by American missionary W.A.P. Martin. It was later introduced to Korea under the title *Manguk kongbŏp*. On the politics of translation and the spread of international legal texts during this period, see Liu, 1999b.

15 The heavy involvement of China in Korean affairs began after Japanese annexation of the Ryukyūs in 1879 and the increasing threat from Russia. See Chung, 2004b: 161.
16 Moreover, the Mins had aided King Gojong in opening Korea to outside powers and initiating modernizing reforms, overturning the previous policy of seclusion instituted and enforced by the Daewon-gun.
17 Other scholars (Nelson, 1946: 87–88; Kang, 2004; Ku, 1988) have characterized Korea's *sokguk* or *sokbang* status as not the equivalent of a vassal kingdom or fief in the Western legalistic sense, but a dependent kin concept which defined *sadaejaso* relations between great and small powers in the Sinocentric order.
18 It should be noted that Koreans did not attach the same meaning to the treaty as the Japanese did. The Koreans considered Article 1, which stated that Korea was an independent state enjoying the same sovereign rights as Japan, a mere reaffirmation of the traditional relations between Korea and China, in which Korea had autonomy of rule over its territory. Consistent with Korea's *sadae gyorin* policy, Korea did not seek Chinese counsel during its negotiations with Japan since Korean-Japanese relations were not viewed to be within the realm of "diplomacy" – an exclusive right of China. Additionally, Korean officials demanded that Japan add the respectful "great" (*dae*), used only toward China, to *Joseon-guk* (Kingdom of Joseon) in order to emphasize Korean superiority over Japan. See Deuchler, 1977: 49.

Bibliography

Beasley, W.G. (1995) *Japan Encounters the Barbarian: Japanese Travelers in America and Europe*. New Haven: Yale University Press.
Bowden, Brett, and Leonard Seabrooke. (2006) Civilizing Markets through Global Standards. In Brett Bowden and Leonard Seabrooke, eds., *Global Standards of Market Civilization*. New York: Routledge.
Bull, Hedley, and Adam Watson, eds. (1984) *The Expansion of International Society*. New York: Oxford University Press.
Burbank, Jane, and Frederick Cooper. (2010) *Empires in World History: Power and the Politics of Difference*. Princeton and Oxford: Princeton University Press.
Buzan, Barry, and George Lawson. (2015) *The Global Transformation: History, Modernity and the Making of International Relations*. Cambridge: Cambridge University Press.
Cassel, Pär Kristoffer. (2012) *Grounds of Judgment: Extraterritoriality and Imperial Power in Nineteenth-century China and Japan*. Oxford: Oxford University Press.
Choe, Dong-hi. (1993) 1880 nyeondae Joseon ui munje wa gumi yeolgang gwa ui oegyo gwan-gye [Issues in Foreign Relations with the Western Powers in 1880s Joseon]. In Han-guk jeongchi oegyosa hakhoi [The Korean Diplomatic History Association], ed., *Han-guk oegyosa* [*The History of Korea's Foreign Relations*]. Seoul: Jimmundang.
Chung, Yong-Hwa. (2004a) Geundae han-guk ui ju-gwon gaenyeom ui suyong gwa jeok-yong [The Adoption and Application of the Sovereignty Concept in Modern Korea] *Segye jongchi* [*World Politics*] 25(1): 43–69.
Chung, Yong-Hwa. (2004b) *Munmyeong ui jeongchi sasang: Yu Giljun gwa geundae han-guk* [*The Political Ideology of Civilization: Yu Giljun and Modern Korea*]. Seoul: Munhak kwa jisongsa.
Craig, Albert M. (1961) *Chōshū in the Meiji Restoration*. Cambridge, MA: Harvard University Press.

Deuchler, Martina. (1977) *Confucian Gentlemen and Barbarian Envoys: The Opening of Korea, 1875–1885*. Seattle: University of Washington Press.

Dudden, Alexis. (1999) Japan's Engagement with International Terms. In Lydia Liu, ed., *Tokens of Exchange: The Problem of Translation in Global Circulations*. Durham and London: Duke University Press, 165–191.

Fujimura, Michio. (1977) Japan's Changing View of Asia. *Japan Quarterly* 24(4): 423–431.

Gluck, Carol. (1985) *Japan's Modern Myths: Ideology in the Late Meiji Period*. Princeton: Princeton University Press.

Gong, Gerrit W. (1984a) China's Entrance into International Society. In Hedley Bull and Adam Watson, eds., *The Expansion of International Society*. New York: Oxford University Press.

Gong, Gerrit W. (1984b) *The Standard of 'Civilization' in International Society*. Oxford: Oxford University Press.

Gordon, Andrew. (2003) *A Modern History of Japan: From Tokugawa Times to the Present*. New York: Oxford University Press.

Hamashita, Takeshi. (2002) Tribute and Treaties: East Asian Treaty Ports in the Era of Negotiation, 1834–1894. *European Journal of East Asian Studies* 1(1): 59–87.

Hara, Takemichi. (1998) Korea, China, and Western Barbarians: Diplomacy in Early Nineteenth-century Korea. *Modern Asian Studies* 32(2): 389–430.

Hevia, James. (1995) *Cherishing Men from Afar: Qing Guest Ritual and the Macartney Embassy of 1793*. Durham: Duke University Press.

Howland, Douglas R. (2002) *Translating the West: Language and Political Reason in Nineteenth-century Japan*. Honolulu: University of Hawaii Press.

Huber, Thomas M. (1975) *Chōshū Activists in the Meiji Restoration*. PhD diss., University of Chicago.

Hunsberger, Warren S. (1997) Introduction: Japan's International Rankings and Roles. In Warren Hunsberger, ed., *Japan's Quest: The Search for International Role, Recognition, and Respect*. Armonk, NY: M. E. Sharpe.

Hwang, In K. (1978) *The Korean Reform Movement of the 1880s*. Cambridge, MA: Schenkman Publishing Company.

Ikenberry, G. John, and Takashi Inoguchi. (2003) Introduction. In G. John Ikenberry and Takashi Inoguchi, eds., *Reinventing the Alliance: U.S.-Japan Security Partnership in an Era of Change*. New York: Palgrave.

Iriye, Akira. (1989) Japan's Drive to Great-Power Status. In Marius B. Jansen, ed., *The Cambridge History of Japan, volume 5: The Nineteenth Century*. Cambridge: Cambridge University Press.

Jansen, Marius B. (1985) Meiji Ishin: The Political Context. In Michio Nagai and Miguel Urrutia, eds., *Meiji Ishin: Restoration and Revolution*. Tokyo: United Nations University.

Kang, Jae-eon. (1994) *Seoyang gwa Joseon: geu yimunhwa gyeoktu ui yeoksa* [*The West and Joseon Korea: A History of the Clash between Civilizations*]. Seoul: Hakgojae.

Kang, Jae-eon. (2003) *The Land of Scholars: Two Thousand Years of Korean Confucianism*. Paramus, NJ: Noma & Sekye Books.

Kaufmann, Chaim. (2001) Possible and Impossible Solutions to Ethnic Civil Wars. *International Security* 20(4): 136–175.

Keene, Edward. (2014) The Standard of 'Civilization', the Expansion Thesis and the 19th-century International Social Space. *Millennium: Journal of International Studies* 42(3): 651–673.

Kim, Dalchoong. (1976) 1880 nyeon dae han-guk guk-nae jeongchi wa oegyo jeongchaek: Min ssi jeongchi jidoryeok mit oegyo jeongchaek jaepyong-ga [Korean Domestic Politics and Foreign Policy in the 1880s: A Reevaluation of the Min Clan's Political Leadership and Foreign Policy]. *Han-guk jeongchi hakhoebo* [*Korean Political Science Journal*] 10: 231–251.

Kim, Key-Hiuk. (1980) *The Last Phase of the East Asian World Order: Korea, Japan, and the Chinese Empire, 1860–1882*. Berkeley and Los Angeles: The University of California Press.

Kim, Yeong-jak. (1989) *Hanmal naesheoneollijeum yeongu* [*The Study of Nationalism in Late Joseon Korea*]. Seoul: Cheong-gye yeon-guso.

Kohno, Masaru. (2001) On the Meiji Restoration: Japan's Search for Sovereignty? *International Relations of the Asia-Pacific* 1(2): 265–283.

Ku, Dai Yeol. (1988) Dongseoyang gukje jilseo-gwan ui chungdol gwa saeroun jilseo-gwan ui hyeongseong [Clash of Eastern and Western Views of the International Order and the Formation of a New Worldview]. *Gukje jeongchi nonchong* [*Review of International Politics*] 28(1): 3–21.

Lake, David A., and Donald S. Rothchild. (1996) Containing Fear: The Origins and Management of Ethnic Conflict. *International Security* 21(2): 41–75.

Larsen, Kirk Wayne. (2008) *Tradition, Treaties, and Trade: Qing Imperialism and Choson Korea, 1850–1910*. Cambridge, MA: Harvard University Press.

Legro, Jeffrey W. (2005) *Rethinking the World: Great Power Strategies and International Order*. Ithaca: Cornell University Press.

Liu, Lydia H. (1999a) Legislating the Universal: The Circulation of International Law in the Nineteenth Century. In Lydia Liu, ed., *Tokens of Exchange: The Problem of Translation in Global Circulations*. Durham: Duke University Press.

Liu, Lydia, ed. (1999b) *Tokens of Exchange: The Problem of Translation in Global Circulations*. Durham: Duke University Press.

Mahoney, James. (2001) *The Legacies of Liberalism: Path Dependence and Political Regimes in Central America*. Baltimore and London: The Johns Hopkins University Press.

Mahoney, James and Dietrich Rueschemeyer, eds. (2003) *Comparative Historical Analysis in the Social Sciences*. New York: Cambridge University Press.

Mitani, Hiroshi. (2006) *Escape from Impasse: The Decision to Open Japan*. Trans. David Noble. Tokyo: International House of Japan.

Nahm, Andrew C. (1988) *Korea: Tradition and Transformations*. Elizabeth, NJ: Hollym International Corp.

Najita, Tetsuo. (1985) Conceptual Consciousness in the Meiji Ishin. In Michio Nagai and Miguel Urrutia, eds., *Meiji Ishin: Restoration and Revolution*. Tokyo: The United Nations University.

Oh, Bonnie B. (1980) Sino-Japanese Rivalry in Korea, 1876–1885. In Akira Iriye, ed., *The Chinese and the Japanese: Essays in Political and Cultural Interactions*. Princeton: Princeton University Press.

Oksenberg, Michel. (2001) The Issue of Sovereignty in the Asian Historical Context. In Stephen D. Krasner, ed., *Problematic Sovereignty: Contested Rules and Political Possibilities*. New York: Columbia University Press.

Osiander, Andreas. (2001) Sovereignty, International Relations and the Westphalian Myth. *International Organization* 55(2): 251–287.

Park, Seo-Hyun. (2017) *Sovereignty and Status in East Asian International Relations*. Cambridge: Cambridge University Press.

Pyle, Kenneth B. (1989) Meiji Conservatism. In Marius B. Jansen, ed., *The Cambridge History of Japan, volume 5: The Nineteenth Century.* Cambridge: Cambridge University Press.

Robinson, Michael. (1991) Perceptions of Confucianism in Twentieth-century Korea. In Gilbert Rozman, ed., *The East Asian Region: Confucian Heritage and Its Modern Adaptation.* Princeton: Princeton University Press.

Samuels, Richard J. (2003) *Machiavelli's Children: Leaders and Their Legacies in Italy and Japan.* Ithaca: Cornell University Press.

Schmid, Andre. (2000) Decentering the 'Middle Kingdom': The Problem of China in Korean Nationalist Thought, 1895–1910. In Timothy Brook and Andrew Schmid, eds., *Nation Work: Asian Elites and National Identities.* Ann Arbor: University of Michigan Press.

Schmid, Andre. (2007) Tributary Relations and the Qing-Chosŏn Frontier on Mount Paektu. In Diana Lary, ed., *The Chinese State at the Borders.* Vancouver: UBC Press.

Scott, David. (2004) *Conscripts of Modernity: The Tragedy of Colonial Enlightenment.* Durham: Duke University Press.

Shin, Gi-Wook. (2006) *Ethnic Nationalism in Korea: Genealogy, Politics, and Legacy.* Stanford: Stanford University Press.

Shin, Yong-ha. (2000) *Modern Korean History and Nationalism.* Seoul: Jimoondang Publishing Company.

Smith, Anthony D. (1996) The Origins of Nations. In Geoff Eley and Ronald Suny, eds., *Becoming National: A Reader.* New York: Oxford University Press.

Stern, John Peter. (1979) *The Japanese Interpretation of the 'Law of Nations', 1854–1874.* Princeton: Princeton University Press.

Stirk, Peter M.R. (2012) The Westphalian Model and Sovereign Equality. *Review of International Studies* 38(3): 641–660.

Suganami, Hidemi. (2007) Understanding Sovereignty through Kelsen/Schmitt. *Review of International Studies* 33(3): 511–530.

Suzuki, Shogo. (2009) *Civilization and Empire: China and Japan's Encounter with European International Society.* London: Routledge.

Toby, Ronald P. (1977) Reopening the Question of Sakoku: Diplomacy in the Legitimation of the Tokugawa Bakufu. *Journal of Japanese Studies* 3(2): 323–363.

Toby, Ronald P. (1984) *State and Diplomacy in Early Modern Japan: Asia in the Development of the Tokugawa Bakufu.* Princeton: Princeton University Press.

Totman, Conrad D. (1980a) *The Collapse of the Tokugawa Bakufu, 1862–1868.* Honolulu: University of Hawaii Press.

Totman, Conrad D. (1980b) From Sakoku to Kaikoku: The Transformation of Foreign-Policy Attitudes, 1853–1868. *Monumenta Nipponica* 35(1): 1–19.

Tōyama, Shigeki. (1985) Independence and Modernization in the Nineteenth Century. In Michio Nagai and Miguel Urrutia, eds., *Meiji Ishin: Restoration and Revolution.* Tokyo: United Nations University.

Tsuzuki, Chushichi. (2000) *The Pursuit of Power in Modern Japan 1825–1995.* Oxford: Oxford University Press.

Vlastos, Stephen. (1989) Opposition Movements in Early Meiji, 1868–1885. In Marius B. Jansen, ed., *The Cambridge History of Japan, volume 5: The Nineteenth Century.* Cambridge: Cambridge University Press.

Wakabayashi, Bob Tadashi. (1986) *Anti-foreignism and Western Learning in Early-modern Japan: The New Theses of 1825.* Cambridge, MA: Council on East Asian Studies, Harvard University.

Winichakul, Thongchai. (1997) *Siam Mapped: A History of the Geo-Body of a Nation.* Honolulu: University of Hawaii Press.

Womack, Brantly. (2006) *China and Vietnam: The Politics of Asymmetry.* New York: Cambridge University Press.

Zarakol, Ayse. (2011) *After Defeat: How the East Learned to Live with the West.* New York: Cambridge University Press.

Zhou, Fangyin. (2007) The Role of Ideational and Material Factors in the Qing Dynasty Diplomatic Transformation. *Chinese Journal of International Politics* 1(3): 447–474.

10 An evil of ancient date

Piracy and the two Pax Britannicas in nineteenth-century Southeast Asia

Mark Shirk

Introduction

Piracy in the islands of Southeast Asia was a thorn in the side of colonial governance and regional trade since the rise of the Dutch East Indian Company (VOC) in the 17th century. It became an even larger problem as western-led trade expanded in the early 19th century. By the 1820s it was recognized as a problem in the British Straits Settlement. Here a couple puzzles present themselves. First, this 'wave' of piracy (Starkey, 2001) was part of a political project that was unrecognized by the British. Pirates were often acting on behalf of local chiefs or sultanates that only formed after the arrival of Europeans. Thus piracy became a way for local leaders to fight back against colonial intrusion. This goes a long way toward explaining the lack of success of British counter-piracy operations. Second, piracy in the region did not stop until Britain decided to take direct control over its Straits Settlement – present-day Malaysia – in 1874, more than half a century after piracy was recognized as a problem. In addition, many colonial officials and merchants had been in favor of this policy for decades. Thus, the questions arise: Why could the British not recognize the political content of piracy? Why did it take so long for them to come to a solution that appeared to be right in front of them?

Both of the puzzles above can be explained by the nature of the Pax Britannica in Southeast Asia. The Pax's liberal universalism in the first half of the 19th century goes a long way toward explaining why the British never recognized the political project of Malay piracy. The British narrative on piracy was that it showed the natural/cultural defects of the Malay people, it was a deviation from civilization. Thus, it could not have political content. In addition, it was a shift in the nature of the Pax that led to Britain directly governing the Straits Settlement, and thus ending piracy. The early to middle of the 19th century was the apex of liberal ideas such as unilateral free trade and the empire's civilizing mission (Bell, 2007b; Semmel, 1986). However, the free trade aspect of the British Empire was questioned starting in the 1860s and a consensus within Britain began to fall apart by the 1870s (Howe, 2007). In addition, following the 1857

Sepoy Rebellion in India many liberals started to question the civilizing mission behind colonialism, preferring instead to reason that the 'backwardness' of the natives – a position built on liberal assumptions – was the reason for British rule. "Orientals" obviously could not rule themselves and order had to be kept (Mantena, 2007). In addition, starting in the 1850s, other European rivals were either consolidating or expanding power in Southeast Asia in the face of the fall of the Sinocentric system that had governed the region. Liberal universalism gave way to a middle ground that prioritized law and order. Because of this shift, piracy became an example of how local rulers could not keep the peace, necessitating British intrusion to keep liberal goals such as trade afloat.

In sum, the liberal nature of the early Pax made it hard for the British to understand the political content of piracy and seriously contemplate taking control of local politics. This understanding never arrived; instead, the British stumbled upon an effective policy because of a shift in the nature of the Pax Britannica. The early Pax saw little competition in the region, a focus on unilateral free trade, and a civilizing mission, but it included piracy. The later Pax was able to do away with piracy, but saw the use of naval power to protect (no longer unilateral) free trade, the end of the civilizing mission, and a lot of competition, though little to no conflict, between European rivals. It was a fully Eurocentric peace. This shift ultimately facilitated the rise of a dominant 'internationalism' (Long and Schmidt, 2005) and the second wave of globalization (Robertson, 2002). In other words, the liberalism of the end of the long 19th century was due in part to Britain's more pragmatic take on the relationship between liberalism and empire developed in the 1860s.

This chapter proceeds as follows. First, I describe the shift in the liberal nature of empire and the Pax Britannica caused by rising protectionism, a faltering of the civilizing mission, and geopolitical competition. Second is an historical section on Malay piracy from the 1820s to the 1870s, giving the reader a feel for both piracy and the political situation in the region – peaceful coexistence between the British, the Dutch, and the Spanish. I then discuss the narratives constructed around piracy by the British and the pirates, to demonstrate why British counter-piracy strategy was so lacking in this period. Finally, I describe how the British finally came across a successful strategy and lay out the general political situation of the latter half of the 19th century. What changed in the middle of the 19th century was not the British narrative on Malay piracy but other narratives about colonized peoples and the best uses of British power. This is indicative of a deeper shift in the relationship between liberalism, empire, and the Pax that explains not only Britain's choice to end piracy by formally colonizing the Straits Settlement but also the 'struggle for Asia' in the period of the 'New Imperialism' (Buzan and Lawson, 2015; Gong, 1984; Hobsbawm, 1987; Koskenniemi, 2002; Osterhammel, 2014).

Pax Britannica

The era of the Pax Britannica is often studied because of the preponderance of global/naval power held by the British. The British beat back challenges from other major European powers, extended their empire, and prevented great power conflict while keeping the seas safe for trade. However, we can also study this period by taking seriously the ways in which British statesmen and thinkers thought that their power should be used. The character of this peace is important for two reasons. First, it tells us what statesmen and politicians argued about during this period. What do we do with this power, how do we keep it, etc.? Second, if we want to understand what happened in specific cases during this period we cannot simply rely on "British Power" as a variable since power manifests itself in different ways across time and space. Thus, it is important to look at the character of the Pax Britannica and to view it as a set of narratives about Britain's role in the world. And the content of this Pax and Britain's empire was liberal.

Liberalism and the Pax

The Pax Britannica was not a term or concept used by those who created and maintained the resulting peace. However, even though the Pax is a post hoc creation it had two important building blocks: empire and liberalism. Political theorist Uday Mehta (1999: 4) argues that "liberal involvement with the British Empire is broadly coeval with liberalism itself." Classical liberal thinkers such as John Locke (1999: 160–181) wrote to justify colonial rule and as early as the 18th century, England's empire was justified as, "Protestant, commercial, maritime, and free" (Armitage, 2000: 8; see also 125–145). This may seem a paradox. How can a political philosophy of individual freedom justify the world's largest colonial empire? A recent spate of scholarship has linked liberalism to empire (Anghie, 2005; Armitage, 2000; Mantena, 2007; Mehta, 1999; Pitts, 2005; Wilson, 2000). Mehta (1999: 20) argues that there is a tension between the universal claims of liberalism and the actualization of those claims. Most colonized people did not show the traits liberals believe to be universal, and this encounter with strangeness led them to assume that while they may not be naturally inferior, they demonstrate a lower level of human development.

John Stuart Mill (2004: 13–14) argued that liberty "applies only to human beings in the maturity of their faculties. We are not speaking of children ... For the same reason, we may leave out of consideration those backward states of society in which the race itself may be considered in its nonage." Thus he could claim that, "Despotism is a legitimate mode of government in dealing with barbarians, providing the end be their improvement, and the means justified by actually effecting that end." James Mill considered it "Britain's duty as a civilized and progressive nation to impose its rule on India" (Pitts, 2005: 125). Viscount Palmerston articulated British imperial identity as "a benevolent giant guiding, first fellow Europeans, and later non-Europeans, towards the virtues of constitutional government and free trade" (Chamberlain, 2014: 181).

Contention and shift

While liberalism was a major factor in the Pax, its manifestation was contested, as anti- and quasi-liberal voices always had prominent places. In the 1850s and 1860s, the Pax shifted from a peace built on liberal universalism to one built on a more muscular, pragmatic liberalism. This is important for the case at hand because while the liberal nature of its empire shielded British authorities from the political content of piracy, the shift to a more pragmatic liberalism opened up space for intervention in the Straits Settlement. I contend that there were three reasons for this shift. Two – growing uneasiness with universal free trade and the civilizing mission – will be covered below. The third – growing competition from European rivals – will be covered in respect to Southeast Asia in the next section.

It was not until the 1830s that a group of British politicians led by Richard Cobden effectively articulated the model of an empire run by unilateral free trade (Howe, 2007). In 1846 the Corn Laws were repealed and in 1849 the same happened to the Navigations Act. In 1851, England proclaimed the virtues of unilateral free trade at its Great Exhibition (Howe, 2002). This meant free trade not just for the British but for all. There were even calls for a Europe united by free trade (Howe, 2002) and a global state (Bell, 2007a). However by the 1860s this policy was met with stiff opposition by protectionists and Tories (Cain, 2002). Much of this opposition was a response to the increase in global colonial competition in Africa and Asia. Thus, the Tories wanted naval power, not merchant ships, to be the foundation of Britain's empire to protect trade (Semmel, 1986), forcing even liberals such as Gladstone into a more pragmatic policy (Cain, 2007). Following conflicts on the continent, increased colonial competition, and the depression of 1873, free trade would no longer be unilateral and would need to be ensured by naval power.

A series of events challenged the empire's civilizing mission as well. The Sepoy Rebellion of 1857 forced Britain to take control of India away from the East India Company (EIC) and soured many on the possibility of reforming the Indian people in Britain's image. That same year, conduct of the Second Opium War sparked a parliamentary debate over the 'standard of civilization' ultimately won by conservatives who saw the Chinese as barbarous (Phillips, 2012). John Stuart Mill failed to bring charges against Jamaican Governor Edward Eyre following the latter's ruthless treatment of local rebels. To many – including luminaries such as Alfred Tennyson and Charles Dickens – the 'Eyre Affair' was further proof the colonized were incorrigible (Mantena, 2007: 121–122).

These events mirrored an intellectual movement that focused on the complexities of colonial rule and colonized people. As Henry Maine stated after the 1857 rebellion, "The thinker or scholar who approaches it [India] in a serious spirit finds it pregnant with difficult questions, not to be disentangled without prodigious pains …" (Mantena, 2007: 128). Maine concluded that it would be far from simple, if not impossible, to reform the Indian people along Western lines. While British/European civilization was universal, colonized societies were "particular" (Anghie, 2005: 4). Many used Darwin's recently published work to argue that the backwardness of the people themselves and the complexity involved became a justification for British rule (Hyam, 2002: 156–157). If India could not be reformed, then reform could not be the justification for ruling it. In the words of Karuna Mantena (2007: 131), "The lessons of 1857 prioritised a practical and strategic concern for questions of law and order over issues of imperial legitimacy and moral purpose." It is no coincidence that this period sees renewed emphasis on settler colonies as 'Greater Britain' (Bell, 2011; Bellich, 2009). Thus, the nature of the Pax, how power was used and peace was created and maintained, changed. This transformation holds not just at the general level covered above, but also for Southeast Asia, where we see the effects of this shift in British policy toward piracy.

Nineteenth-century Southeast Asian piracy

For much of the 19th century, in addition to areas ruled by local sultans and chiefs, the islands of Southeast Asia had three prominent European colonies. To the east and the north, the Spanish claimed what is today the Philippines; to the south the Dutch colony of Java roughly matches present-day Indonesia. Nestled in between was the British Straits Settlement, covering much of present-day Malaysia and Singapore. The first major British settlement in the region was on the island of Penang. In 1811, British traders were able to gain the ear of imperial policymakers, and Singapore – at the southern tip of the Malay Peninsula and the gate to the quickest route from China to Europe – became the base of operations (Lewis, 1997). It grew quickly from a population of only 5,000 in 1819 to 80,000 by 1860. It would become the major port for trade to Calcutta and Canton, giving the EIC a major advantage over both the VOC and local traders. By 1826, Singapore, Malacca, and Penang were consolidated into the Straits Settlements, under the government of India (Gough, 2014: 118–124).

Despite periodic trade disputes, relations between the British and the Dutch were cordial. There was little sense of direct competition as would become prevalent later in the century. For instance, in the 1824 Anglo-Dutch treaty the Dutch gained Sumatra for concessions in Malaya and India.[1] Conservative MP John Wodehouse commented that it was, "in many ways advantageous that the Dutch should possess the [Indonesian] archipelago" (Tarling, 2001). This is similar to how Britain ruled its own territory. Local leaders kept control, and there was little attempt to govern directly. The empire was meant to civilize and facilitate trade, not rule. Colonel Stamford Raffles – who became the Lt. Gov. of the colony – hoped to rescue the Malay from piracy, proclaiming that it was by "commerce alone that we may best promote our own interests for their advancement" (Turnbull, 1972: 223). This was a period marked by a less active, less competitive colonial rule in Southeast Asia focused on ports, open trade, and civilizing native peoples. Naval power and direct control were not a part of the early Pax.

However, piracy was persistent during this period, a blight on the Pax. Each colonial power had problems with piracy. Iranun, Samal, and Tirun pirates raided around the Philippine islands while Buginese pirates raided Java. Pirates from the sultanates of Johore and Riau-Linga attacked along the Strait of Malacca and Dayak pirates attacked the island of Borneo, which had both English and Dutch settlements. Piracy was also very transnational. C.M. Turnbull (1972: 243–244) recounts that many Malay pirates attacked east coast peninsular trade in April and May, sailed around Johore from June to September, cruised along the Strait of Malacca from October to January – often attacking ships stuck during the frequent 'calms' – and then headed back to fish and plan for the next year's journey in February and March. Philippine pirates moved similarly, heading to the Northern Philippine islands from March to October and then south to Mindanao and the Strait of Malacca in late fall (Loyre, 1997: 80). Thus, pirates were very flexible and mobile, something it took a long time for the British to come to grips with. Seasonal patterns created rivalries among pirate groups. For instance, pirates from the Sulu region of the Philippines were fierce rivals with those from the Riau archipelago in Malaysia (Hall, 1981: 570). By the middle of the 19th century, piracy had become largely a British problem: "Now England derives more benefit from the use of the seas of the Archipelago than any other nation ... her means of action far superior to [Holland and Spain]" (1849a: 465).

Raiding was mostly small-scale. It never organized along the lines of the great Chinese pirate confederations who were rough contemporaries (Antony, 2003; Konstam, 2008; MacKay, 2013; Murray, 1997). That said, it was not unheard of for pirate fleets to number 30 'prahu' vessels with 36 oarsmen each. Pirates often attacked the native shipping 'downstream' of ships sent to Europe and China (often based on 'illegal' trade), as these ships were easier targets (Turnbull, 1972: 176). As a result, the number of native craft that arrived in Singapore fell from 2,856 to 1,484 between 1828 and 1834 – to choose one period – and was not replaced by European square rigged vessels (Newbold, 1971: 369). Recorded statistics often underrated the costs of piracy as shipping companies wanted to avoid the higher fees involved with state protection (Anderson, 1997). Often the arms trade based out of Singapore and other major ports actually perpetuated piracy even as pirates attacked shipping into and out of these ports. Profits were derived from stolen goods and a kidnapping and ransom business, much of which came from raids of villages and outposts as opposed to attacking ships at sea (Atsushi, 2010: 136). All told, while piracy was never described as a crisis for the region's colonial empires – there were debates on the seriousness of the threat (1849a; Campo, 2003; St. John, 1849; Trocki, 2008) – it was a near permanent problem. Many merchants and colonial officials in the Straits Settlements advocated for direct control over the colony, but it took decades for this to actually happen.

British narrative of piracy

In order to understand why this happened, it is necessary to look at the narratives constructed by pirates and counter-pirates alike to give piracy meaning. Violence and threat are narrative constructions (Balzacq, 2010; Buzan et al., 1998; Waever, 1995; Watson, 2012; for works on piracy see Bueger, 2013; Mabee, 2009; Shirk, 2017). As Richard Jackson and Matt McDonald argue, "... acts of political violence do not necessarily 'speak for themselves'; they have to be narrated and interpreted in meaningful ways within a particular social, cultural, and historical context," (Jackson and McDonald, 2009: 18). There is no single action that is 'piracy': it is always constructed for political purposes in similar ways to 'terrorism' (Jackson et al., 2009; Stump and Dixit, 2012) or 'crime' (Tilly, 1985). Instead there are multiple actions that are narrated as piracy (and similar actions that are not) and assigned multiple meanings. Often multiple narratives are constructed that compete with each other (Shirk, 2016). In this case we see a counter-pirate narrative that piracy was innate to the Malay people and evidence that they were not as civilized as Europeans/British, and a pirate narrative of piracy as a political tool to gain local power and fight colonial intrusion. This particular narrative configuration made it hard for the British to recognize the political underpinnings of piracy and develop policies to counter them.

The British (and to a lesser degree the Dutch and the Spanish) narrated piracy as a force against the rising tide of civilization and trade. Like many colonized peoples, the locals were cast as barbarians for whom nefarious deeds were innate to their society. There is logic to this if we are to assume the liberal starting point. Singapore was already a pirate base when the British arrived (Turnbull, 1972: 243) and as early as 1775 an entire colonial settlement was wiped out by Sulu pirates in Malaysia (Hall, 1981: 536). Thus, the Malay and others were considered natural pirates. One anonymous commenter (1837: 464) summed up this position nicely, "plunder and bloodshed seems the invariable object of every Malay." Raffles – who saw himself, "as a liberal progressive, a force for good ... the personification of Pax" (Gough, 2014: 119) – stated that piracy was, "an evil of ancient date, and intimately connected with the Malayan habits," while an EIC official stated that, "From the earliest times ... piracy has been a distinguishing feature in the Character of the Malays" (Layton, 2011: 83, 84). A merchant by the name of Dalton complained that "All Bugis [a prominent Indonesian people] are pirates" and that "they paralyze the exertions of thousands of individuals who would otherwise be active ... Indeed the Bugis, are the most mercenary, blood-thirsty, inhuman race of the whole ... the most deadly foes to all Europeans whenever they get them into their power" (Moor, 1837: 15, 29). Singapore Governor Samuel Bonham described one prominent local chief, the Temenggong Ibrahim, as "completely illiterate, not a remove higher on the scale of civilization than the meanest of his followers" out of frustration with his participation in piracy (Trocki, 2008: 79). Colonial Official J.R. Logan said of local leaders that they were "indolent debauchees and greedy monopolists," out to "drain and paralyse the industry of their people ..." (Logan, 1847: 17–18).

The fault of piracy was laid at the hands of local peoples. Dutch official H. W. Mutinghe claimed that piracy was not motivated by profit but instead "unwillingness to perform useful labor" (Campo, 2003: 202). It was also claimed that piracy, though an obvious deviance to a civilized man, was considered honorable among the Malay (Hall, 1981: 362–367; Layton, 2011: 83). There were also more calculated concerns about piracy. In addition to costing money, pirates also proved a barrier to the solidification of the empire. Dalton's problem with the Bugis pirates stems from their ability to build up an informal empire in areas where the Dutch had little control and thus become a competitor in trade with the English (Tarling, 1978: 113). This is why Wodehouse's quote above is so interesting – better the Dutch than the pirates. Nearly all local politics were soon tagged as piracy. As contemporary Horace St. John proclaimed, "All Malay political activity is piracy" (St. John, 1853: 160–162; see also Trocki, 2008: 76–77). Since local chiefs were often set up at the mouths of rivers to tax trade, conflicts between them often disrupted trade (Tarling, 1957: 14–15; Trocki, 2008: 77). Thus Simon Layton (Layton, 2013: 213) claims, "What the British called 'piracy' was not so much a characterization of any particular crime but rather an axiom of empire that tried to criminalize entire sets of seafaring peoples, thereby justifying the expropriation of trade."

Pirates' political project(s)

The narrative above has as much to do with the liberal nature of the Pax as it does historical interactions with the Malay. First, there were many who saw difference and were predisposed to see the Malay as deficient. Second, even though many liberals rejected natural inequality, local people were developmentally inferior. The practical differences between racial theories and liberal theories of development were often negligible (Pitts, 2005: 19). The liberal starting position made it hard for the British to recognize the political claims and projects inherent in Malay piracy. This had not always been the case. Writing in 1680, explorer and privateer/pirate William Dampier claimed that the Malay "in general are a bold people, and yet I do not find any of them addicted to Robbery ... the Pirates who lurk on this coast, seem to do it as much to revenge themselves on the Dutch, for restraining their Trade, as to gain this way what they cannot obtain in war of Traffick" (Tarling, 1978: 10–11). Dampier's writings were widely distributed and read in his time, so this information was accessible. Instead of being natural to the Malay people, "piracy" in the region grew with the influx of Dutch trading ships in the late 18th century. As one anonymous contemporary observer remarked, "The rigid monopoly maintained by the Dutch [forced locals into] ... less commendable pursuits, in which piracy and slave dealing held a principle place" (1849b). Dianne Lewis (1997) argues that the founding of Singapore shattered the rising trade port of Riau, causing the traditional Malay state structure to splinter. Local peoples across the region were put under pressure to move inland, where they often fought with groups who already held this land (Watson Andaya, 1997). This does not capture the whole story, however. Carl Trocki argues that what really changed was not necessarily a rise in piracy but a recognition of local politics as piracy when Europeans took over the local trading system.

Contemporary observers provide some hint that their motives were neither barbaric nor solely economic. Often they were characterized as anticolonial. One English observer (1837) drew a comparison between the Malay and "our northern forefathers ... the Romans were to them as the Europeans are to the Malay – intruders, conquerors, tyrants ... [They] attacked indiscriminately everything which bore an affinity to the Roman name." The same observer (1837: 484) also notes a strong "hatred of Europeans, in which, however [they] may differ on other subjects, they all agree." Another observer (1849b: 464) remarked that "there are very few of the Native Rulers, not under European influence and control, who are not more or less participant." Historians have emphasized the political aspects of piracy: "Origins were not to be found in the moral turpitude of the Malays, but rather in commercial and political changes, and their motivations less in mere greed than in objects of political ambition and prestige" (Tarling, 1978: 11). Others have argued that while piracy was caused by European intrusion, "colonialism altered the rules of political and economic life in several ways" (Loyre, 1997: 81). Even claims that piracy had long been used by the Malay missed that 'piracy' was a western concept. Here we see the contested nature of the term. To local leaders, they ruled parts of the ocean and whatever was on them. This is not piracy, which has traditionally been viewed in the west as a deviation from legitimate activity. It is merely a different form of taxation based on a different concept of legitimacy (Trocki, 2008: 68).

Sultanates that controlled piracy in the Philippines postdate the rise of piracy and the presence of Europeans (Loyre, 1997). Piracy had long been a governing tool, but during this period it reconfigured local politics. Balances of power shifted. For instance, Buginese pirate bands in the Strait of Malacca became prominent after the fall of the powerful Macassar fleet at the hands of the Dutch (Hall, 1981: 362). For local leaders who predated the presence of Europeans, piracy became a way to fight the intruders and pursue personal or political interests in this new world. To many it was a symbol of resistance against Europeans. Alliances and relationships between leaders were often determined by piracy, as local leaders and villages who worked with the Europeans became targeted and villagers regularly felt the brunt of raiding activity. Simon Layton argues that pirates grew in number due to the ruptures to local history and politics caused by colonial intrusion. He quotes one condemned pirate at his trial in Singapore as justifying his actions thus, "If we had *not* been pirates, our own chiefs would have killed us; and, because we *are* pirates, you kill us: it is the same to us, whatever we do – either way: we die" (Layton, 2011: 93).

We can see these claims in the story of the Temenggongs of Johor in the first half of the century: Abdul Rahman and his son, Ibrahim. Local Malay rulers claimed a hereditary feudal right to the seas. Those that had a title from the Temenggong were legitimate, those that did not were illegitimate, what were called *perompak* (Trocki, 2008: 68). To the British, it was all piracy. When the British enlisted Temenggong Abdul Rahman to protect shipping into and out of Singapore, he cracked down on *perompak*. However, this did not prove profitable enough for the Temenggong and he had to resort to raiding for his own purposes. Thus piracy never really went away. Frustrated, the British removed Abdul Rahman from power shortly before his death in 1825, leading to a rapid decline in his seat's power. This vacuum forced all local leaders, including the Temenggong's son Ibrahim, to resort to raiding for their own purposes. By 1830, Ibrahim found that "his only political resource, his only subjects, were the pirates themselves" (Trocki, 2008: 78). Ignored in the criticism of Ibrahim by Bonham above was that his kingdom of Johor was largely a jungle with little opportunity for agriculture. If Ibrahim wanted to build his own polity back to what his father had, he had to control the sea and this meant piracy. Eventually in 1837, Ibrahim was enlisted by Bonham to suppress piracy. His contacts in Singapore helped gain him an edge against local leaders. However, raiding did not stop. Ibrahim's help was important but nominal (Turnbull, 1972: 247). For instance, those that he relocated to Singapore to keep an eye on actually made it a base for raiding (Tarling, 1978: 102). In addition, the Temenggong had enemies who did not accept this arrangement, and one conflict in the early 1850s saw 'piracy' – in this case a fight for control over parts of the Straits by local leaders – surge (Trocki, 2008: 84).

What the Malay saw as legitimate governance based on hereditary rights, the British saw as piracy. Ibrahim and his competitors were looking to expand their control by methods that were a) traditional and b) available to them. In addition, the British also recognized competition as piracy. Many who were considered *perompak* opposed the British and their allies, giving piracy an anti-colonial edge. Many polities were squeezed between the British intrusions on the coast and the presence of inland peoples. What we see here are local politics, whether for the gain of a particular ruler, his opposition, or opposition to the British. And often it was all considered piracy. This was masked by the liberal universalism of the Pax Britannica.

British counter-piracy policy

Nicholas Tarling (1969) claims that British involvement in the Malay states was a consequence of their wish to deal with piracy. While this claim ignores how British involvement in the 18th and early 19th centuries fractured Malay politics and led to an increase in piracy (Lewis, 1997), I argue that piracy was a reason why the British developed an interventionist policy in the Straits Settlement in 1873. Recognizing piracy as a problem as early as the 1820s, Raffles claimed that, "The practice of piracy is now an evil so extensive and formidable, that it cannot be put down by the strong hand [i.e., naval action] alone" (Layton, 2011: 83). Instead, he recommended that to solve the problem, Britain would have to rule Malaysia (Tarling, 1957: 45). However, it was not until 1873 that the British finally took this seriously and, in conjunction with similar actions by the Dutch in Indonesia and the Spanish in the Philippines, ended the pirate threat. Why did it take so long? Why were so many other avenues tried before formal colonization? Certainly it was not a lack of piracy, as there were many years with heavy raiding activity between 1827 and 1874. Nor did piracy peak in the late 1860s. It also was not because no one saw this as a possible solution. In addition to Raffles, by the 1850s most merchants in Singapore favored intervention in local politics. Instead, it was a shift in the nature of the use of British power, i.e., the Pax, which made intervention much more likely.

It is instructive to first look at what did not work. Piracy became a recognized problem in the 1820s. In addition to its political ramifications, the 1824 Anglo-Dutch treaty also laid out a pathway for counter-piracy cooperation. However, the treaty's counter-pirate clauses were not put into effect until 1836 and ended soon thereafter over British mistrust of Dutch incentives (Turnbull, 1972: 248). Dutch initiatives to give new sources of income to local leaders worked immediately but proved fruitless in the medium term (Atsushi, 2010: 138). As of 1830, the British had no mechanism for trying captured pirates in the Straits (Turnbull, 1972: 245). In 1837 the accused could only be tried for piracies within three miles of the coast. Extending this further would have been inimical to Britain's free trade orthodoxy. The 1830s saw a major increase in piracy and it was only at this time that the British began to use Naval ships to cruise the straits (Turnbull, 1972: 246). This, of course, cost local British merchants in taxes, and therefore when the Chinese Emperor reached out to the British for help with piracy they declined, considering the inevitable taxes and higher insurance premiums too expensive (Turnbull, 1972: 245). In 1845, the British convinced Temenggong Ibrahim to give up piracy in exchange for trading rights (Turnbull, 1972: 276). This quelled piracy for a few years but by 1850 it returned.

The fallback counter-piracy tactic was to attack pirate bases and protect ships. However, cruising and direct protection were more "a palliative than a cure" (Anderson, 1997). Usually, it consisted of an attempt to attack a pirate base, killing and scattering pirates – one famous attack in Sarawak in 1843 killed nearly 800 pirates (1849c; Gosse, 1932: 290–293) – and then holding that area to prevent their return. These attacks, however, were sporadic and had the effect of driving pirate communities elsewhere, effectively simulating the carnival game 'whack-a-mole'. One contemporary critic (1849b: 581) opined that, "Vigorous efforts followed by lengthened periods of inaction, have proved over and over again to be inadequate." This is actually a common problem in cases where we see this particular narrative configuration. Relationships between pirates and local sultanates or other leaders facilitated flexibility among pirate gangs, relationships often ignored by

Europeans who denied the political content of piracy (Shirk, 2016). The situation was such that one observer stated that, "It is only by engaging all of the powers in the western part of the Archipelago to act in concert, that effectual measures can be taken" (1849a: 464).

Ultimately this led to the Straits Settlement being governed through the colonial office in 1867. This shift was not due to any single event but instead a series of longer processes, and it took some time to implement. In many ways the timing had more to do with bureaucratic procedure than events in the Straits. Prior to 1867, the Straits Settlement was under the rule of the Government of India, ruled for much of this time by the EIC. Many British living and working in the Straits were unsatisfied with this situation, complaining that India treated it as an extension of the subcontinent. The Sepoy Rebellion, a Chinese rebellion in the Straits province of Sarawak, and complaints over taxes and duties led to a petition for British control signed by Singapore merchants in 1857. Mentioned in this petition was a failure to "wipe out piracy" (Turnbull, 1972: 349). Still, it took ten years and some very persistent lobbying by colonial officials – by no means representing a majority – who were in favor of the move. Once taking control, the early policy from the colonial office was, like the Indian government before it, non-intervention designed to stay out of local disputes (Tarling, 1978: 229–230), which were often viewed as piracy. However, the one aspect of the 1857 petition that had not been rectified was turmoil in the Malay states. Two merchants complained that traders cannot "anticipate that the British government will intervene to enforce their contracts …" (Turnbull, 1972: 388). It was not until 1873, after the ouster of the Strait's first colonial office governor, Samuel Ord, that the British took an interventionist policy towards the colony (Turnbull, 1972: 381–391). This decision won praise from the *Straits Times* for, "put[ing] an end to these disturbances" (Turnbull, 1972: 389). Part of the reason for this interventionism was the "suppression of piracy" (Tarling, 1978: 231) and, in conjunction with the Dutch colonization of Indonesia and the creeping Spanish influence over the Philippines (Hall, 1981: 617, 571), it finally proved effective in ending piracy. J.L. Anderson sums up the situation nicely: "Whatever the morality of the matter, the economics were sound" (Anderson, 1997: 97).

The shift in liberalism's relationship to empire was important to this decision. The narrative about piracy did not change; it was an inherent part of the Malays that stood in the way of the growth of civilization and free trade. Piracy was not at an historical high, as there had been multiple periods with considerable piracy over the previous five decades. Nor was there a shift in opinion among British officials and merchants with experience in the region, since men like Logan and Raffles had long favored intervention. What did change was the link between liberalism and empire, changing the meaning of the British narrative on piracy and changing minds in London. One could blame the Malay's nature or Malay culture or the Malay's progress toward civilization. Even in the latter camp one could argue that the Malay is not naturally deficient but still be skeptical that the British could turn him around. This is essentially Maine's argument about the Indian above. It was this shift, from the civilizing mission to skepticism toward it, that led to an emphasis on law and order with piracy as a major flashpoint. This new emphasis made it much more likely that intervention and direct control over local politics would become an option. Despite Raffles' remarks that defeating piracy would necessitate the vast majority of local leaders working together, it still took seven years for intervention to happen after London took control from Calcutta. In other words, working with local leaders to help them solve problems was still viewed as desirable; the early version of the Pax was not overturned overnight. Since "suppression of piracy" was given as a reason for intervention, it appears that law and order won the day.

The decision to consolidate control of the Straits Settlement in London was also part of a larger context. The Dutch and the British had gotten along as well as could be expected in the first half of the 19th century. The Dutch never developed settler colonies or centralized control over Indonesia. As British naturalist Alfred Russel Wallace (1869: 149) observed during his travels in the 1850s, "The mode of government now adopted in Java is to retain the whole series of native rulers." However, the Dutch began consolidating power in Indonesia in the 1830s. Wars with local leaders led to the Dutch subjugating the Javanese in 1830, the Mingangkabau in 1838, Bali in 1849, and the Kalimantan Sultan in 1863. Consolidation over Aceh in 1871 specifically scared the British (Tarling, 2001). While Dutch expansion was in part an attempt to better protect trade from rivals and pirates, it was also meant to consolidate power in the face of increasing European intrusion into the region (Ricklefs, 2001: 131). In addition, the Spanish were slowly gaining more control over the local politics of the Mindanao and Sulu regions in the 1850s (Hall, 1981: 571).

While the Dutch and Spanish were consolidating power in pre-existing colonies, France and Germany were beginning to extend their own empires into the region. In the early 19th century, French presence in Southeast Asia was largely comprised of Catholic missionary posts. In 1857, Napoleon III ordered Admiral Charles Rigault de Genouilly to attack Da Nang (Milza, 2004; Tarling, 2001; Tucker, 1999). While the attack was ostensibly for the protection of Catholic missionaries, Napoleon also "hoped to secure a port there [Vietnam] on the model of Hong Kong" (Tucker, 1999: 29). This was for national prestige, as French colonialism often lacked an economic context and was often undertaken by peripheral officers with little central planning or execution (Andrew and Kanya-Forstner, 1988). While the attack did not succeed, Genouilly led an expedition that captured Saigon in 1859. By 1862 the French controlled Cochinchina. In 1863 Cambodian King Norodom sought a protectorate treaty to balance against his traditional Siamese rivals. Admiral P.P.N. de la Grandiere annexed the western provinces of Indochina in 1867 against explicit orders from Paris (Tarling, 2001: 114–131). France also took part in the Second Opium War on the side of the British from 1857–1860. While it was not until 1887 that full power was consolidated over Indochina, French expansion ramped up during the 1850s and 1860s. Their behavior became more aggressive in Indochina and Cochinchina following defeat in the Franco-Prussian War.

The victors of that war also stepped into the region during this time (Kundrus, 2008; Naranch, 2014; Wehler, 1970). Despite Bismarck claiming in 1868 that, "advantages claimed for colonies were illusory" (Henderson, 1993: 32), Germany would eventually rule the northern half of Papua New Guinea in 1887 and control the Chinese city of Qingdao in 1897 in addition to winning access to a number of Chinese treaty ports. Elsewhere, the United States entered Japan in 1854 and would take the Philippines from the Spanish in 1898. From 1868 to 1873, Italy repeatedly attempted to set up a penal colony in Borneo, much to the consternation of the British and the Dutch (Squires, 2009). Despite losing territory in present-day Cambodia, Laos, and on the Straits, Siam was the only local power to resist European intrusion. This was in part due to its relationship with the British and later its diplomatic skill in remaining a 'buffer state' between the British and the French. Their relationship with the British in particular caused problems for French expansion in Indochina in the 1860s (Tuck, 1995).

All of this happened as the historical superpower in the region was beginning to fall apart. A Chinese tributary system that ruled much of East and Southeast Asia for centuries (Ringmar, 2012; Zhang, 2001; Zhang and Buzan, 2012) started to lose its grip. Loss in the First Opium War gave control over Hong Kong to the British and access to five treaty ports – including Shanghai – in 1842. The Second Opium War created more treaty ports, ending with almost 80. Eventually foreign traders were given travel rights throughout China. China also experienced two rebellions in the latter half of the 19th century, the Taiping rebellion (1850–1864) by a millennium Christian sect and the Boxer Rebellion (1899–1901) by Chinese nationalists, which strengthened the hand of the Europeans.

These developments give further context to the British decision to take a 'law and order' approach to colonial governance and piracy. They saw the fall of the Sinocentric system in the middle of the 19th century, largely of their own doing, being replaced by European expansion into and/or consolidation of Indonesia, China, Indochina, Cambodia, and Papua New Guinea. Thus the pragmatists had a strengthened hand to protect British holdings and trade through the use of force not just from local threats but also from European rivals. This in part explains taking responsibility for the Straits in 1867 and developing an interventionist policy that culminated in direct rule starting in 1873. Tarling gives 1870 as an inflection point in the region and claims that by this point local states "all succumbed to the Europeans, save Siam [present-day Thailand] ... The renewed rivalry of the Europeans ... dislodged the compromises Britain had made when it was virtually unchallenged" (Tarling, 2001: 42). European competition had replaced competition between and with local polities in the region. However, there were not major conflicts between European powers over Southeast Asia. There was still a Pax, but its content had changed.

Conclusion

The early version of the Pax Britannica in Southeast Asia was built on unilateral free trade, a civilizing mission, and low levels of European competition. It was characterized by trading posts and a willingness to allow local or native rulers autonomy. However, it was also characterized by piracy – a blight on any claims to be protecting trade. The later version of the Pax found a way to defeat piracy. However, the civilizing mission, unilateral free trade, and the general absence of competition between European powers receded, although increased competition never led to outright hostilities. Such a shift reminds us that the Pax, if it ever existed at all, was neither complete nor singular. At the peak of the liberal universal Pax, Britain could never control piracy. Once it got a handle on piracy, it was facing increased intervention in the region by other European powers. Thus, the most we can say about the Pax is that it was Eurocentric and never really brought peace to the interactions between Europeans and locals.

This is why it is important to think of the Pax not simply as an historical fact that we can test but instead as a way to look at the purpose of British power. Doing so helps us recognize a change in the content of the Pax. At its peak Southeast Asia was governed by trade, not rule and there was little European geopolitical competition. But the British could not control what they called piracy. The shift in the Pax in the 1850s and 1860s meant more direct, centralized colonization. It meant ramping down the civilizing mission and unilateral free trade in exchange for law and order and a trade protected by force. From 'trade, not rule' to 'trade through rule'. It meant dealing with the incursions of France and Germany and consolidation in the Dutch and Spanish colonies. It is both a response to and a cause of the 'New Colonialism' and the 'struggle for Asia'. It suggests that the great period of internationalism and globalization that typified the second half of the long 19th century was built on a pragmatic liberalism, not the liberal universalism that first gave such a world a voice.

It also explains the puzzles set out at the beginning of this chapter about British counter-piracy policy in 19th-century Southeast Asia. The early Pax was a hindrance to the British. The liberal assumptions about native peoples and indirect rule made it hard for many officials to recognize, let alone solve, the political problems that led to and sustained piracy. This is why I have taken the time to show both the British and pirate narratives. However, the 'answer' did not come when the British finally recognized the political content of piracy and found a just solution to the problem. It came when a shift in the use of British power made it easier to defeat piracy once and for all by intervening and directly ruling the Straits Settlement. In conjunction with similar moves from the Dutch and the Spanish, the leaders who kept piracy alive no longer had the space or capacity to continue doing so. The political project of pirates ultimately failed to keep the colonizers at bay for reasons largely out of their control. Finally, if this was the last great 'wave' of early modern piracy this only reinforces the claim that the shift in the nature of the Pax was instrumental in creating the late 19th-century global world.

Note

1 The treaty also contained the origins of the current Malaysia/Indonesia border in the Strait and the formalization of British control over the Malay peninsula (1849a; Turnbull, 1972).

Bibliography

Anderson, J.L. (1997) Piracy in the Eastern Seas: 1750–1850: Some Economic Implications. In David J. Starkey et al., eds., *Pirates and Privateers: New Perspectives on the War on Trade in the Eighteenth and Nineteenth Centuries.* Exeter: University of Exeter Press.

Andrew, C.M. and A.S. Kanya-Forstner. (1988) Centre and Periphery in the Making of the Second French Colonial Empire, 1815–1920. *Journal of Imperial and Commonwealth History* 16(3): 9–34.

Anghie, Anthony. (2005) *Imperialism, Sovereignty, and the Making of International Law.* Cambridge: Cambridge University Press.

Anonymous. (1837) The Malay Pirates: With a Sketch of Their System and Territory. *United Service Journal and Naval and Military Magazine* 1: 458–466.

Anonymous. (1849a) Malay Amoks and Piracies: What Can We Do to Abolish Them? *Journal of the Indian Archipelago and Eastern Asia* 3: 463–467.

Anonymous. (1849b) Piracy and the Slave Trade of the Indian Archipelago. *Journal of the Indian Archipelago and Eastern Asia* 3: 581–588.

Anonymous. (1849c) Destruction of the Fleet of the Sarabas and Sakarran Pirates by the Expedition of Sarawak on the Night of 31st July 1849. *Journal of the Indian Archipelago and Eastern Asia* 3: 589–593.

Antony, Robert J. (2003) *Like Froth Floating on the Sea: The World of Pirates and Seafarers in Late Imperial South China.* Berkeley: Institute for East Asian Studies.

Armitage, David. (2000) *The Ideological Origins of the British Empire.* Cambridge: Cambridge University Press.

Atsushi, Ota. (2010) The Business of Violence: Piracy around Riau, Lingga, and Singapore. In Robert J. Antony, ed., *Elusive Pirates, Pervasive Smugglers: Violence and Clandestine Trade in the Great China Sea.* Hong Kong: Hong Kong University Press.

Balzacq, Thierry. (2010) *Understanding Securitisation Theory: How Security Problems Emerge and Dissolve.* New York: Routledge.

Bell, Duncan. (2007a) The Victorian Idea of a Global State. In Duncan Bell, ed., *Victorian Visions of Global Order: Empire and International Relations in Nineteenth-century Political Thought.* Cambridge: Cambridge University Press, pp. 159–185.

Bell, Duncan, ed. (2007b) *Victorian Visions of Global Order: Empire and International Relations in Nineteenth-century Political Thought.* Cambridge: Cambridge University Press.

Bell, Duncan, ed. (2011) *The Idea of Greater Britain: Empire and the Future of World Order, 1860–1900.* Princeton: Princeton University Press.

Bellich, James. (2009) *Replenishing the Earth: The Settler Revolution and the Rise of the Anglo-World, 1789–1939.* Oxford: Oxford University Press.

Bueger, Christian. (2013) Practice, Pirates and Coast Guards: The Grand Narrative of Somali Piracy. *Third World Quarterly* 34(10): 1811–1827.

Buzan, Barry and George Lawson. (2015) *The Global Transformation: History, Modernity and the Making of International Relations.* Cambridge: Cambridge University Press.

Buzan, Barry, Ole Wæverand Jaap de Wilde. (1998) *Security: A New Framework for Analysis*. Boulder: Lynne Rienner.

Cain, Peter. (2002) Wealth, Power, and Empire: The Protectionist Movement in Britain, 1880–1914. In Patrick Karl O'Brien and Armand Clesse, eds., *Two Hegemonies: Britain 1846–1914 and the United States 1941–2001*. Burlington: Ashgate.

Cain, Peter. (2007) Radicalism, Gladstone, and the Liberal Critique of Disraelian "Imperialism". In Duncan Bell, ed., *Victorian Visions of Global Order: Empire and International Relations in Nineteenth-century Political Thought*. Cambridge: Cambridge University Press.

Campo, Joseph N.M.F. (2003) Discourse without Discussion: Representation of Piracy in Colonial Indonesia, 1816–1825. *Journal of Southeast Asian Studies* 34(2): 199–214.

Chamberlain, Muriel E. (2014) *Pax Britannica? British Foreign Policy 1789–1914*. New York: Routledge.

Gong, Gerrit W. (1984) *The Standard of Civilization in International Society*. Oxford: Oxford University Press.

Gosse, Philip. (1932) *The History of Piracy*. New York: Tudor.

Gough, Barry. (2014) *Pax Britannica*. London: Palgrave Macmillan.

Hall, D.G.E. (1981) *A History of Southeast Asia*. New York: St. Martin's.

Henderson, W.O. (1993) *The German Colonial Empire, 1884–1919*. London: Cass.

Hobsbawm, Eric J. (1987) *The Age of Empire: 1875–1914*. New York: Random House.

Howe, Anthony. (2002) Free-Trade in Britain, 1846–1914. In Patrick Karl O'Brien and Armand Clesse, eds., *Two Hegemonies: Britain 1846–1914 and the United States 1941–2001*. Burlington: Ashgate.

Howe, Anthony. (2007) Free Trade and Global Order: The Rise and Fall of a Victorian Vision. In Duncan Bell, ed., *Victorian Visions of Global Order: Empire and International Relations in Nineteenth-century Political Thought*. Cambridge: Cambridge University Press.

Hyam, Ronald. (2002) *Britain's Imperial Century, 1815–1914: A Study of Empire and Expansion*. London: Palgrave Macmillan.

Jackson, Richard and Matt McDonald. (2009) Constructivism, US Foreign Policy, and the "War on Terror". In Inderjeet Parmar, et al., eds., *New Direction in US Foreign Policy*. New York: Routledge.

Jackson, Richard, Mary Breen Smyth, and Jeroen Gunning, eds. (2009) *Critical Terrorism Studies: A New Research Agenda*. New York: Routledge.

Konstam, August. (2008) *Piracy: The Complete History*. New York: Osprey.

Koskenniemi, Marti. (2002) *The Gentle Civilizer of Nations: The Rise and Fall of International Law, 1870–1960*. Cambridge: Cambridge University Press.

Kundrus, Birthe. (2008) Germany and Its Colonies. In Prem Poddar et al., eds., *A Historical Companion to Postcolonial Literatures: Continental Europe and Its Empires*. Edinburgh: Edinburgh University Press.

Layton, Simon. (2011) Discourses of Piracy in an Age of Revolutions. *Itinerario* 35(2): 81–97.

Layton, Simon. (2013) Hydras and Leviathans in the Indian Ocean World. *International Journal of Maritime History* 25(2): 213–225.

Lewis, Diane. (1997) British Policy in the Straits of Malacca to 1819 and the Collapse of the Traditional Malay State Structure. In Brook Barrington, ed., *Empires, Imperialism and Southeast Asia*. Clayton, Australia: Monash Asia Institute.

Locke, John. (1999) *Political Essays*. Cambridge: Cambridge University Press.

Logan, James Richardson. (1847) *The Journal of the Indian Archipelago and Eastern Asia*.

Long, David and Brian C. Schmidt, eds. (2005) *Imperialism and Internationalism in the Discipline of International Relations.* Albany: SUNY Press.

Loyre, Ghislaine. (1997) Living and Working Conditions in Philippine Pirate Communities, 1750–1850. In David J. Starkey et al., eds. *Pirates and Privateers: New Perspectives on the War on Trade in the Eighteenth and Nineteenth Centuries.* Exeter: University of Exeter Press.

Mabee, Bryan. (2009) Pirates, Privateers, and the Political Economy of Private Violence. *Global Change, Peace, and Security* 21(2): 139–152.

MacKay, Joseph. (2013) Pirate Nations: Maritime Pirates as Escape Societies in Late Imperial China. *Social Science History* 37(4): 551–573.

Mantena, Karuna. (2007) The Crisis of Liberal Imperialism. In Duncan Bell, ed., *Victorian Visions of Global Order: Empire and International Relations in Nineteenth-century Political Thought.* Cambridge: Cambridge University Press.

Mehta, Uday S. (1999) *Liberalism and Empire: A Study in Nineteenth-century British Liberal Thought.* Chicago: University of Chicago Press.

Mill, John S. (2004). *On Liberty and Other Writings.* Cambridge: Cambridge University Press.

Milza, Pierre. (2004) *Napoléon III.* Paris: Perrin.

Moor, J.H. (1837) *Notices of the Indian Archipelago, and Adjacent Countries: Being a Collection of Papers Relating to Borneo, Celebes, Bali, Java, Sumatra, Nias, The Philippine Islands, Sulus, Siam, Cochin China, Malayan Peninsula.* http://seasiavisions.library.cornell.edu/catalog/sea:075.

Murray, Dian. (1997) Living and Working Conditions in Chinese Pirates Communities 1750–1850. In David J. Starkey et al., eds., *Pirates and Privateers: New Perspectives on the War on Trade in the Eighteenth and Nineteenth Centuries.* Exeter: University of Exeter Press.

Naranch, Bradley, ed. (2014) *German Colonialism in a Global Age.* Durham: Duke University Press.

Newbold, T.J. (1971) *Political and Statistical Account of the British Settlements in the Straits of Malacca.* Oxford: Oxford University Press.

Osterhammel, Jurgen. (2014) *The Transformation of the World: A Global History of the Nineteenth Century.* Princeton: Princeton University Press.

Phillips, Andrew. (2012) Saving Civilization from Empire: Belligerency, Pacifism and the Two Faces of Civilization during the Second Opium War. *European Journal of International Relations* 18(1): 5–27.

Pitts, Jennifer. (2005) *A Turn to Empire: The Rise of Imperial Liberalism in Britain and France.* Princeton: Princeton University Press.

Ricklefs, M.C. (2001) *A History of Modern Indonesia since c. 1200.* Stanford: Stanford University Press.

Ringmar, Erik. (2012) Performing International Systems: Two East-Asian Alternatives to the Westphalian Order. *International Organization* 66(1): 1–25.

Robertson, Robbie. (2002) *The Three Waves of Globalization: A History of a Developing Global Consciousness.* New York: Zed Books.

Semmel, Bernard. (1986) *Liberalism and Naval Strategy: Ideology, Interest and Sea Power during the Pax Britannica.* Crows Nest, Australia: Allen & Unwin.

Shirk, Mark A. (2016) Busting Blackbeard's Ghost: Somali Piracy in Historical Context. *Global Change, Peace, and Security* 28(1): 17–34.

Shirk, Mark A. (2017) How Does Violence Threaten the State? Four Narratives on Piracy. *Terrorism and Political Violence* 29(4): 656–673.

Squires, Nick. (2009) Italy planned penal colony in Borneo. *The Telegraph.* October 12. www.telegraph.co.uk/news/worldnews/europe/italy/6307840/Italy-planned-penal-colony-in-Borneo.html.

St. John, Horace StebbingRoscoe. (1853) *The Indian Archipelago; Its History and Present State.* London: Longman, Brown, Green.

St. John, Spencer. (1849) Piracy in the Indian Archipelago. *Journal of the Indian Archipelago and Eastern Asia* 3: 251–260.

Starkey, David J. (2001) Pirates and Markets. In C.R. Pennell, ed., *Bandits at Sea: A Pirates Reader.* New York: New York University Press.

Stump, Jacob L. and Priya Dixit. (2012) Toward a Completely Constructivist Critical Terrorism Studies. *International Relations* 26(2): 199–217.

Tarling, Nicholas. (1957) British Policy in the Malay Peninsula and Archipelago, 1824–1871. *Journal of the Malayan Branch of the Royal Asiatic Society* 30(3): 3–228.

Tarling, Nicholas. (1969) *British Policy in the Malay Peninsula and Archipelago, 1824–1871.* Oxford: Oxford University Press.

Tarling, Nicholas. (1978) *Piracy and Politics in the Malay World: A Study of British Imperialism in Nineteenth-century Southeast Asia.* Nendeln, Liechtenstein: Kraus.

Tarling, Nicholas. (2001) *Imperialism in Southeast Asia: "A Fleeting, Passing Phase".* New York: Routledge.

Tilly, Carles. (1985) War Making and State Making as Organized Crime. In Peter B. Evans, et al., eds., *Bringing the State Back In.* Cambridge: Cambridge University Press.

Trocki, Carl A. (2008) *Prince of Pirates: The Temenggongs and the Development of Johor and Singapore, 1784–1885.* Singapore: NUS Press.

Tuck, Patrick. (1995) *The French Wolf and the Siamese Lamb: The French Threat to Siamese Independence, 1858–1907.* Bangkok: White Lotus.

Tucker, Spencer. (1999) *Vietnam.* Lexington: University Press of Kentucky.

Turnbull, C.M. (1972) *The Straits Settlements 1826–1867: Indian Presidency to Crown Colony.* Oxford: Oxford University Press.

Waever, Ole. (1995) Securitization and Desecuritization. In Ronnie D. Lipschutz, ed., *On Security.* New York: Columbia University Press.

Wallace, Alfred Russel. (1869) *The Malay Archipelago: The Land of the Orang-Utan and the Bird of Paradise.* London: Macmillan.

Watson, Scott D. (2012) "Framing" the Copenhagen School: Integrating the Literature on Threat Construction. *Millennium: Journal of International Studies* 40(2): 279–301.

Watson Andaya, B. (1997) Raiding Cultures and Interior-coastal Migration in Early Modern Island Southeast Asia. In Brook Barrington, ed., *Empires, Imperialism, and Southeast Asia.* Clayton, Australia: Monash Asia Institute.

Wehler, Hans Ulrich. (1970) Bismarck's Imperialism 1862–1890. *Past and Present* 48 (1): 119–155.

Wilson, Kathleen. (2000) Citizenship, Empire, and Modernity in the English Provinces, c. 1720–1790. In Catherine Hall, ed., *Cultures of Empire: Colonizers in Britain and the Empire in the Nineteenth and Twentieth Centuries.* New York: Routledge.

Zhang, Yongjin. (2001) System, Empire and State in Chinese International Relations. *Review of International Studies* 27(5): 43–63.

Zhang, Yongjin and Barry Buzan. (2012) The Tributary System as International Society in Theory and Practice. *Chinese Journal of International Politics* 5(2): 3–36.

11 Conclusions
The value of our new historical narrative

Daniel M. Green

This volume has developed and provided evidence for a rather novel narrative for the global nineteenth century, dividing it into two halves, a first era of British laissez-faire hegemony outside of Europe, and a second of multiple great powers all engaged in a competitive imperial scramble to consume the globe. In the middle is a period of significant changes, in which one mode of ordering the world is under attack and withering away, in the face of power shifts, policy choices and ideational developments. The main implication is to suggest further efforts to understand two different eras in a nineteenth century often thought of as homogeneous. It also highlights the second phase of frenzied imperialism and its violence, and the unusual birthing of a system of empires, problematizing and historicizing British 'hegemony', IR's most common lens for the century as a whole. While the presence of British great-power influence may endure across the century, its implications for international behavior vary markedly. Rather than re-summarize the book's findings, this short concluding chapter will discuss the most fundamental message of our volume – that grappling with grand narratives of large swathes of history is a worthwhile endeavor for IR scholarship. Is it a good and valuable thing to have engaged in this activity of constructing a new narrative for the century? Should anyone really care about historical narratives and periodizations? We argue that in fact they are vitally important.

To begin, what do we mean by a 'grand' narrative or indeed any narrative of international relations history? Here it is useful to look back to arguments about the scale of claims that one might make about history (e.g., Hobson and Lawson, 2008). At the most expansive, 'mega-macro' scale such a very grand narrative might be the familiar realist one: "Because of human nature/anarchy, life is always a violent struggle for survival." Or the liberal-idealist mega-narrative: "As freedom, human rights, and democracy gradually spread, the world will become peaceful." Both are about the traditional central concern of IR, the incidence of war and peace and the prospects for conflict and cooperation. But they are at a huge and timeless scale, amounting to approximations of old-school 'Great Plan of History' arguments, and clearly do massive, irreparable damage to any treatment of the details of history itself. A slightly lesser scale 'macro' narrative might be that of hegemonic stability theory: "A series of dominant great powers has provided security, stability, and order in the international system across history, to aid in global flourishing." This narrative covers four-five centuries, still too expansive, but it is slightly more explanatory and detailed, and lingers as an important touchstone in IR thinking until today. Our narrative in this volume is best labeled a meso-narrative of history: "The first half of the nineteenth century was like this, but then key events happened and it became qualitatively different in the second half, and each half needs to be understood on its own terms." We contend that this scale of narrative is the most useful and the least damaging, hitting the analytic 'sweet spot'. It is still at a somewhat grand scale, allowing us to engage with broader patterns beyond the micro, but it challenges the narratives at higher levels of abstraction, even fatally, neither relying on them nor buttressing them. Simply stated, mega-macro narratives make claims in terms of millennia, macro claims are in terms of centuries, meso narrative claims are in terms of decades, and micro claims are about months and perhaps years. For central topics in international relations history – regarding the incidence of war/mass violence/conquest, peace, conflict, and cooperation – meso is best.

There is a necessary connection between history, narratives, and IR's academic work because history and theory are co-constitutive: "If theory is always 'from somewhere', then the universal 'somewhere' is history. Not only because theorists write in historical contexts they cannot escape, but because the theories invariably rest on historical propositions" (Reus-Smit, 2016: 422). Yet IR's mode of theorizing for the last 40 years at least has largely pushed history aside and, with a ruined history, we are inevitably burdened with weak theories, especially at the macro level. If we do not avail ourselves of richer, varied accounts of history, our debates and cumulation suffer – and this has been IR's experience. Fortunately, there is a solution to this problem.

This concluding chapter proceeds in three steps to explain why constructing our narrative has been a worthwhile undertaking. First, it argues that respect for methodological and metatheoretical advice actually requires IR scholars to construct such narratives and periodizations, or to be working on them. Indeed, critics of business-as-usual in IR's relationship with history need to make that point clearer. Second, we point out that such narratives are in fact omnipresent in our discipline and in life, and are needed, for good reasons. Finally, we assert that ours is a good and useful one, that relieves us of some of the time-bound prejudices and distortions of previous narratives of the nineteenth century. Our account illuminates more than just balancing patterns, a sustained hegemony, or an era of peace. Instead, we unveil key historical processes previously neglected by IR, spotlighting the oddity of the first half of the century and the tectonic shifts and imperial violence in the second half.

Methodological strictures require engagement with historical narratives

To begin, a read through IR method and metatheory tracts of the last 40 years brings one inexorably to the conclusion that IR must get properly serious about history. There are a number of reasons, but two receive attention here. First, this is because we in fact have an historical narrative in IR, one which may have waned but has now returned, and it is highly problematic. And second, history liberates our thinking and theorizing.

IR's default narrative is problematic

First, we must care about grand historical narratives in IR because our default one is problematic and, though we may think it moribund, it is not. Methodological good sense, articulated in various places since the 1980s at least, more or less presses us into engaging properly with historical narratives and historical contextualization. This can be seen in the critiques of IR's received ahistorical and transhistorical realist-rationalist narrative. Any IR scholar who has taken seriously the last four decades of critiques of IR's treatment of history recognizes that the ahistorical approach is mistaken (Ashley, 1986; Hobson, 2002; Hobson and Lawson, 2008; Reus-Smit, 2002; Walker, 1993). All lament IR's transhistorical realist-rationalism that erases historical difference.

Well-known advice from IR's methods and metatheory literatures has long counseled our field to accept what amounts to the challenge of wrestling with historical narratives. This is repeatedly made clear in critiques of the damage done by the Waltzian and Westphalian 'hangovers' that have afflicted us for some time. The target is an agglomerate of the Westphalia/1648 narrative, Kenneth Waltz's 1979 book and its particular positions, the greater neorealism or structural realism research program, plus the general utilitarian rationalism implicated in much of the above and in neoliberal IR theory. These have made the discipline's predominant world image dangerously and dysfunctionally oversimplified. Waltz's 1979 *Theory of International Politics* is pivotal (Donnelly, 2015). In pursuit of parsimonious theory-building and to explain what he held to be key transhistorical continuities, Waltz burdened us with the deadly hyper-simplifications of the 'like-unit assumption' and the 'anarchy assumption'. These constitute a "fixed ahistorical view" (Cox, 1981: 131) and created a structural realism that was static, in which history disappears entirely (Buzan, Jones, and Little, 1993: 85–101; Teschke, 2003: 15). The legacy of those assumptions is a debilitating Waltzian hangover we are still trying to get over.

Grappling with and countering Waltz brought forth crucial critical projects. Neorealism's utilitarianism and rationalism were indicted as part of an historical erasing (Ashley, 1986; Cox, 1981). The assumption of a transhistorical 'common rationality' was crucially enabling but dangerous, requiring the embrace of historical complexity as a solution (Cox, 1981). Waltz came under attack for myriad reasons, but IR has seen especially brave efforts to fix the historical worldview, first correcting the like unit assumption (Doyle 1983; Hobson, 2002: 15–16; Lake, 1992; Moravcsik, 1997; Teschke, 1998), and more recently dethroning the anarchy assumption (Donnelly, 2015; Gunitsky, 2013; Lake, 2009; Mattern and Zarakol, 2016).[1] Of course the problem is also larger. Stefano Guzzini (2013: 527–529) reminds us, taking on much of twentieth-century IR, that the quest for regularity and 'science' in IR scholarship ended up focusing on reason of state thinking, geopolitics, and balance of power and shut everything else out.

IR writings provide repeated warnings against symptoms of the realist-Waltzian hangover, such as 'anarchophilia' and the sovereignty obsession (Buzan and Little, 2000). Alongside are critiques condemning general 'rationalist modes of theorizing' that logically accompany the 'atemporal structuralism' of neorealism and neoliberalism (Reus-Smit, 2002: 120). All these rely upon a particular historical narrative for their existence and salience, and it is the realist-rationalist/Westphalian one.

These arguments link in with other terms invented to diagnose our use of history, such as Hobson's (2002) 'tempocentrism' and 'chronofetishism'. Chronofetishism is 'the assumption that the present can adequately be explained only by examining the present' (Hobson, 2002: 6). This tendency means that historical analysis is not used to problematize the present, and thereby reifies and naturalizes it (pp. 5–6). Tempocentrism is the smoothing over and homogenization of history so that it all relates seamlessly to one's present interests and problems (Hobson 2002: 9–11). Tempocentrism creates the 'isomorphic illusion' (Hobson 2002: 7) that past historical systems are homologous, thereby preventing recognition of unique features. In sum, chronofetishism is what we do to analyzing the present; tempocentrism is what we thereby also do to the past. By both we are rendered uninterested in developing a thick account of history.

The post-paradigmatic turn is not helping

Mindful of this record and heritage of critique, the failure to be self-consciously aware of one's broader narrative of international relations history is indefensible. Yet, despite great effort, we have not necessarily made bounds of progress in recent years, and indeed are perhaps descending anew into darkness. It has been suggested that the momentous end of the Cold War reintroduced change into IR, spawning more sophisticated approaches to history (Elman and Elman, 2008; Reus-Smit, 2008). Yet while constructivism and liberal IR theory were breaths of fresh air indeed for 10–15 years, since then the field has become post-paradigmatic – these no longer constitute bold 'challengers'. Work within them continues but has been sidelined out of the mainstream and channelized into mid-range empirical theorizing.

The new post-paradigmatic trend has been popular (e.g., Lake, 2011), but damaging. Essentially it means that "working with one of the isms has become considered outmoded, 'been there,' if not outright harmful" (Guzzini, 2013: 522).

This pushes out leading, contending theoretical approaches such as feminist, postcolonial, and Marxist IR and their accounts of history; these in the past provided crucial alternatives to jar mainstream thinking and in the future might have become predominant. (This is also an embrace of problem-solving, not critical theory in Coxian terms.) Second, post-paradigmatic methodological proclivities are focused on the micro: "We are urged to trace 'processes' and 'mechanisms' at the micro-level" (Berenskötter, 2017 online). Accounts of IR history are squeezed by a homogenization of research down to "quantitative-followed-up-by-qualitative" work in which "all there is to theory is reached when some robust empirical generalization can be made under specific scope conditions" (Guzzini, 2013: 522). The post-paradigmatic turn to 'practical knowledge' and micro-level analysis also has an underlying supposition of the old realist-rationalist mega-narrative.

On a related point, one might object that the old realist-Westphalia-1648 narrative of IR history has already been done in by critiques during the post-Cold War age of free thinking, so what is there to return too? The Westphalia-1648 narrative has indeed been well-trampled in the last 30 years (de Carvalho et al., 2011; Glanville, 2013; Kayaoglu, 2010; Krasner, 1999; Nexon, 2009; Osiander, 2001; Teschke, 2003). The sovereign state model is critiqued as a central conceptualization and model of international relations that is so routinely violated as to be highly suspect (Krasner, 1999). Some wonder whether a true 'sovereign-territorial state system', so central to IR thought and theorizing, ever even existed in reality (Nexon, 2009: 287; Schmidt, 2011: 601). The 1648-turning-point narrative is similarly cast as a lie that clouds our thinking (de Carvalho et al., 2011), an 'ideology' (Osiander, 2001), and political project, charged with a multitude of political sins: valorizing states, state leaders, and their pursuit of power (Ashley, 1986); endorsing a world of nation-states desired by nineteenth- and twentieth-century nationalists (Osiander, 2001); portraying the West as the enlightened creator of the proper order of things, and teacher of others (Hobson, 2012, Kayaoglu, 2010). But if we now return to de facto realist-rationalism with the post-paradigmatic turn, what good were these efforts? The Westphalia-1648 narrative was already massively transhistorical because it encompassed 400 years. Abandoning the 1648 date for an entirely transhistorical rationalist narrative is perhaps an easy step, but in the wrong direction.

In sum, transhistorical thinking makes it seem as if nothing has changed, when in fact understanding what is unique about the present and past is fundamentally essential to IR as a discipline. Transhistorical rationalism does not reveal different contexts, but obscures them. What is thereby missing is any sense of history and of historical discontinuities. If our arguments are transhistorical and our theoretical devices trans-contextual, then by definition we must be working with a very straitened, mega-macro narrative of history, and it is not the liberal, feminist, or Marxist one but the old realist-rationalist one, still alive.

History liberates our thinking, theorizing, conceptualizing

Thus, the diluted realist, rationalist, and statist/Westphalian narrative of the present day is much the same as before and still imposes upon us its dysfunctional modes of analysis. Concomitantly, we still suffer under the zombie-like, haunting presence of key 'time invariant' concepts that are along for the ride, such as the state, anarchy, sovereignty, and polarity that plague historical IR – "timeless analytic entities" (Lawson, 2007: 346; McDonald, 2015). States, polarity, and the rise and fall of great powers are still at the heart of analyses of today's international developments, functionally perpetuating a particular international relations.

Conversely, what a liberation throwing off these blinders would be! This is the answer to our troubles, on all fronts. To defeat transhistoricity in all its dimensions and reform our time-invariant concepts, we must chop history up into appropriately sized chunks. Hobson (2002: 7) notes that eschewing tempocentrism and the isomorphic illusion that the past and present are the same means that we can finally trace 'the fundamental difference between past and present' and thereby understand what is unique about both. A new temporally sophisticated IR would emerge. Digging into history tells us what concepts have meant, though this cannot be about finding "essences" that instrumentally define concepts for present purposes (Guzzini, 2013: 536). Even if we remain interested in tracing causal mechanisms, placing these in context is the key to seeing their workings (Falleti and Lynch, 2009).

To summarize, a new "orrery of errors" (Ashley, 1986) walks amongst us or, more accurately, it is the same old one but grown even more hegemonic in the mainstream of the discipline, as we have become post-paradigmatic. The solution this book suggests is that sustained reflection about historical narratives is precisely the 'golden ticket' to escape the entire orrery. Scholars getting serious about historical narratives would profoundly disrupt the possibility for ahistorical, transhistorical thinking. In this new frontier we should not see only commonalities that enable transhistorical research, but search for the differences that bind events in a particular context and make processes timebound. A lack of interest and will to engage with constructing one or a couple of robust, vetted, perhaps discontinuous, historical narratives of international history enables the backward slide into atemporal, ahistorical work and keeps us there.

Grand narratives are omnipresent anyway

Conversely, only worsening the situation would be to somehow refuse to have historical narratives at all, adopting a poststructuralist sensibility that embraces infinite, ongoing complexity. This has been called "Radical Historicism" (Hobson and Lawson, 2008; Yetiv, 2011) and would entail constant micro-contextualization and deconstruction of meanings, because larger narratives are methodologically bad and politically dangerous and oppressive. In response to this argument it bears pointing out that historical narratives of IR history are actually omnipresent and cannot be avoided, because they play such crucial roles in academic work.

There is no neutral position (Cox, 1981) or mode of inquiry that has no account of history implicitly or explicitly.[2] Broad narratives are essential to the functioning of any IR perspective. Everyone has narratives, about everything (Suganami, 2008; White, 1980). Periodizations and macro-scale historical narratives establish the very parameters in which IR scholars labor, speculate, and theorize. Therefore, we should be highly attentive to how we produce these narratives. Yet there is a surprising lack of reflection on general practices in such matters.

Similarly, it bears repeating that the rationalist-realist one IS a historical narrative, of timelessness and repetition, and it does damage, as the above section illustrated (Mearsheimer and Walt, 2013). If we think we do not have them, we are fooling ourselves – the point is to be reflexive about our narratives, their scale, and impacts. Attempting to avoid meso-narratives returns us to the default position of the timeless realist-rationalist one of eternal repetition, falling back into transhistorical power discussions of hegemony, polarity issues, and distribution of material power, as if these are always appropriate. And thereby, as Rob Walker observed, "The lived meaning of history is excluded" (1993: 114).

Second, large-scale narratives are ubiquitous because they are so important. Historical narratives are crucial to setting the parameters for all subsequent inquiry. They can be the inspiration for more fruitful grand theory disputes and paradigm wars, or for cumulation that avoids them. As the historian William A. Green observed years ago (1995: 99):

> Periodization is both the product and begetter of theory. The organizing principles upon which we write history, the priorities we assign to various aspects of human endeavor, and the theories of change we adopt to explain the historical process: all are represented in periodization. Once firmly established, periodization exerts formidable, often subliminal, influence on the refinement and elaboration of theory.

Thus, by definition, we have to confront the issue. (Relatedly, one can see how the 1648 date imposed a singular, simple agenda on us, for covering almost 400 years of history.)

The solution? Embrace and construct narratives of IR history

People have already written about solutions to this problem, but IR has not necessarily implemented them. All IR work should be historically situated; in effect, we all need a rich account of history in our heads. Historical narratives make the world more intelligible by sorting information and simplifying infinite complexity. Narratives at the appropriate scale do this without doing great damage to our efforts to understand history as 'accurately' as is feasible. This calls on IR to develop an attentiveness to both periodizations and the related question of continuities and (the certainty of) discontinuities. In effect, these two are intimately connected, since periodization is "about the criteria for defining what constitute major continuities and major changes in any story that evolves over time" (Buzan and Little, 2000: 386). We must be attentive to "the fundamental differences between past and present international systems and institutions, to thereby reveal the unique constitutive features of the present" (Hobson, 2002: 7).

Addressing periodization is also likely a way to settle and make cohere dimensions of disparate research programs in IR. In some ways it is no surprise we have had the 'great debates' we have had, given our laboring under such a flawed approach to theory and history. Our great debates have been a sign of engagement in a conflictual way, but historical narrative has the potential to foster engagement in a collaborative way, to further our cumulation and even some convergence. Given the intimate connections between theory and history, how else might this occur, if not around historical narratives? Getting narratives right could be the basis for the next step: grand theories (Berenskötter, 2017).

Relatedly, reflexivity about the scale of narratives is crucial. We should be careful about the real limits to generalizations in the social sciences (Mearsheimer and Walt, 2013: 432). There is for example a certain rationalism that is useful, but it is highly situational. We should not use it as a crutch to erase history. Similarly, as Suganami has observed so sensibly (2008: 341): "Why should the story be about *regular* outcomes?" If one is positing stability and continuity in events and concepts, one needs to make a strong case for it (Büthe, 2002; Jervis, 2001).

Wrapping up

The above provides a basis for how scholars ought to take history honestly and seriously in IR. When we follow these provisos, we situate things historically and put them in their own ideational-normative contexts. Just as important, we become alert to the possibility of discontinuities, one of the most important things an improved IR approach to history can contribute.

As periodizations and the contours of discontinuities become more prominent, an emergent issue is how useful the international relations past actually is or might be for understanding the present. How disruptive are discontinuities? What are the continuities across them, if any? Important issues all, but there is much to do. The mapping of unique highly situated processes as such, for example, has barely begun in IR. Similarly, the mapping of the impacts of certain normative turning points is not well understood. We have a better sense of the impacts of technological changes, in some ways – perhaps a model to follow. Musgrave and Nexon (2016) offer some observations on this, cautioning that we might best store historical things in the attic to discuss later (p. 442), in deference to immediate presentist issues. But this also would imply, given all the above arguments, that one's ahistorical inquiries using time-invariant concepts simply render such work confused; closeting history and locking it away has high costs. They warn that making the case for "any particular macro-transformation" (p. 443) means studying the past becomes less valuable, but failing to also means studies of the present will always be lacking, perhaps seriously so.

In sum, narratives of history are arguably the most important subject for IR scholars to be reflexive about. We think this book makes contributions in the right direction, in asking for a global narrative and in finding a discontinuity that divides historical processes and materializes two historical 'worlds' in the nineteenth century. The realist-statist/Westphalian narrative is ahistorical and Eurocentric and desperately needs replacing. One important corrective is to construct narratives of IR as if everyone in the world matters, not just white people from the West, and not hiding away the fact of the devastating conquest of the non-European world. But in key ways that was an odd explosion of activity, so addressing its origins and understanding the international relations that came before is necessary. In that narrative there is also resistance, adaptation, and reconfiguration, in the lingering import of the Sinosphere, in the choices made by political leaders everywhere. We pin our thesis on a discontinuity, in the pivot period, putting 1869–1914 in its own context, rather than simply as the pre-WWI era. Of course, coming to consensus conclusions regarding IR's historical narrative(s) is unlikely, but that should not dissuade us from the effort, as a learning opportunity and as steps on a better path than the one most trod now. We hope this book can launch a thorough and fruitful discussion in the IR discipline, about a crucial – even pivotal! – century.

Notes

1 See Lake (2011: 467) for a report on the growing literature going after the anarchy assumption.
2 This conundrum resembles the decades-long debates in the discipline of history about the possibility of objectivity (Novick, 1988), which has seen objectivity suffer and fall from its throne.

Bibliography

Ashley, Richard K. (1986) The Poverty of Neorealism. In Robert O. Keohane, ed., *Neorealism and Its Critics*. New York: Columbia University Press.
Berenskötter, Felix. (2017) Deep Theorizing in International Relations. *European Journal of International Relations* (Online First): 1–27.
Büthe, Tim. (2002) Taking Temporality Seriously: Modeling History and the Use of Narratives as Evidence. *American Political Science Review* 96(3): 481–493.
Buzan, Barry, Charles Jones, and Richard Little. (1993) *The Logic of Anarchy: Neorealism to Structural Realism*. New York: Columbia University Press.
Buzan, Barry and Richard Little. (2000) *International Systems in World History: Remaking the Study of International Relations*. Oxford: Oxford University Press.
de Carvalho, Benjamin, Halvard Leira, and John M. Hobson. (2011) The Big Bangs of IR: The Myths That Your Teachers Tell You about 1648 and 1919. *Millennium: Journal of International Studies* 39(3): 735–758.

Cox, Robert W. (1981) Social Forces, States and World Order: Beyond International Relations Theory. *Millennium: Journal of International Studies* 10(2): 126–155.

Donnelly, Jack. (2015) The Discourse of Anarchy in IR. *International Theory* 7(3): 393–425.

Doyle, Michael. (1983) Kant, Liberal Legacies, and Foreign Affairs: Parts One and Two. *Philosophy and Public Affairs* 12: 205–235, 325–353.

Elman, Colin and Miriam Fendius Elman. (2008) The Role of History in International Relations. *Millennium: Journal of International Studies* 37(2): 357–364.

Falleti, Tulia G. and Julia F. Lynch. (2009) Context and Causal Mechanisms in Political Analysis. *Comparative Political Studies* 42(9): 1143–1166.

Glanville, Luke. 2013. The Myth of 'Traditional' Sovereignty. *International Studies Quarterly* 57(1): 79–90.

Green, William A. (1995) Periodizing World History. *History and Theory* 34(2): 99–111.

Guzzini, Stefano. (2013) The Ends of International Relations Theory: Stages of Reflexivity and Modes of Theorizing. *European Journal of International Relations* 19(3): 521–541.

Hobson, John M. (2002) What's at Stake in 'Bringing Historical Sociology Back into International Relations'? Transcending 'Chronofetishism' and 'Tempocentrism' in International Relations. In Stephen Hobden and John M. Hobson, eds., *Historical Sociology of International Relations*. Cambridge: Cambridge University Press.

Hobson, John M. (2012) *The Eurocentric Conception of World Politics: Western International Theory, 1760–2010*. Cambridge: Cambridge University Press.

Hobson, John M. and George Lawson. (2008) What Is History in International Relations? *Millennium: Journal of International Studies* 37(2): 415–435.

Jervis, Robert. (2001) Variation, Change, and Transitions in International Politics. *Review of International Studies* 27(5): 281–295.

Kayaoglu, Turan. (2010) Westphalian Eurocentrism in International Relations Theory. *International Studies Review* 12(2): 193–217.

Krasner, Stephen D. (1999) *Sovereignty: Organized Hypocrisy*. Princeton: Princeton University Press.

Lake, David A. (2009) *Hierarchy in International Relations*. Ithaca: Cornell University Press.

Lake, David A. (2011) Why 'Isms' Are Evil: Theory, Epistemology and Academic Sects as Impediments to Understanding and Progress. *International Studies Quarterly* 55(2): 465–480.

Lawson, George. (2007) Historical Sociology in International Relations: Open Society, Research Programme and Vocation. *International Politics* 44(4): 343–368.

Mattern, Janice Bially and Ayse Zarakol. (2016) Hierarchy in World Politics. *International Organization* 70(3): 623–654.

McDonald, Patrick. (2015) Great Powers, Hierarchy, and Endogenous Regimes: Rethinking the Domestic Causes of Peace. *International Organization* 69(3): 557–588.

Mearsheimer, John J. and Stephen M. Walt. (2013) Leaving Theory Behind: Why Simplistic Hypothesis Testing Is Bad for International Relations. *European Journal of International Relations* 19(3): 427–457.

Moravcsik, Andrew. (1997) Taking Preferences Seriously: A Liberal Theory of International Politics. *International Organization* 51(4): 513–553.

Musgrave, Paul and Daniel Nexon. (2016) The Global Transformation: More Than Meets the Eye. *International Theory* 8(3): 422–435.

Nexon, Daniel H. (2009) *The Struggle for Power in Early Modern Europe*. Princeton: Princeton University Press.

Novick, Peter. (1988) *That Noble Dream: The 'Objectivity Question' and the American Historical Profession.* Cambridge: Cambridge University Press.

Osiander, Andreas. (2001) Sovereignty, International Relations, and the Westphalian Myth. *International Organization* 55(2): 251–288.

Reus-Smit, Christian. (2008) Reading History through Constructivist Eyes. *Millennium: Journal of International Studies* 37(2): 395–414.

Reus-Smit, Christian. (2016) Theory, History, and Great Transformations. *International Theory* 8(3): 422–435.

Schmidt, Sebastian. (2011) To Order the Minds of Scholars: The Discourse of the Peace of Westphalia in International Relations Literature. *International Studies Quarterly* 55(3): 601–623.

Suganami, Hidemi. (2008) Narrative Explanation and International Relations: Back to Basics. *Millennium: Journal of International Studies* 37(2): 327–356.

Teschke, Benno. (1998) Geopolitical Relations in the European Middle Ages: History and Theory. *International Organization* 52(2): 325–358.

Teschke, Benno. (2003) *The Myth of 1648: Class, Geopolitics and the Making of Modern International Relations.* London: Verso.

Walker, R.B.J. (1993) *Inside/Outside: International Relations as Political Theory.* Cambridge: Cambridge University Press.

Waltz, Kenneth. (1979) *Theory of International Politics.* New York: Random House.

White, Hayden. (1980) The Value of Narrativity in the Representation of Reality. *Critical Inquiry* 7(1): 5–27.

Yetiv, Steve. (2011) History, International Relations, and Integrated Approaches: Thinking about Greater Interdisciplinarity. *International Studies Perspectives* 12(1): 94–118.

Index

Africa 8, 15, 17, 27, 103
Alexander, Tsar 105
American Civil War 14–15, 16
Amherst, Lord William 87–8, 89, 96
Angell, Norman 128, 132–3
Arrow War 1856–1860 88–90
Ashworth, Lucian M. 10, 119–37
Asia 13–14, 15, 18; domestic legitimacy crises in East Asia 161–8; hybrid regional order in East Asia 160–1; international hierarchy in late nineteenth-century East Asia 159–60; Japanese and Korean status-seeking strategies, contrasting outcomes of 168–9; *see also* piracy
Austria 66, 67; antagonism towards Prussia 68–73; Austrian/Prussian territorial shifts within Germany 68–70; constitutional crisis in Germany 71–3; increasing rivalry with Prussia 73–6; Prussian economic hegemony and the Zollverein 70–1, 74, 75
autonomy 158, 159–60, 170; sovereign autonomy 160–1

Banks, David 8, 9, 80–100
Barnett, Michael 28
Bayly, Chris 101, 102
Beaupré, Jean Jayet de 44, 51
Benton, Lauren 47
Berlin Conference 1884–1885 28, 147
Bismarck, Otto von 76, 143, 190
Blaney, David 38
Bowden, Brett 28
Bowman, Isaiah 123
Brailsford, Henry Noel 124, 129, 130–2
Britain: colonies, increase in 111–12; counter-piracy policy 186–90;
diplomatic missions to China 86–8; industrialization 111; and liberalism 179; loss of influence 13, 15–16; narrative of piracy 183–4; naval power 46, 179, 180; relationship with the Dutch 181, 187, 189; role in the Americas 45–6; view of indigenous peoples as backward and uncivilized 177–8, 179, 180, 183–4; world position 17–18, 32
British East India Company 12, 29, 32, 36, 86, 180
Bruce, Frederick 89, 96
Bruce, James, Earl of Elgin 89
Brzezinski, Zbigniew 81
Bull, Hedley 6, 140, 141
Buzan, Barry 2, 6, 11, 119, 120, 122, 126

Cabot, Bailey & Co 52, 53
Canning, George 109
Carey, William 29, 32–3, 36
Caribbean *see* privateering
Castlereagh, Lord 102, 105, 106, 109
Chamberlain, Muriel E. 12
Chang, Michael G. 94
China 8, 14, 28, 111–12; Amherst mission of 1816 87–8, 96; from Amherst to the *Arrow* War of 1856–1860 88–90; autonomy 159–60; competing diplomatic practices in 19th century Europe and East Asia 81–5; declining influence of 190; diplomatic practice and the Sinocentric system 84–5; emperors 84–5; and European international society 86; great powers intervention 1900 148; *koutou* ritual 84–5, 87–8, 89, 91, 94–6; legitimacy, practice and power in Qing China 92–6; Macartney mission of 1793

208 Index

86–7, 91, 95–6; Qing behavior, explanation of 91–2, 95–6; Qing regime 80, 81, 84; Qing rule, precarious nature of 92–3; relationship with Korea 166–7, 169; self-isolation 80; Taiping Rebellion 112; tributary system 85; and Westphalian diplomacy 81–3, 86–90
chronofetishism 199
civilization 12, 168; European 130; hydrocarbon civilization 122, 126–7; missionary conceptions of 28–9, 34–8, 39, 40; standard of 2, 4, 6, 7, 9, 110, 113, 114, 161, 180
colonialism 12, 17, 111–12, 128, 178; and liberalism 179; and missionaries 27–8; neo-colonialism 131; role in nineteenth century political economy 121–2, 124–5, 129–30; view of indigenous peoples as backward and uncivilized 177–8, 179, 180, 183–4
Concert of Europe 9, 77, 101–18, 138, 139; assessment of 103–4; background of a world crisis 101–3; collective action 148; constitutionalism, challenge of 109; effectiveness of 108–10; evolution and changes in practice 144–6, 152–3; fostering peace 104; global managerial practices, emergence of 147–9; and global transformation 110–13; great power status and Concert membership in the 1860s, identity of 141–3; historians' views of 102; inter-and intra-imperial conflicts, escalation of 112–13; legalized hegemony 113–15; multilateral international conferences and organizations 148–9, 150–1; networks of 104; ordering Europe 105–8; repression of reform and radical movements 108, 109; spheres of influence 148; status, continuing relevance and changes in practice 149–52; world outside Europe, neglect of 110
Congress of Vienna 66, 76, 105–8
constitutionalism 9, 65, 71–2, 106, 109
Cox, Jeffrey 29
Cox, Robert 10
Crimean War 12, 13, 70, 103, 109–10, 144

Dampier, William 184
Darwin, Charles 14, 181

Denmark 15, 50
Dickens, Charles 25, 180
diplomacy 80–100, 168–9; Amherst mission of 1816 87–8, 96; from Amherst to the *Arrow* War of 1856–1860 88–90; ceremonial rights and protocol 82–3; China and European international society 86; Chinese resistance to Westphalian diplomacy 86–90; competing diplomatic practices in 19th century Europe and East Asia 81–5; embassies 82, 150; immunity for ambassadors 82; Japanese and Korean status-seeking strategies, contrasting outcomes of 168–9; language use 168; legitimacy, practice and power in Qing China 92–6; Macartney mission of 1793 86–7, 91, 95–6; Qing behavior, explanation of 91–2, 95–6; Qing practice, power of 93–5; Qing rule, precarious nature of 92–3; recognition of rising powers 149–50; Sinocentric system and diplomatic practice 84–5, 157–8; sovereign autonomy 160–1; tributary system 85; Westphalian diplomacy, practice of 81–3
Disraeli, Benjamin 17, 18
Doyle, Michael 6, 27

embassies 82–3, 150
English School, in International Studies 3, 6, 133–4, 139, 140
evangelicalism 30, 31, 36, 39

First World War 127, 131–3
Foreman-Peck, James 121, 124
France 7, 12–13, 14–15, 16, 112; peace negotiations 63; revolutionary wars 60, 62; in Southeast Asia 189
Frederick William III 65, 72
Frederick William IV 74
free trade 12, 14, 16, 75, 123, 177, 180, 191

Galtung, Johan 27
Ganghwa, Treaty of, 1876 168, 172n18
Geneva Convention 112–13
Gentz, Friedrich von 105, 106
Germany 15, 16, 17, 60–79, 127–8, 145; from the 1848 revolutions to the war of 1866 73–6; Austrian/Prussian territorial shifts within Germany 68–70; Austro-Prussian antagonism,

Index

management of 68–73; Carlsbad Decrees 72–3, 75; colonies, increase in 124; constitutional crisis 71–3; Federal Act 69–70, 71; French revolutionary wars, effects of 60–1, 62–3; German Confederation, as political compromise 66–8; German Confederation, establishment of 61–2; *Mittelstaaten* 61, 62, 63, 65, 66, 67, 73, 76; from the old Empire to the Congress of Vienna 62–6; political transformation 64–6; Prussian economic hegemony and the *Zollverein* 70–1, 74, 75; in Southeast Asia 190; territorial transformation 62–3
Getachew, Lullit 27
Gilpin, Robert 3
Gong, Gerrit W. 6
great powers 83, 103, 104, 105, 107, 108, 113, 126, 138–56; collective action 148; definition of 127–8; distinction from world powers 150–1; global managerial practices, emergence of 147–9; great power status and Concert membership in the 1860s, identity of 141–3; and inequality 114–15; institution of great powers, evolution and changes in practice 144–6, 152–3; interaction between grading of powers and their managerial function 139; multilateral international conferences and organizations 148–9, 150–1; patterns of stratification and the institution of great powers 140–1, 142; practices through which the institution of great powers was performed 139; as a product of industrialization 121; recognition of 108; relations between European great powers 129–30; special rights and duties 151–2; spheres of influence 148; status, continuing relevance and changes in practice 149–52
Green, Daniel M. 1–24, 196–206
Green, William A. 202
Gruner, Wolf 69
Guzzini, Stefano 199

Haldén, Peter 68
Hall, Catherine 36, 39
Hall, Rod 4, 6
Hara, Takemichi 159

hegemony 3–4, 5, 7–8, 70–1, 102, 108; collective hegemony 140–1; hegemonic stability theory 197; legalized hegemony 113–15
Hirono, Miwa 28
Hobson, John A. 121–2, 128, 199
Holy Alliance 105–6
Holy Roman Empire 60, 62–3, 64

imperialism 1–2, 4, 6, 10, 111, 112; competitive imperialism 11; inter-and intra-imperial conflicts, escalation of 112–13; and missionaries 38–40; new imperialism concept 11, 103, 128; role in nineteenth century political economy 121–2, 124–5, 129–30
Inayatullah, Naeem 38
India 12, 180, 181
industrialization 10, 110, 111, 119–37, 149; awareness of effects of 119; coal, importance of 122–3, 125–6; communications 123, 125, 126; competition between European and non-European worlds 130; copper, importance of 123; first and second industrial revolutions 122; food supplies 123; in the history of international relations 133–5; how industrialization created the modern world 121–7; importance of to international relations 119–20, 121; international political thought, development of 127–33; relations between European great powers 129–30; resources, importance of 120, 122–6, 132–3; two-tiered global order concept 128–32, 135; war, shock of 131–3
international political economy (IPE) 119, 133
International Prize Court 151–2
Italy 15, 18, 75, 143, 145

Jackson, Richard 183
James, Angell 34, 35
Japan 139, 157, 158, 163–5, 168–9; autonomy 159–60; Japanese and Korean status-seeking strategies, contrasting outcomes of 168–9; regime legitimacy 160, 161–8; *sakoku* policy 159, 160, 161, 162, 163–5; status of 149, 150; transition

to Westphalian statehood 1853–1877 160, 163–5
Johnson, Arthur N. 31–2

Keene, Edward 4
Keynes, John Maynard 132
Korea 157, 158, 162; autonomy 159–60; dual status problem, 1882–1895 166–8; Japanese and Korean status-seeking strategies, contrasting outcomes of 168–9; nationalist identity 169; regime legitimacy 160, 161–8; *sadae* policy 159, 160, 161, 162, 167–8; transition to Westphalian statehood 160

Lankina, Tomila 27
Las Damas Argentinas (ship) 44, 51–4, 55
Lawrence, T.J. 151–2
Lawson, George 2, 6, 9, 11, 101–18, 119, 120, 122, 126
Layton, Simon 184, 185
legitimacy 39, 40, 45, 47, 48, 105–6, 109–10, 144, 158, 181, 185; Japanese and Korean domestic legitimacy crises 159–60, 161–8, 170; in Qing China 91–2, 92–6
Lemke, Tobias 9, 60–79
Lewis, Dianne 184
liberalism: changes in links with empire 188–9; and the *Pax Britannica* 177–8, 179
List, Friedrich 127
Little, Richard 6
Livingstone, David 12, 25–6, 37–8, 40
Locke, John 179

Macartney, George 86–7, 91, 95–6
Mahan, Alfred Thayer 129–30, 131–2
Maine, Henry 180
Mantena, Karuna 181
McDonald, Matt 183
Mearsheimer, John 4, 125, 134
Mehta, Uday 179
Metternich, Klemens von 67, 71–2, 102, 106, 109
Mexico 13, 14–15
Mill, James 179
Mill, John Stuart 179, 180
missionaries 8, 12, 25–42, 189; and the age of empire 38–40; Christianity and the civilizing mission 34–8; civilizing influence of 28–9; and international relations 27–9; middle-class influences 35–6; rise of, in Britain 29–34
Mitchell, Timothy 122, 125–6
Modelski, George 119–20
Monroe Doctrine 8, 15, 46–7, 49, 148
Moon, Parker 125
Morgenthau, Hans, J. 4
Mulich, Jeppe 8, 43–59
Müller, Thomas 10, 138–56
Murphy, Craig N. 119
Musgrave, Paul 203–4

Napoleon III 12, 13, 14–15, 16, 189
narratives of history: default narrative of international relations, problems of 198–9; grand narratives 196–7, 201–2; history as a liberator of thinking, theorizing and conceptualizing 201; history's importance to international relations 203–4; international relations history narratives 202–3; macro narratives 197; meso-narratives 197; methodological strictures and the need for engagement with historical narratives 198–201; periodization 202–3; post-paradigmatic turn 199–200; transhistorical dimensions 200; Westphalia-1648 narrative 200
Nexon, Daniel 203–4
nineteenth century: as a bifurcated century 5, 102, 113–14, 138, 152–3; as a century of continuities 3–4

offensive realism 134
Oliphaunt, Laurence 95
opium trade 86, 89, 91, 111–12
Osterhammel, Jürgen 1, 10–11, 19
Ottoman Empire 13, 110

Palmerston, Lord 15, 16, 179
Paras, Andrea 8, 25–42
Park, Seo-Hyun 10, 157–76
Parliamentary Select Committee on Aborigines 37
Parry, Jonathan 15
Pax Britannica concept 1, 3, 4, 5, 7, 19, 46; contention and shift 180–1; liberal nature of 179; and piracy 177–8, 187, 191; in Southeast Asia 177–8
Peace of Westphalia 81–2
Permanent Court of Arbitration 151
piracy 47, 177–95; British counter-piracy policy 186–90; British narrative of piracy 183–4; distinction from

privateering 48, 54–5; nature of 182; and *Pax Britannica* 177–8, 179, 187, 191; political content of 177, 178, 184–6, 188; in Southeast Asia 177, 181–90; Straits Settlement 177, 180, 181, 188–9; Temenggongs of Johor 186
Porter, Andrew 30, 34, 36
power 10, 108, 126; balance of power 129–31; land power notion 134
privateering 8, 43–59; Atlantic revolutions, age of 44–7; *Las Damas Argentinas*, case of 51–4, 55; letters of marque 47, 48, 51; as a networked order in the Caribbean 48–50; as a strategy of recognition 47–8
Prussia 65, 67; antagonism towards Austria 68–73; Austrian/Prussian territorial shifts within Germany 68–70; constitutional crisis in Germany 71–3; economic hegemony and the Zollverein 70–1, 74, 75; increasing rivalry with Austria 73–6

Quadruple Alliance 106–7

racial issues 14, 16–17, 112
Raffles, Colonel Stamford 181, 183, 186–7
Ratzel, Friedrich 127–8, 130
Reinsch, Paul 128, 148

Schroeder, Paul 7, 144
Schulz, Martin 144
Second Hague Conference 1907 139, 144, 151, 152
Shirk, Mark 10, 177–95
Simpson, Gerry 107, 141, 147
Sinocentric system *see* diplomacy
slavery 8–9, 12, 14, 16–17, 19, 25, 32, 33, 36
Social Darwinism 5

society of states concept 133–4
Society of the Propagation of the Gospel in Foreign Parts (SPG) 30, 31
sovereignty 43, 47, 49, 54, 106, 144, 157–8, 165; sovereign autonomy 160–1; sovereign equality 170
Spain 15; Concert of Europe membership 141–3
St Thomas (Caribbean island) 50, 51–4
Stanley, Brian 29, 30, 34
Suez Canal 13, 18

Tarling, Nicholas 186, 190
tempocentrism 199, 201
Thompson, R. Wardlaw 31–2
Thorne, Susan 25, 35, 36
Thouvenel, Édouard de 142
trade unions 126
Trocki, Carl 185
Turnbull, C.M. 182
Twells, Alison 30, 35
two worlds concept 2–3, 5, 6, 77, 138, 152

United States (US) 16, 46–7, 112, 139, 148; status of 149, 150

Vick, Brian 107, 115–16n6
Vienna Règlement 1815 149–50

Walker, Rob 202
Walls, Andrew 30, 33
Waltz, Kenneth, *Theory of International Politics* 198–9
Wesley, John 30, 31
Wester, Charles 114
Westphalian diplomacy *see* diplomacy
Wicquefort, Abraham de 83
Wight, Martin 140
Woodberry, Robert 27–8

Zollverein see Germany

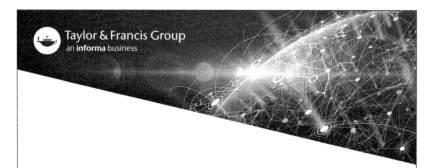